Garfield Treasury

Garfield Treasury

BY: JIM DAVIS

BALLANTINE BOOKS · NEW YORK

Copyright © 1982 by United Feature Syndicate, Inc.

The Sunday strips appearing here in color were previously included in black and white in *GARFIELD At Large, GARFIELD Gains Weight, GARFIELD Bigger Than Life,* and *GARFIELD Weighs In.*

All rights reserved under International and Pan-American Copyright Conventions. Published in the United States by Ballantine Books, a division of Random House, Inc., New York, and simultaneously in Canada by Random House of Canada Limited, Toronto, Canada

Library of Congress Catalog Card Number: 82-90221

ISBN: 0-345-32106-5

First Edition: November 1982

Cover design by Brian Strater and Neil Altekruse

Designed by Gene Siegal

30 29 28 27 26 25 24 23 22 21

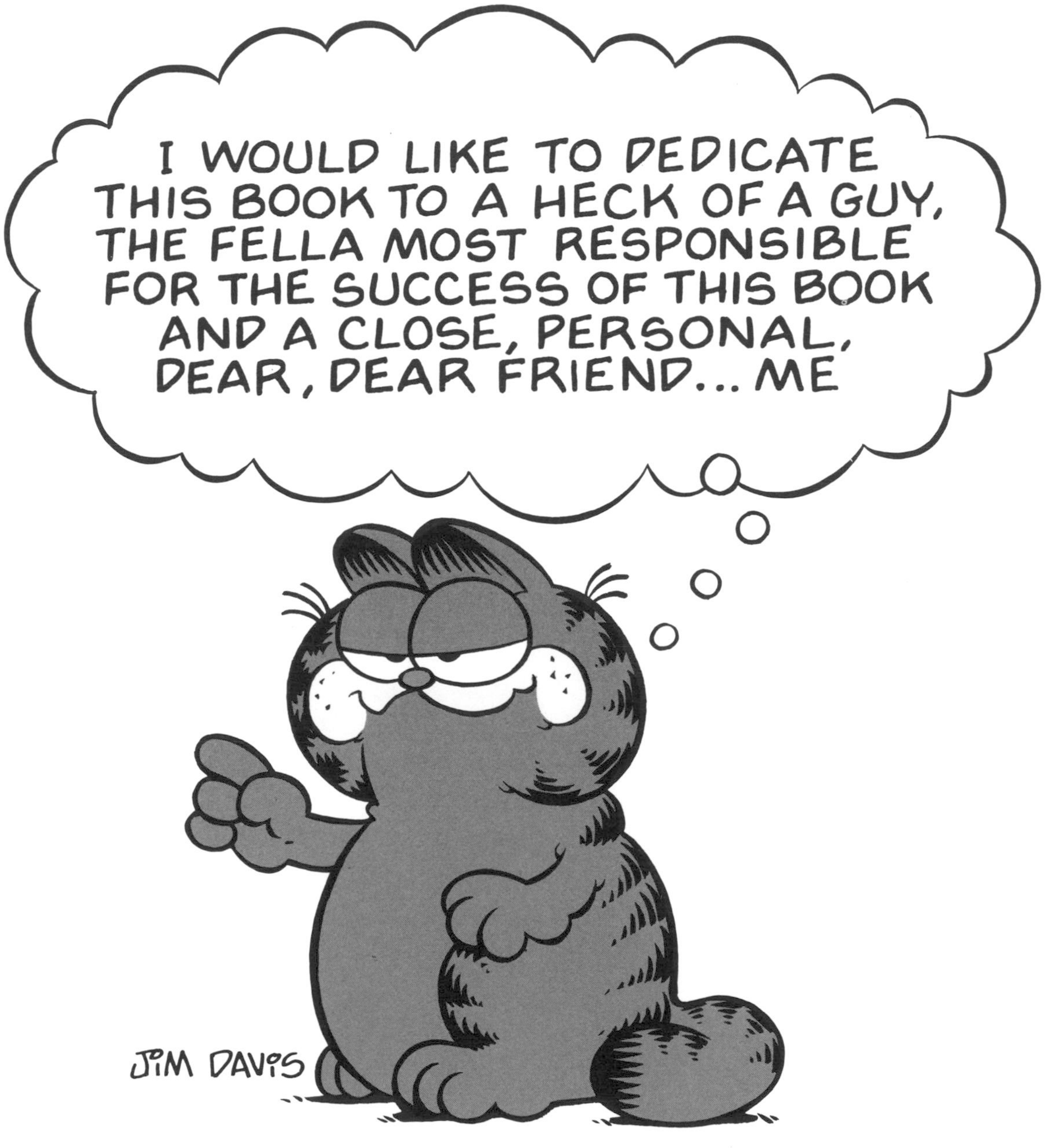
I WOULD LIKE TO DEDICATE THIS BOOK TO A HECK OF A GUY, THE FELLA MOST RESPONSIBLE FOR THE SUCCESS OF THIS BOOK AND A CLOSE, PERSONAL, DEAR, DEAR FRIEND... ME
JIM DAVIS

Garfield
Treasury

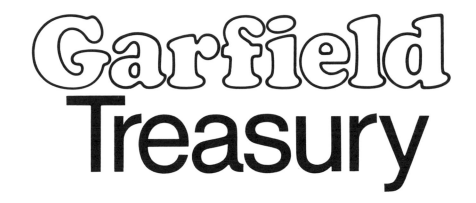

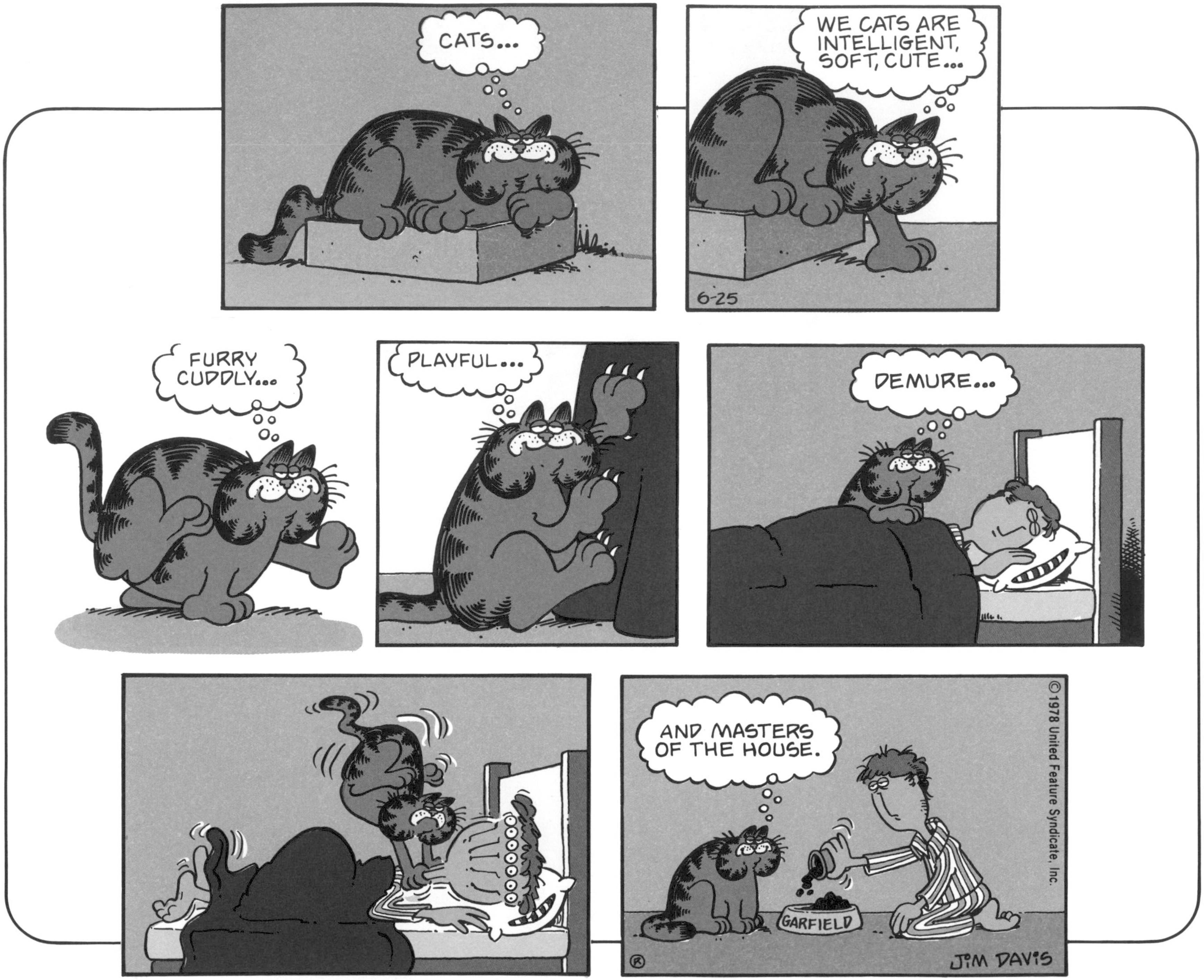

CATS...
WE CATS ARE INTELLIGENT, SOFT, CUTE...
6-25
FURRY CUDDLY...
PLAYFUL...
DEMURE...
AND MASTERS OF THE HOUSE.
GARFIELD
© 1978 United Feature Syndicate, Inc.
JIM DAVIS

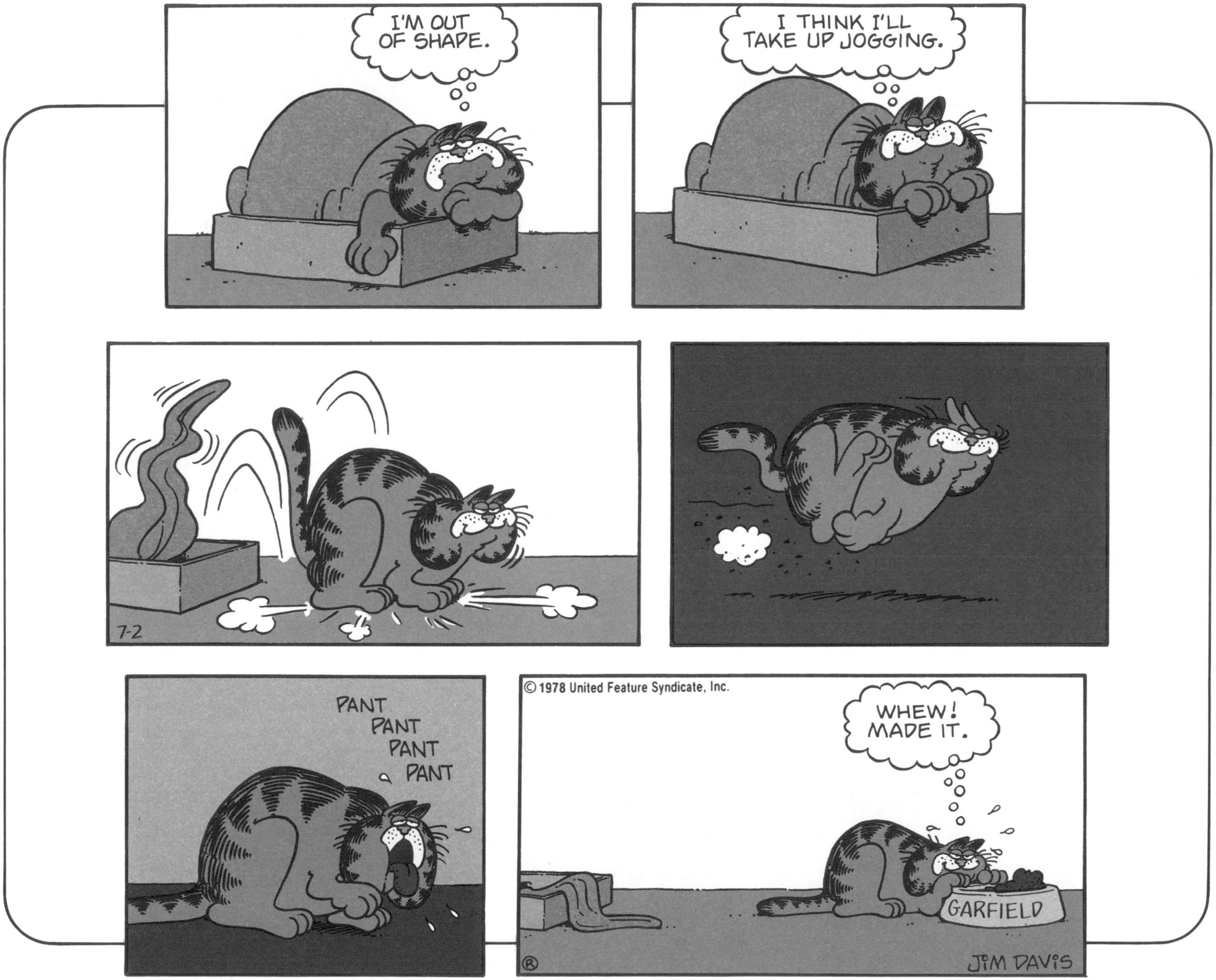
I'M OUT OF SHAPE.
I THINK I'LL TAKE UP JOGGING.
7-2
PANT PANT PANT PANT
© 1978 United Feature Syndicate, Inc.
WHEW! MADE IT.
GARFIELD
®
JIM DAVIS

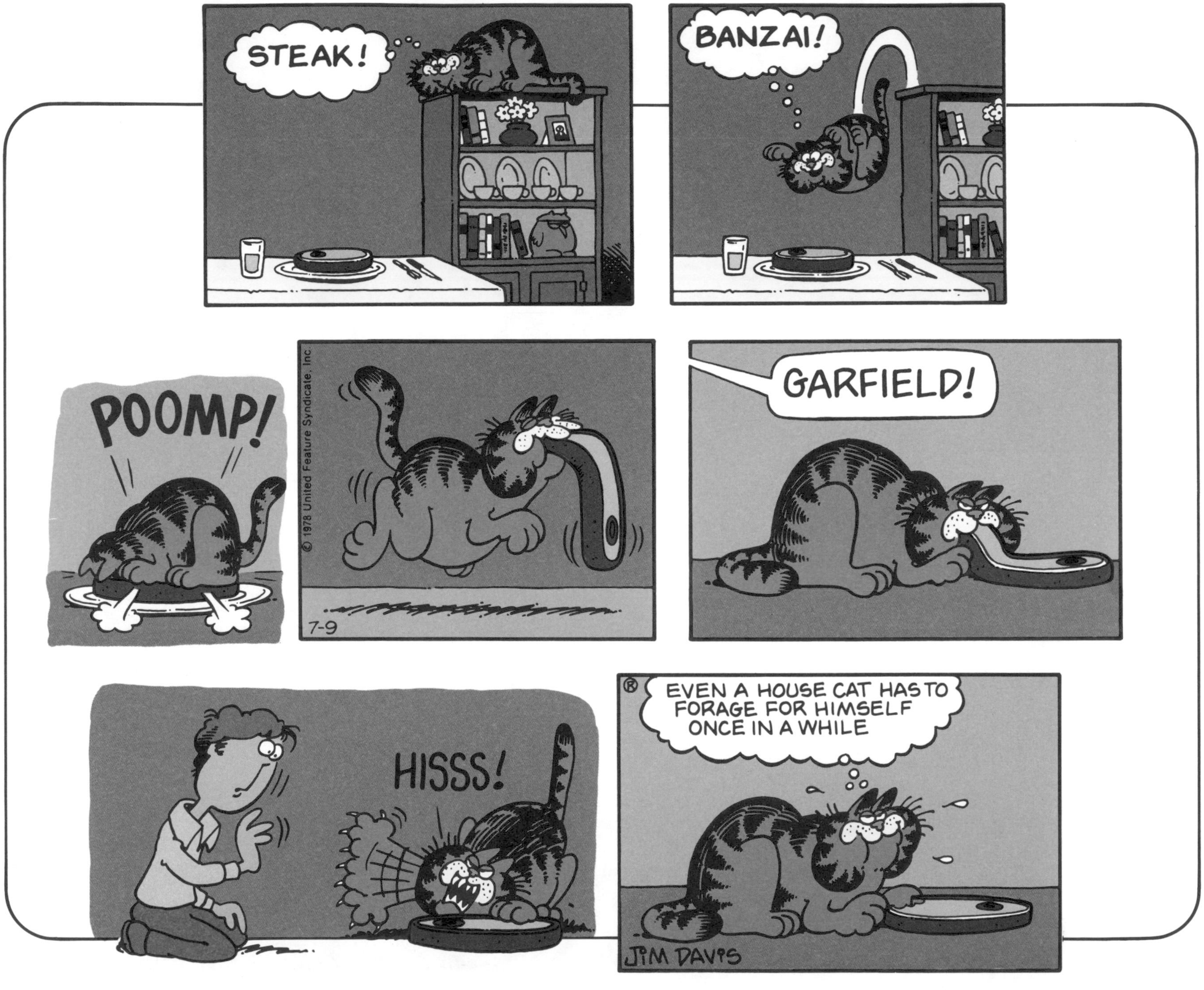
STEAK!
BANZAI!
POOMP!
© 1978 United Feature Syndicate, Inc.
7-9
GARFIELD!
HISSS!
EVEN A HOUSE CAT HAS TO FORAGE FOR HIMSELF ONCE IN A WHILE
JIM DAVIS

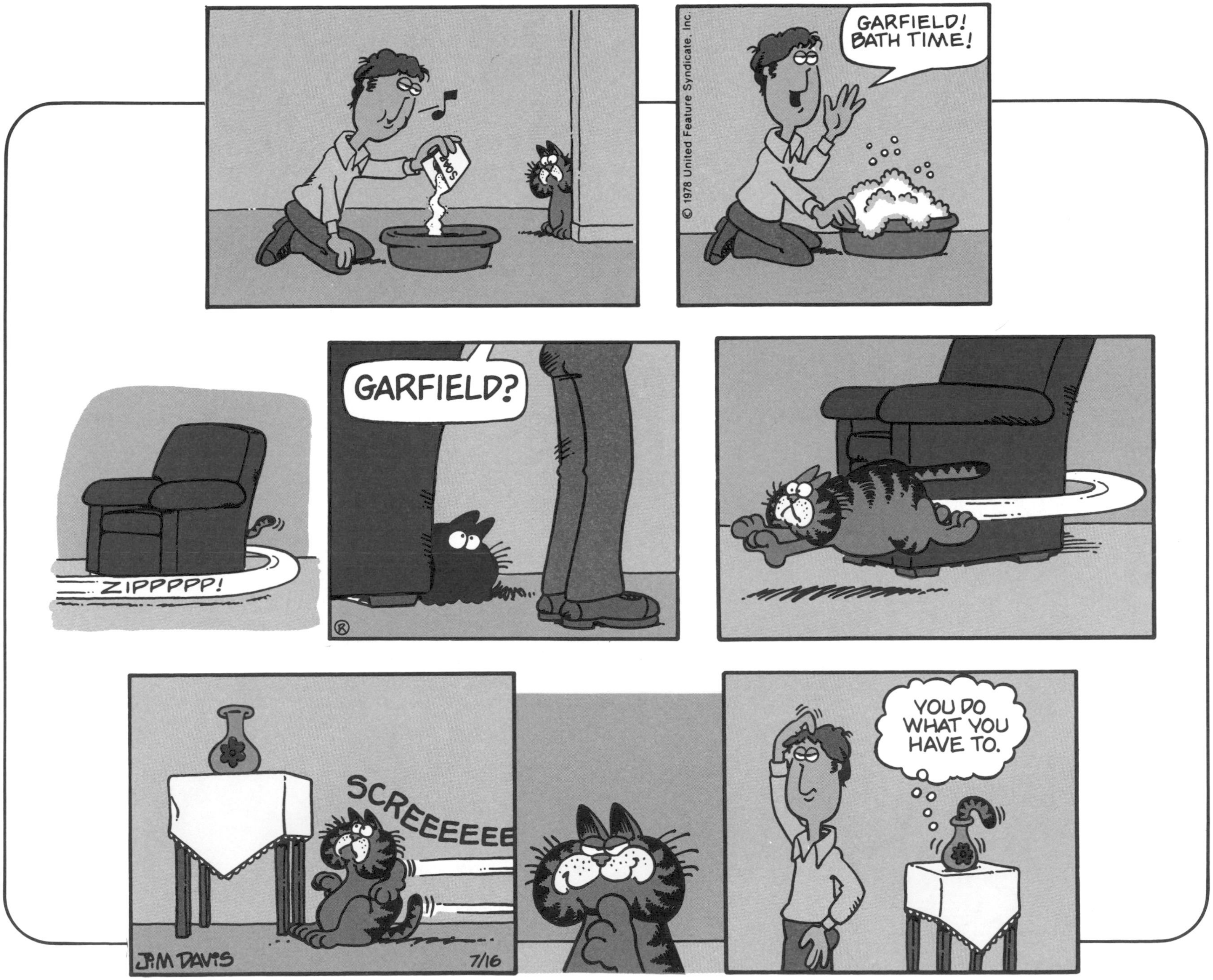
SOAP
© 1978 United Feature Syndicate, Inc.
GARFIELD! BATH TIME!
ZIPPPPPP!
GARFIELD?
SCREEEEEEE
JIM DAVIS
7/16
YOU DO WHAT YOU HAVE TO.

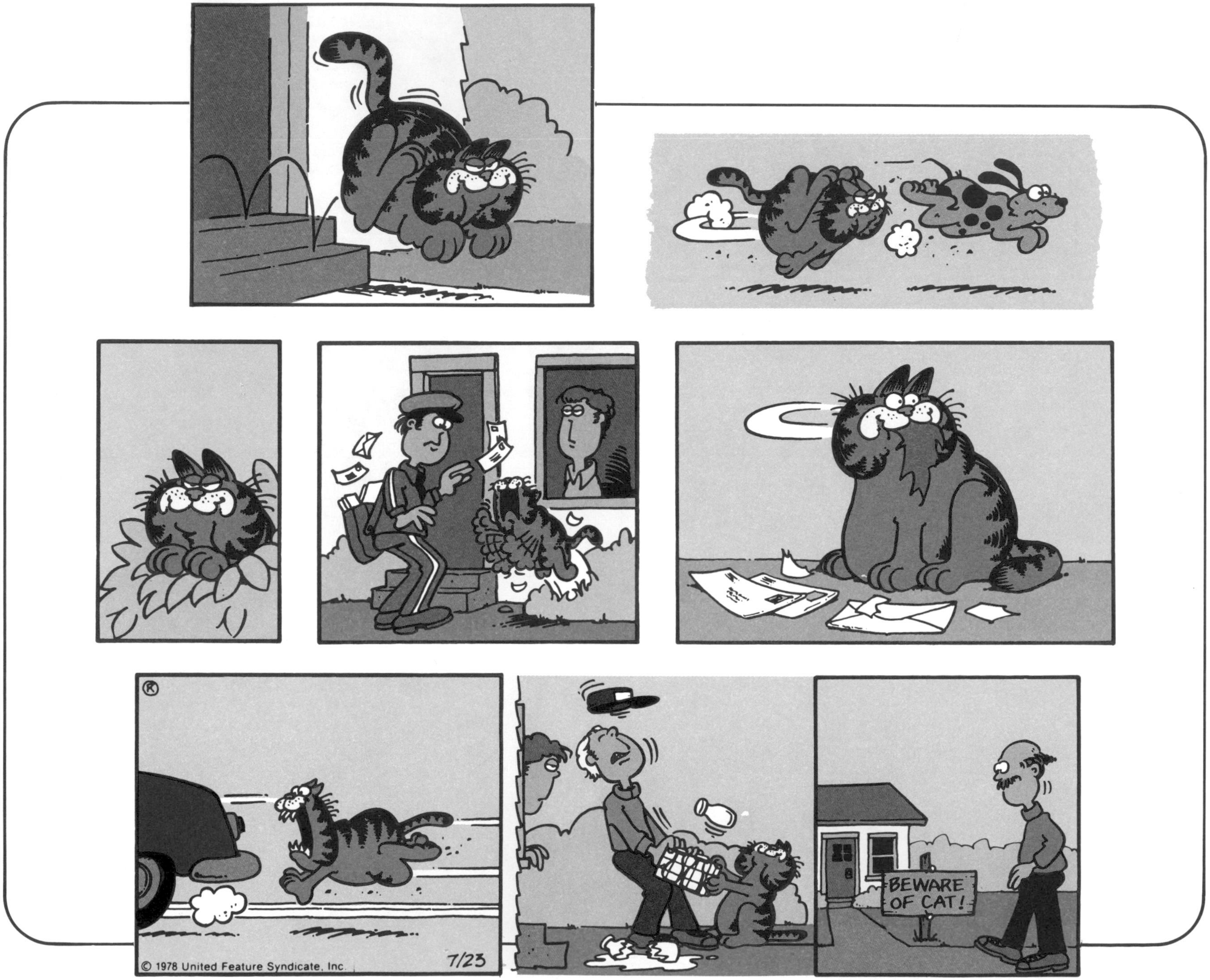
© 1978 United Feature Syndicate, Inc.
7/23
BEWARE OF CAT!

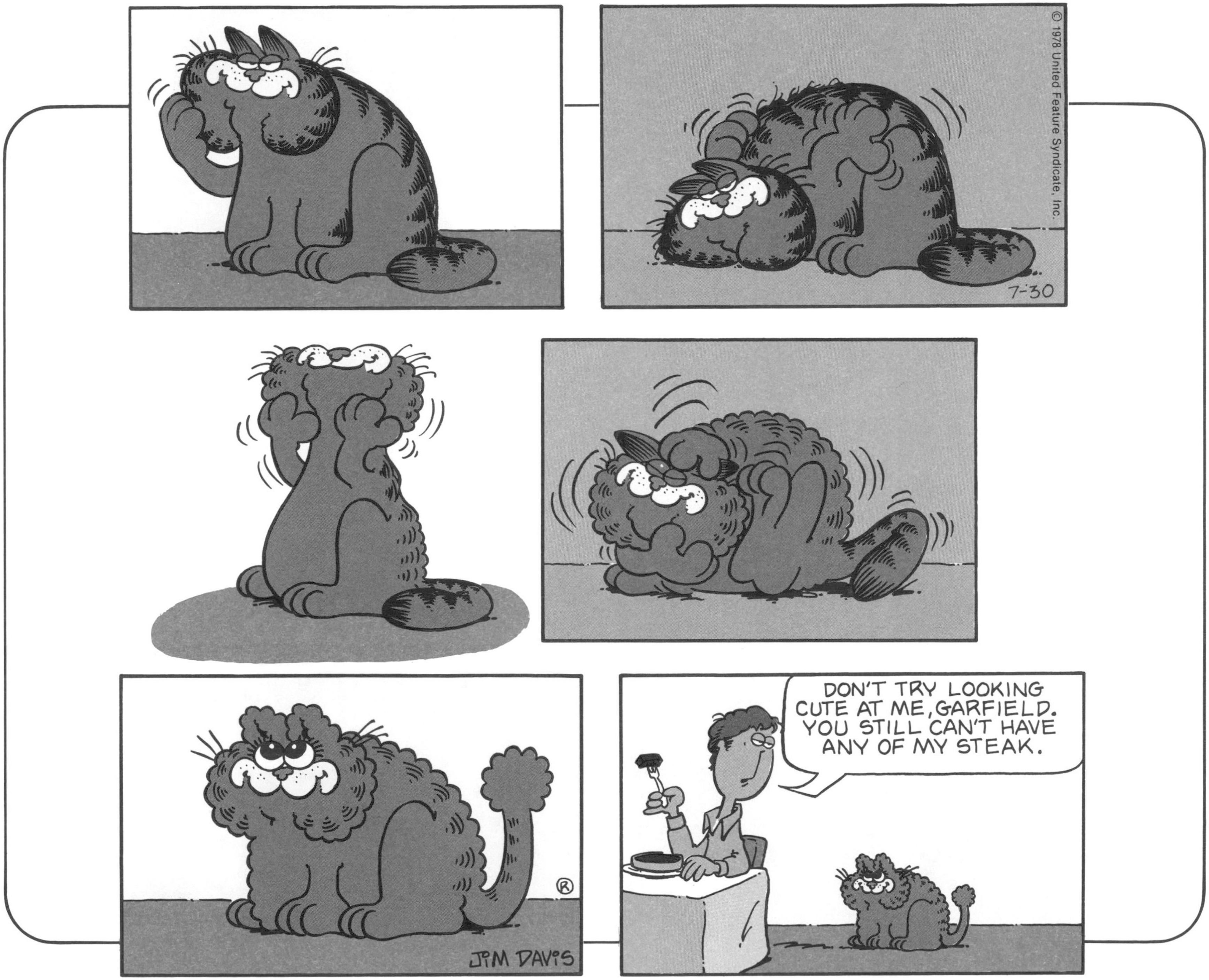
© 1978 United Feature Syndicate, Inc.
7-30
JIM DAVIS
DON'T TRY LOOKING CUTE AT ME, GARFIELD. YOU STILL CAN'T HAVE ANY OF MY STEAK.

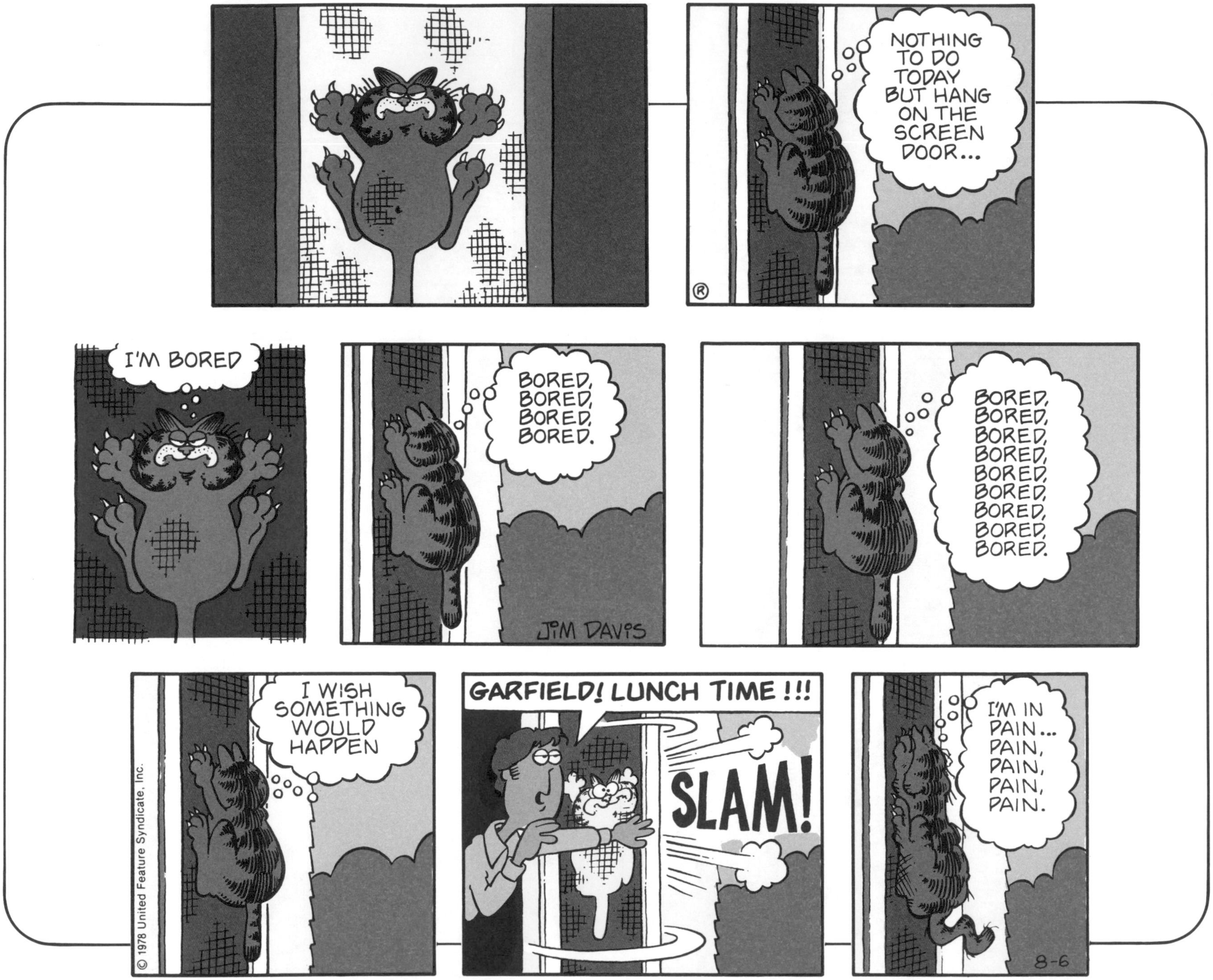

NOTHING TO DO TODAY BUT HANG ON THE SCREEN DOOR...
I'M BORED
BORED, BORED, BORED, BORED.
JIM DAVIS
BORED, BORED, BORED, BORED, BORED, BORED, BORED, BORED, BORED.
I WISH SOMETHING WOULD HAPPEN
© 1978 United Feature Syndicate, Inc.
GARFIELD! LUNCH TIME!!!
SLAM!
I'M IN PAIN... PAIN, PAIN, PAIN, PAIN.
8-6

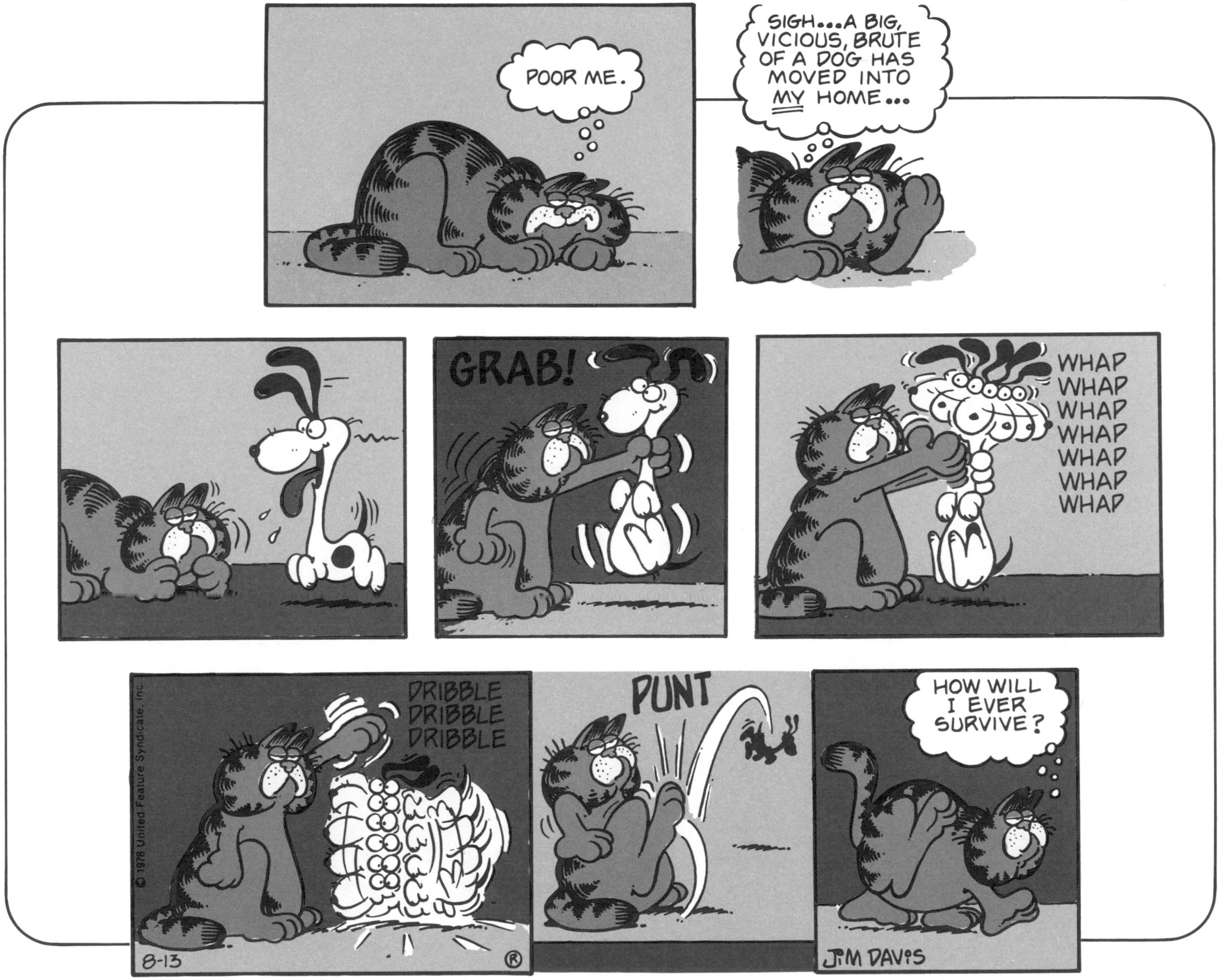
POOR ME.
SIGH...A BIG, VICIOUS, BRUTE OF A DOG HAS MOVED INTO MY HOME...
GRAB!
WHAP WHAP WHAP WHAP WHAP WHAP WHAP
DRIBBLE DRIBBLE DRIBBLE
© 1978 United Feature Syndicate, Inc.
8-13
PUNT
HOW WILL I EVER SURVIVE?
JIM DAVIS

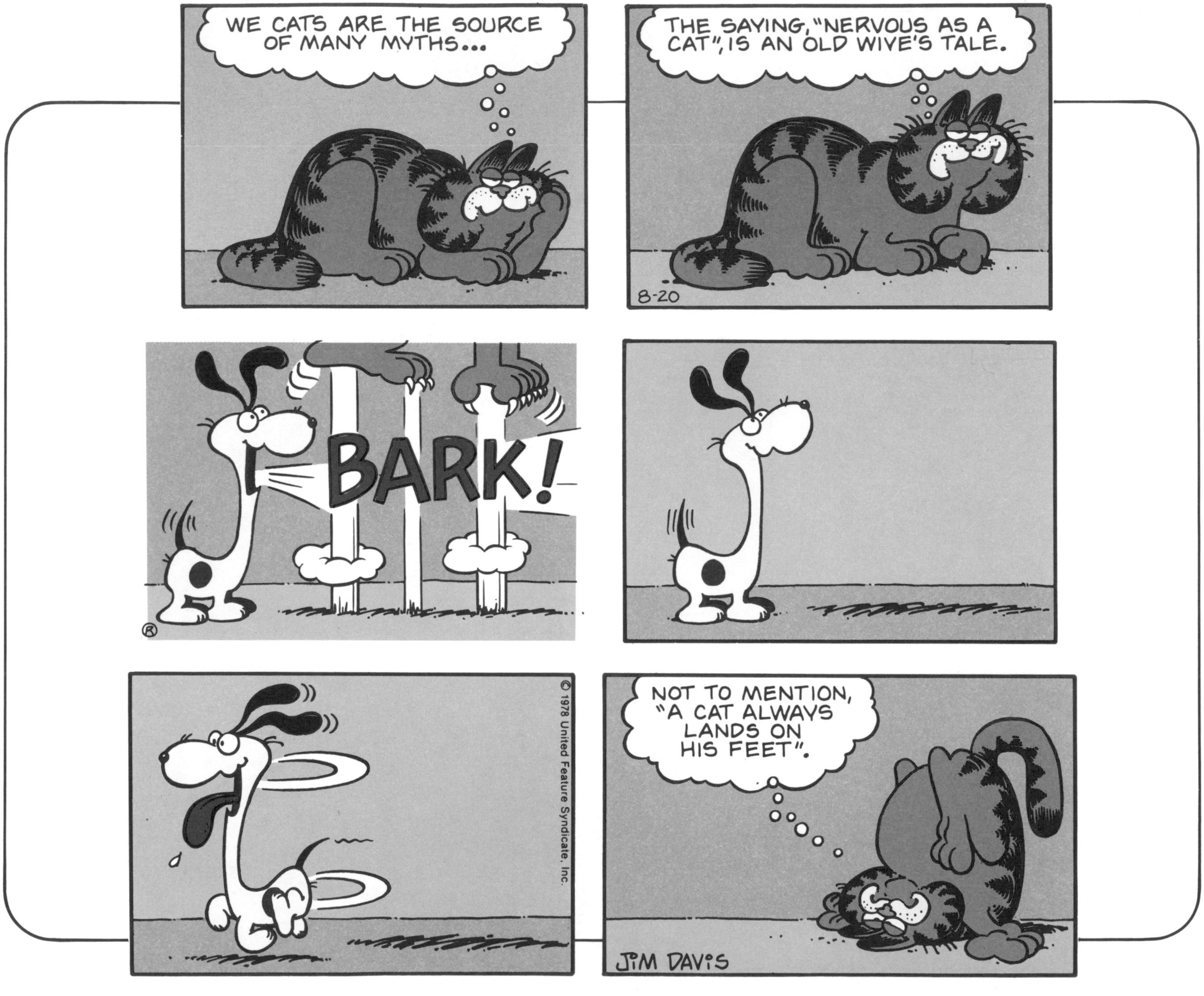
WE CATS ARE THE SOURCE OF MANY MYTHS...
THE SAYING, "NERVOUS AS A CAT", IS AN OLD WIVE'S TALE.
8-20
BARK!
© 1978 United Feature Syndicate, Inc.
NOT TO MENTION, "A CAT ALWAYS LANDS ON HIS FEET".
JIM DAVIS

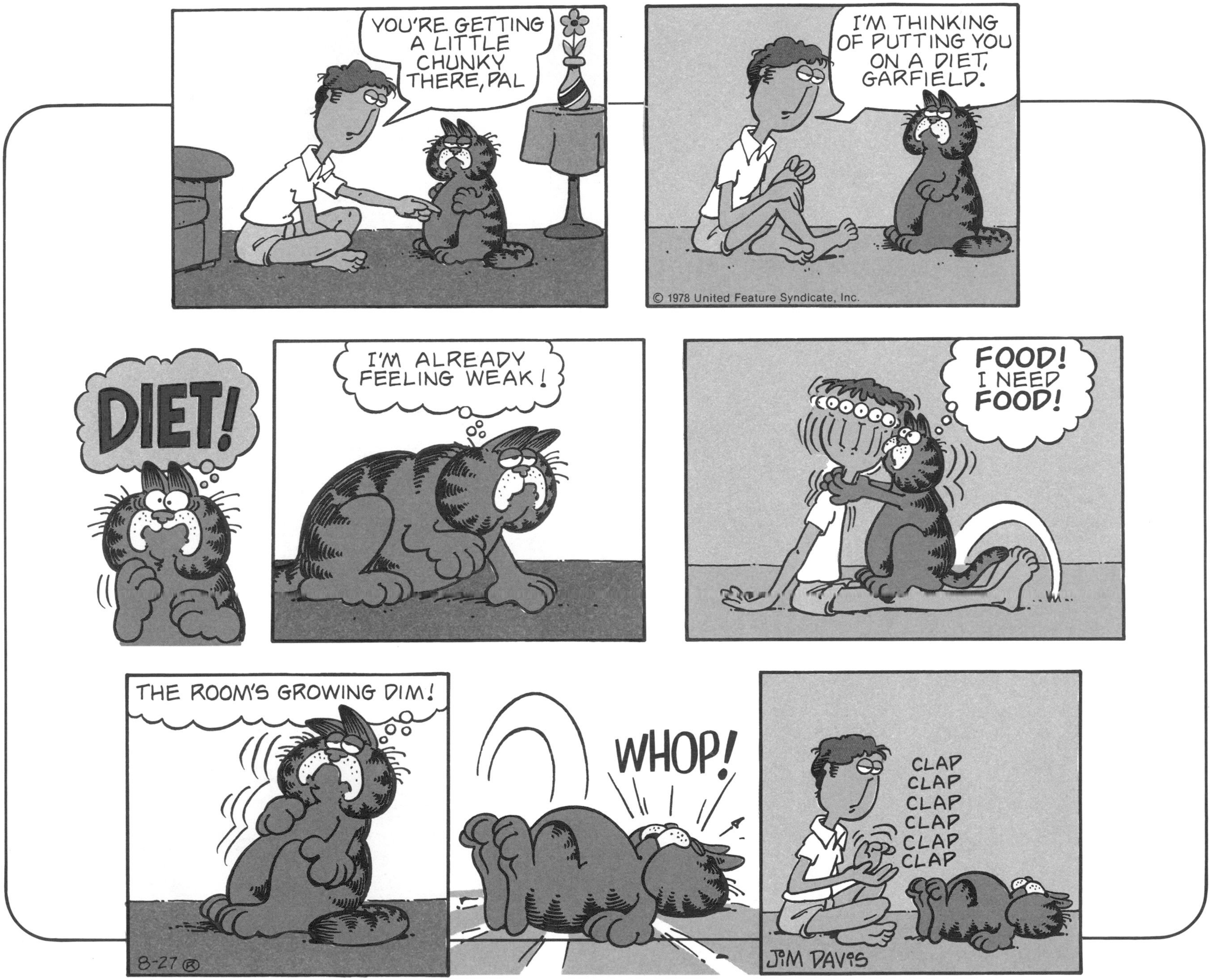
YOU'RE GETTING A LITTLE CHUNKY THERE, PAL
I'M THINKING OF PUTTING YOU ON A DIET, GARFIELD.
© 1978 United Feature Syndicate, Inc.
DIET!
I'M ALREADY FEELING WEAK!
FOOD! I NEED FOOD!
THE ROOM'S GROWING DIM!
8-27 ®
WHOP!
CLAP
CLAP
CLAP
CLAP
CLAP
CLAP
JIM DAVIS

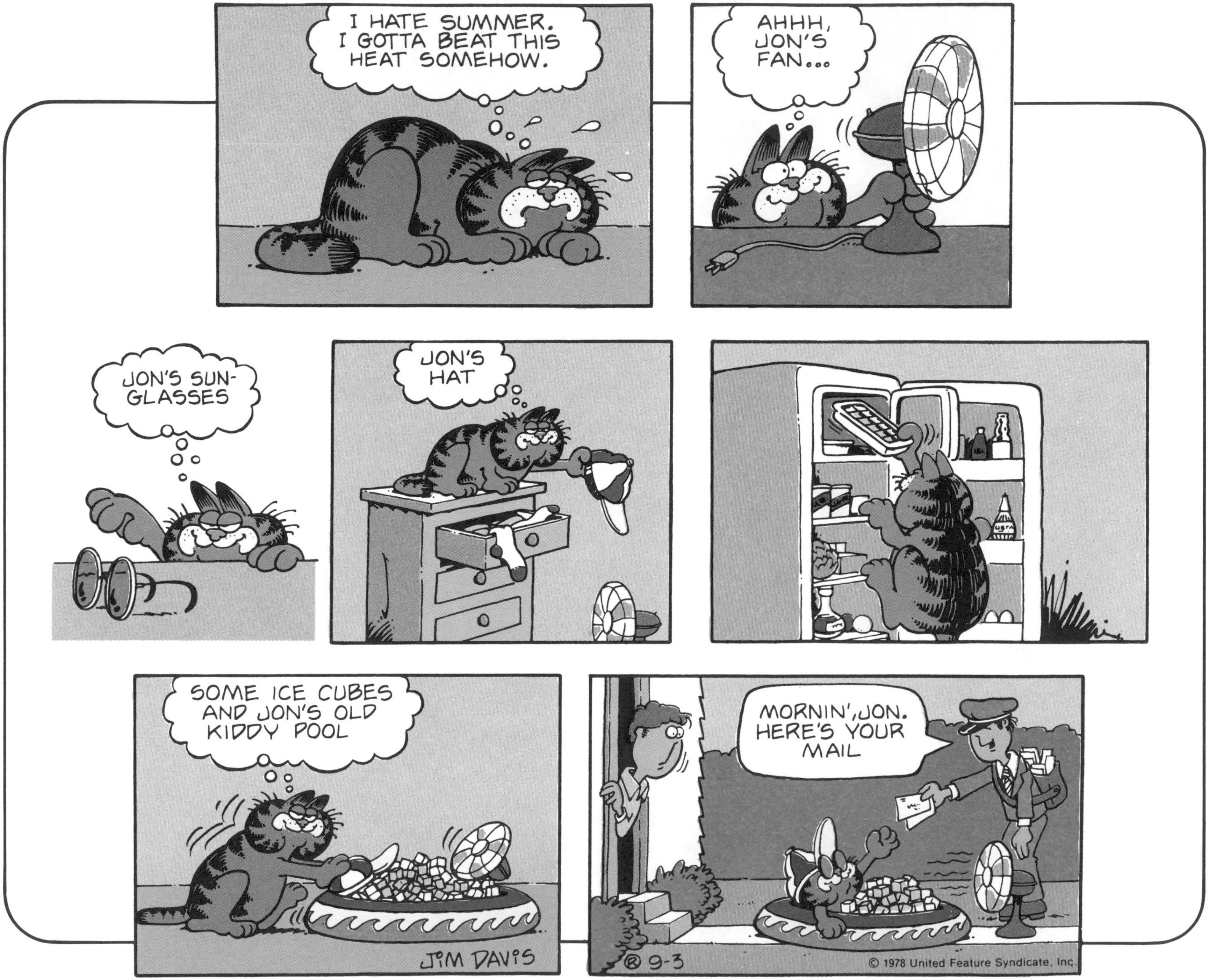
I HATE SUMMER. I GOTTA BEAT THIS HEAT SOMEHOW.
AHHH, JON'S FAN...
JON'S SUN-GLASSES
JON'S HAT
SOME ICE CUBES AND JON'S OLD KIDDY POOL
JIM DAVIS
MORNIN', JON. HERE'S YOUR MAIL
® 9-3
© 1978 United Feature Syndicate, Inc.

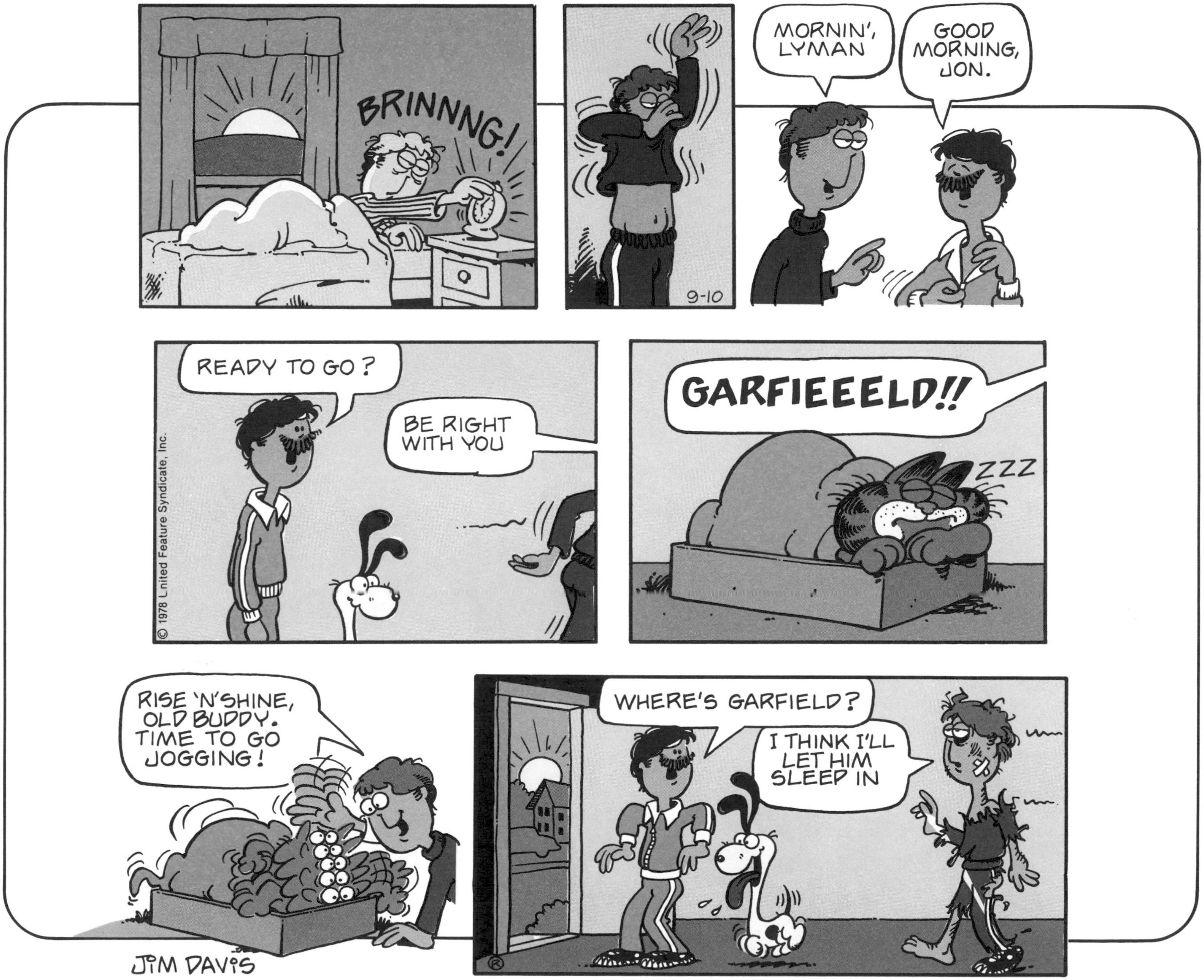
BRINNNG!
9-10
MORNIN', LYMAN
GOOD MORNING, JON.
READY TO GO?
BE RIGHT WITH YOU
© 1978 United Feature Syndicate, Inc.
GARFIEEELD!!
ZZZ
RISE 'N' SHINE, OLD BUDDY. TIME TO GO JOGGING!
WHERE'S GARFIELD?
I THINK I'LL LET HIM SLEEP IN
JIM DAVIS

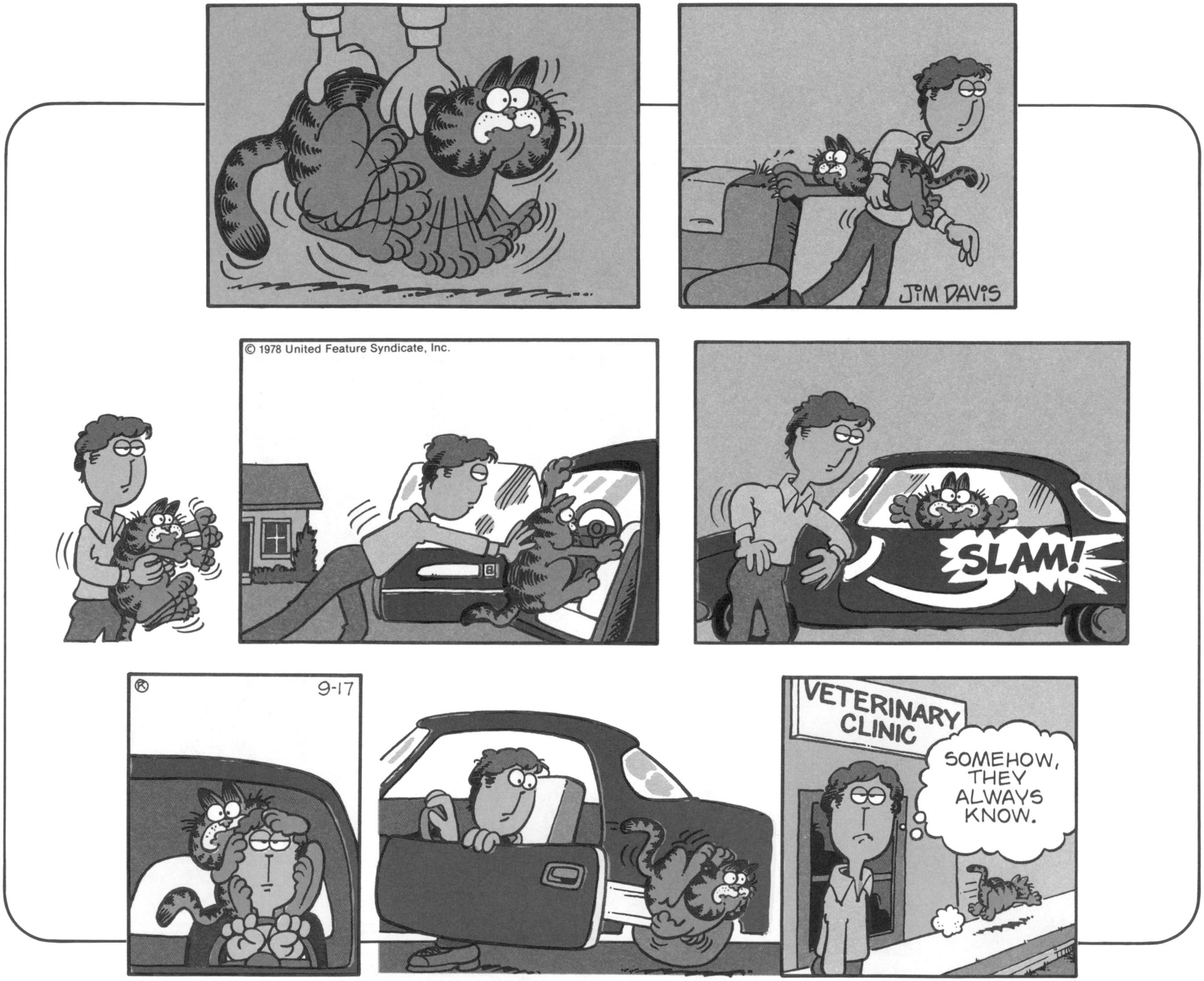
JIM DAVIS
© 1978 United Feature Syndicate, Inc.
SLAM!
9-17
VETERINARY CLINIC
SOMEHOW, THEY ALWAYS KNOW.

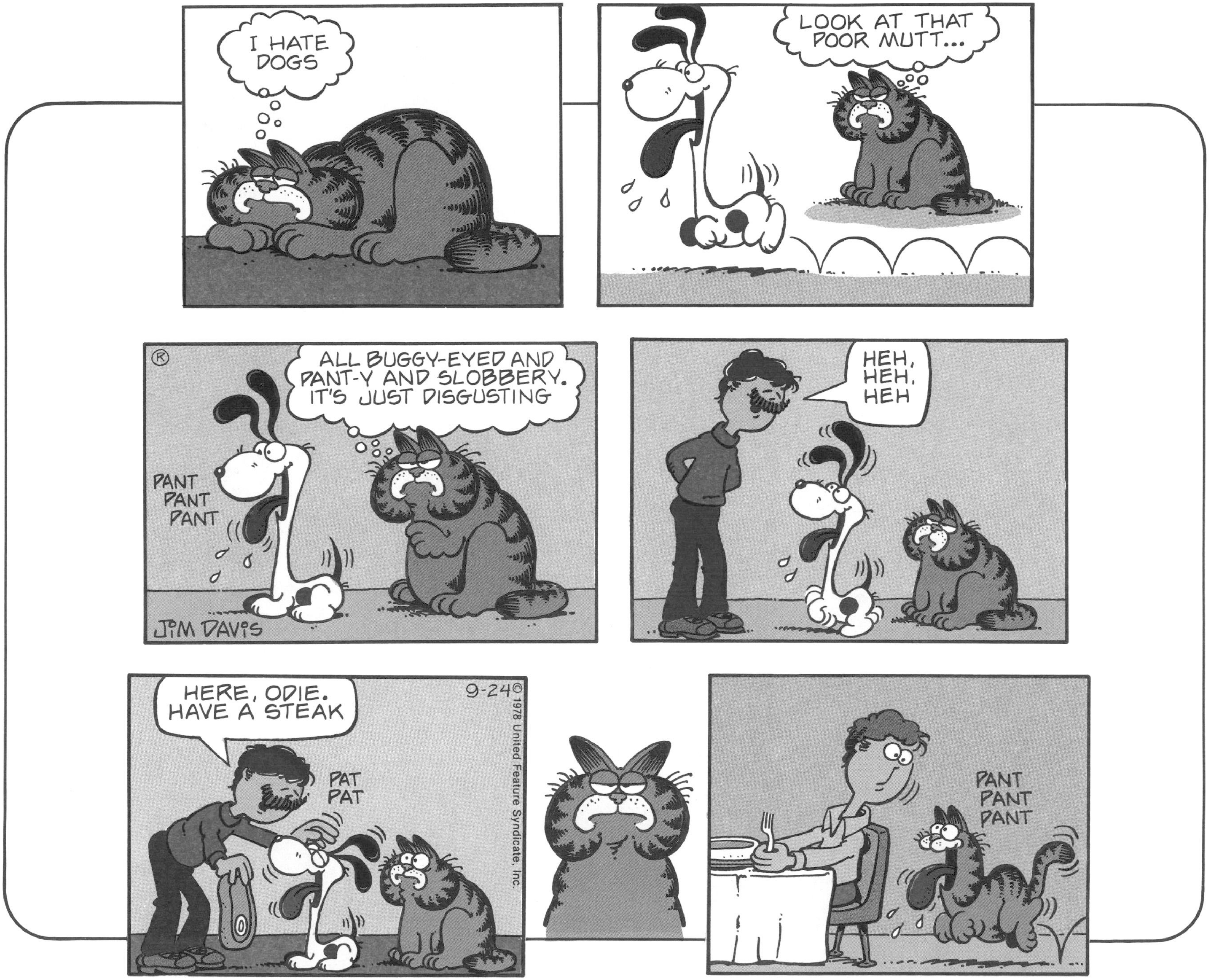

I HATE DOGS
LOOK AT THAT POOR MUTT...
ALL BUGGY-EYED AND PANT-Y AND SLOBBERY. IT'S JUST DISGUSTING
PANT PANT PANT
JIM DAVIS
HEH, HEH, HEH
HERE, ODIE. HAVE A STEAK
9-24 © 1978 United Feature Syndicate, Inc.
PAT PAT
PANT PANT PANT

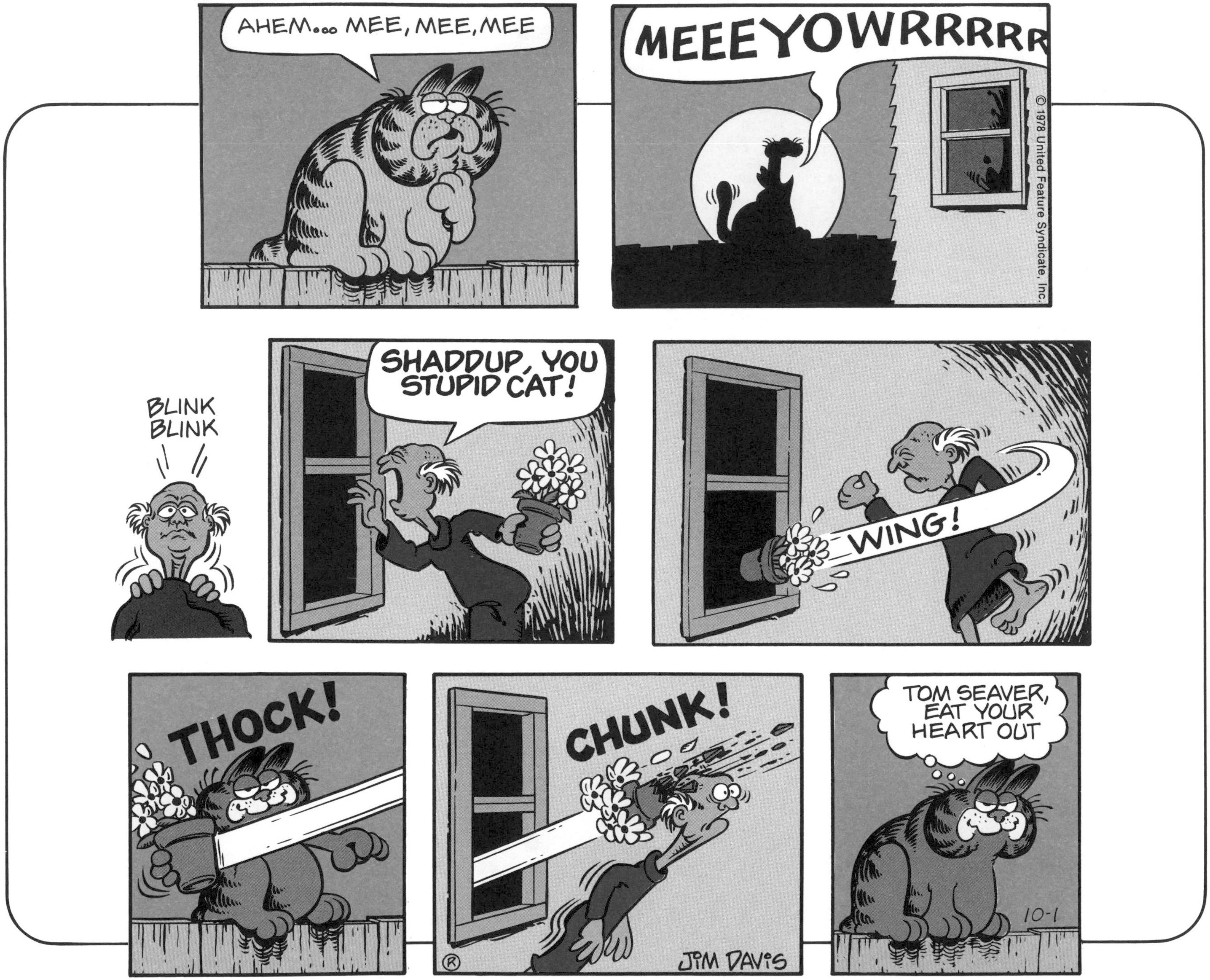
AHEM... MEE, MEE, MEE
MEEEYOWRRRRR
© 1978 United Feature Syndicate, Inc.
BLINK BLINK
SHADDUP, YOU STUPID CAT!
WING!
THOCK!
CHUNK!
JIM DAVIS
TOM SEAVER, EAT YOUR HEART OUT
10-1

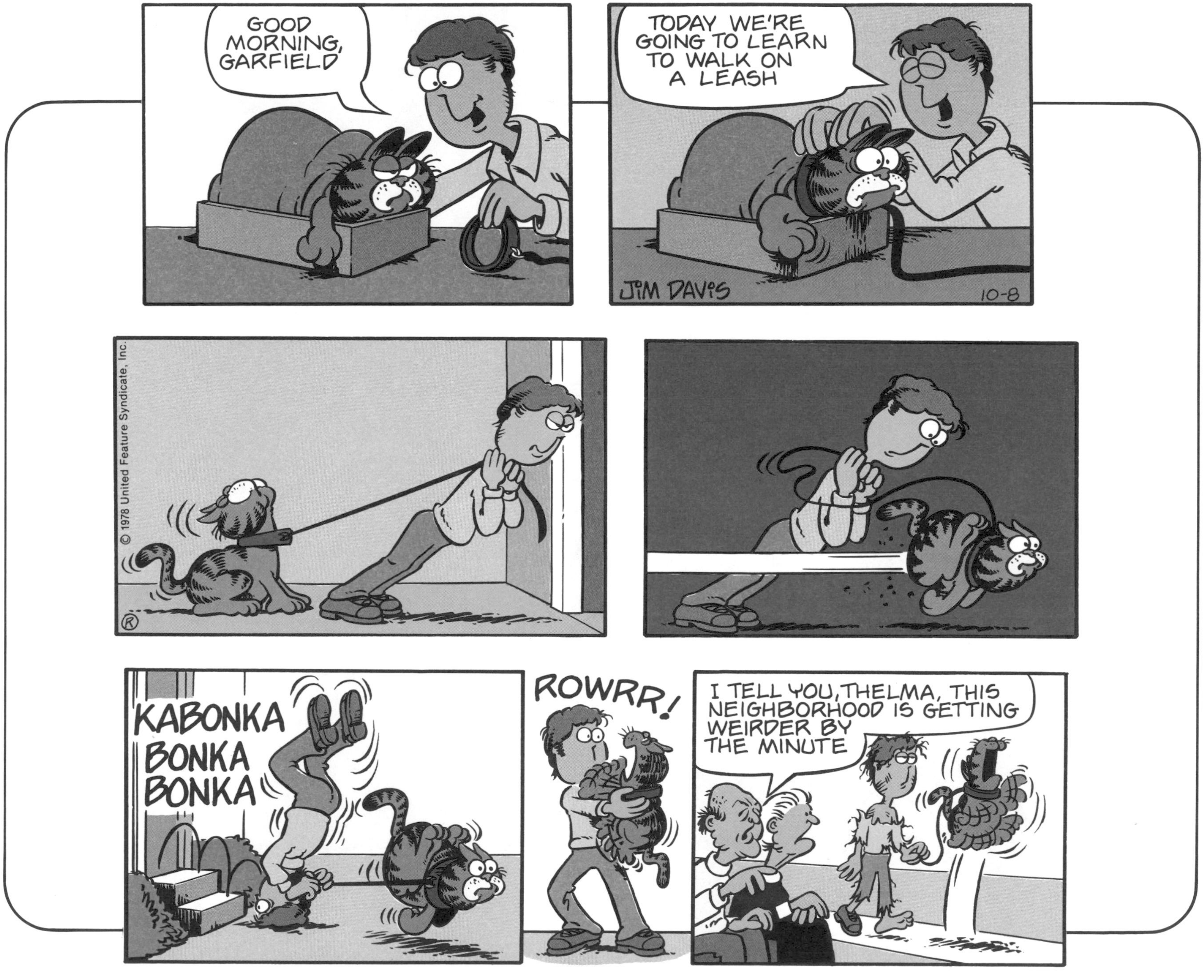
GOOD MORNING, GARFIELD
TODAY WE'RE GOING TO LEARN TO WALK ON A LEASH
JIM DAVIS
10-8
© 1978 United Feature Syndicate, Inc.
KABONKA BONKA BONKA
ROWRR!
I TELL YOU, THELMA, THIS NEIGHBORHOOD IS GETTING WEIRDER BY THE MINUTE

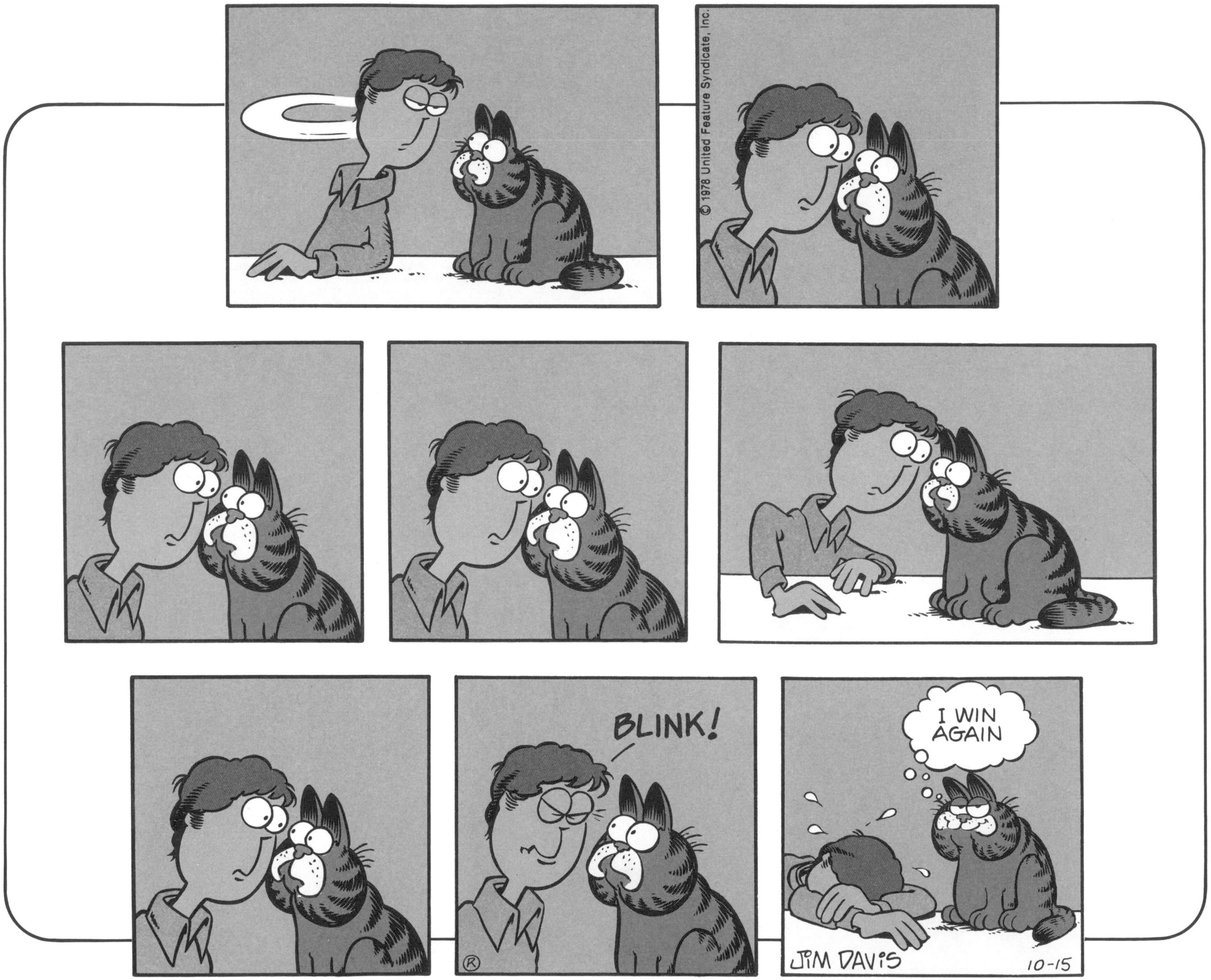
© 1978 United Feature Syndicate, Inc.
BLINK!
I WIN AGAIN
JIM DAVIS
10-15

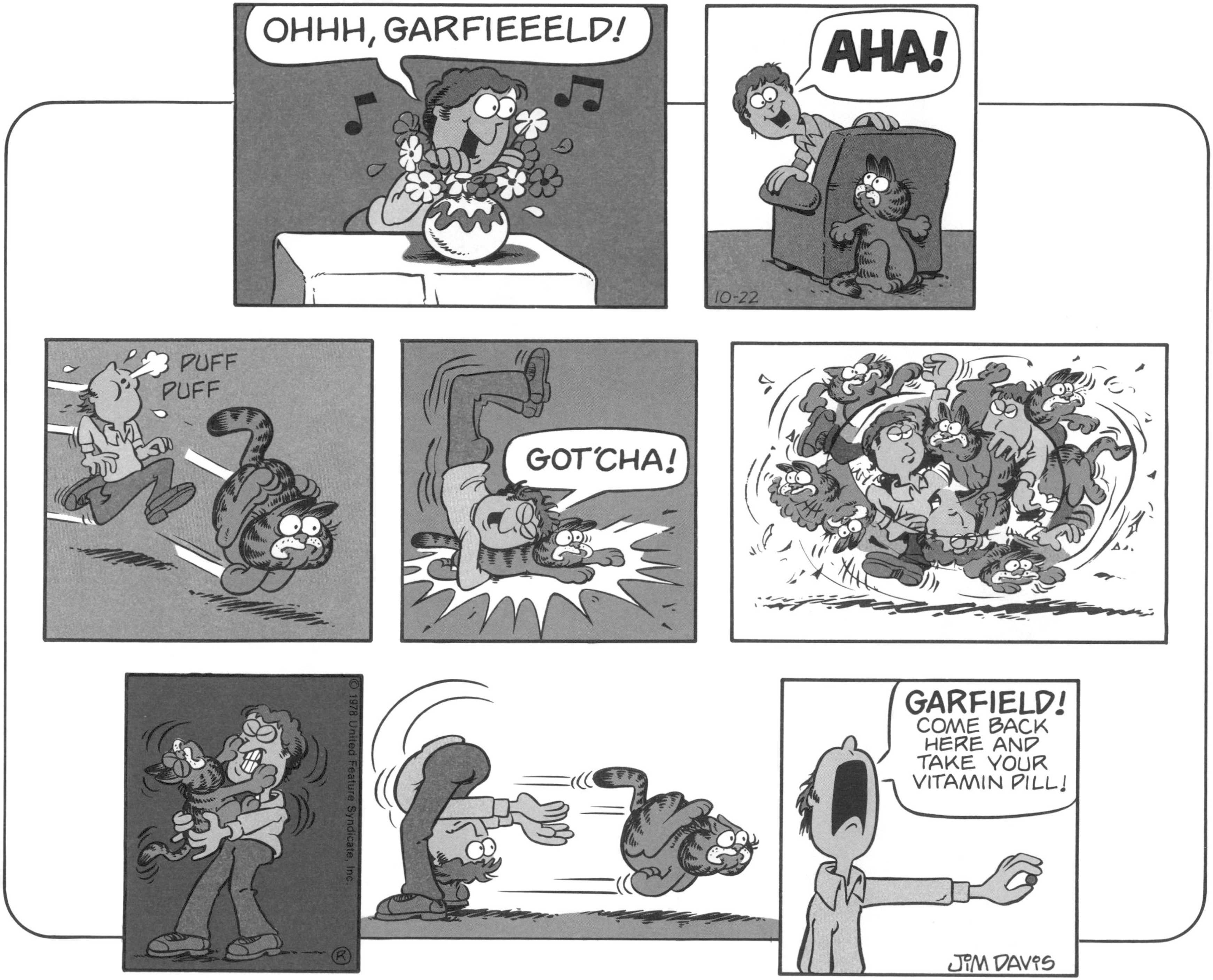
OHHH, GARFIEEELD!
AHA!
10-22
PUFF PUFF
GOT'CHA!
© 1978 United Feature Syndicate, Inc.
GARFIELD! COME BACK HERE AND TAKE YOUR VITAMIN PILL!
JIM DAVIS

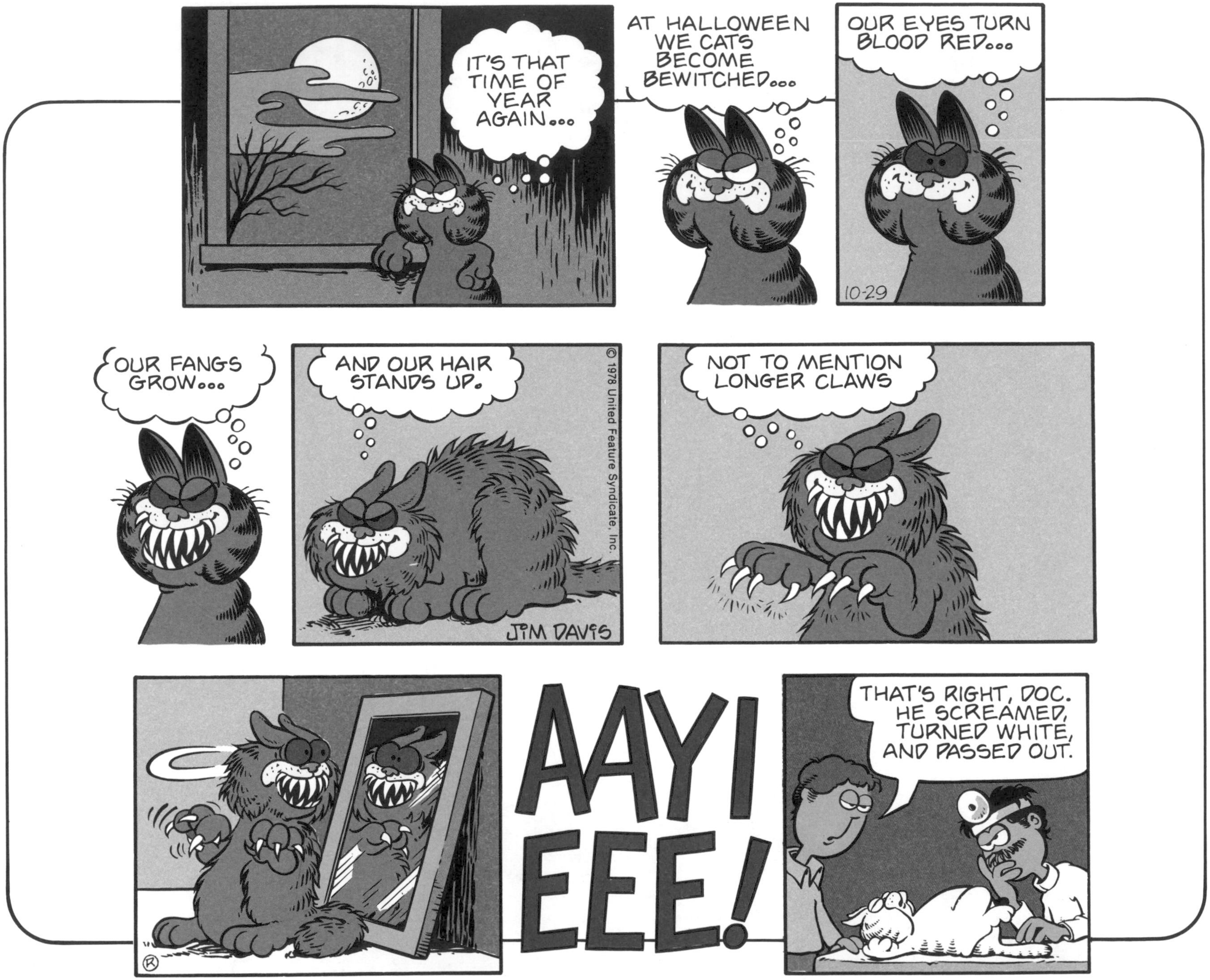
IT'S THAT TIME OF YEAR AGAIN...
AT HALLOWEEN WE CATS BECOME BEWITCHED...
OUR EYES TURN BLOOD RED...
10-29
OUR FANGS GROW...
AND OUR HAIR STANDS UP.
© 1978 United Feature Syndicate, Inc.
JIM DAVIS
NOT TO MENTION LONGER CLAWS
AAYIEEE!
THAT'S RIGHT, DOC. HE SCREAMED, TURNED WHITE, AND PASSED OUT.

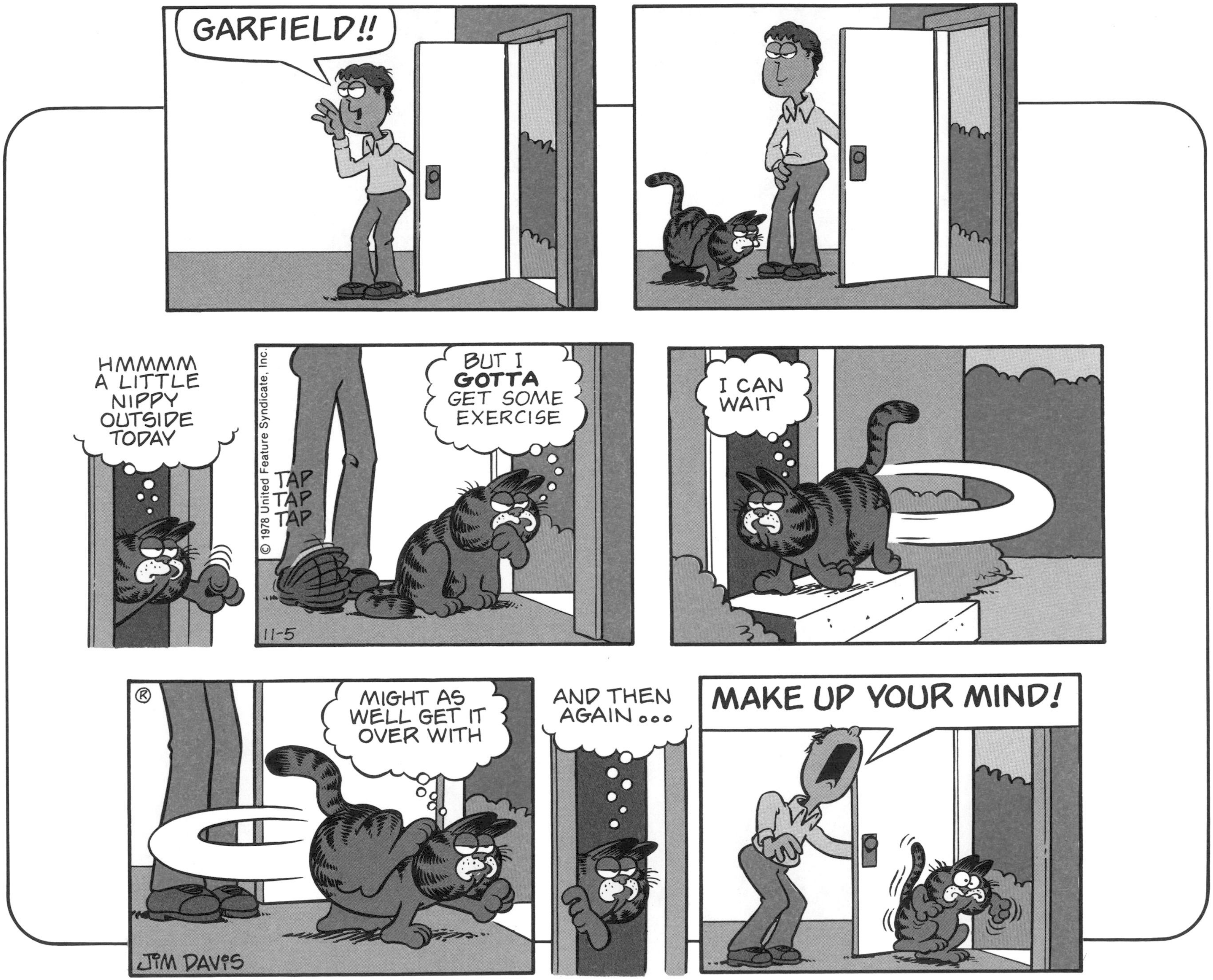
GARFIELD!!
HMMMM A LITTLE NIPPY OUTSIDE TODAY
© 1978 United Feature Syndicate, Inc.
TAP TAP TAP
BUT I GOTTA GET SOME EXERCISE
11-5
I CAN WAIT
®
MIGHT AS WELL GET IT OVER WITH
JIM DAVIS
AND THEN AGAIN...
MAKE UP YOUR MIND!

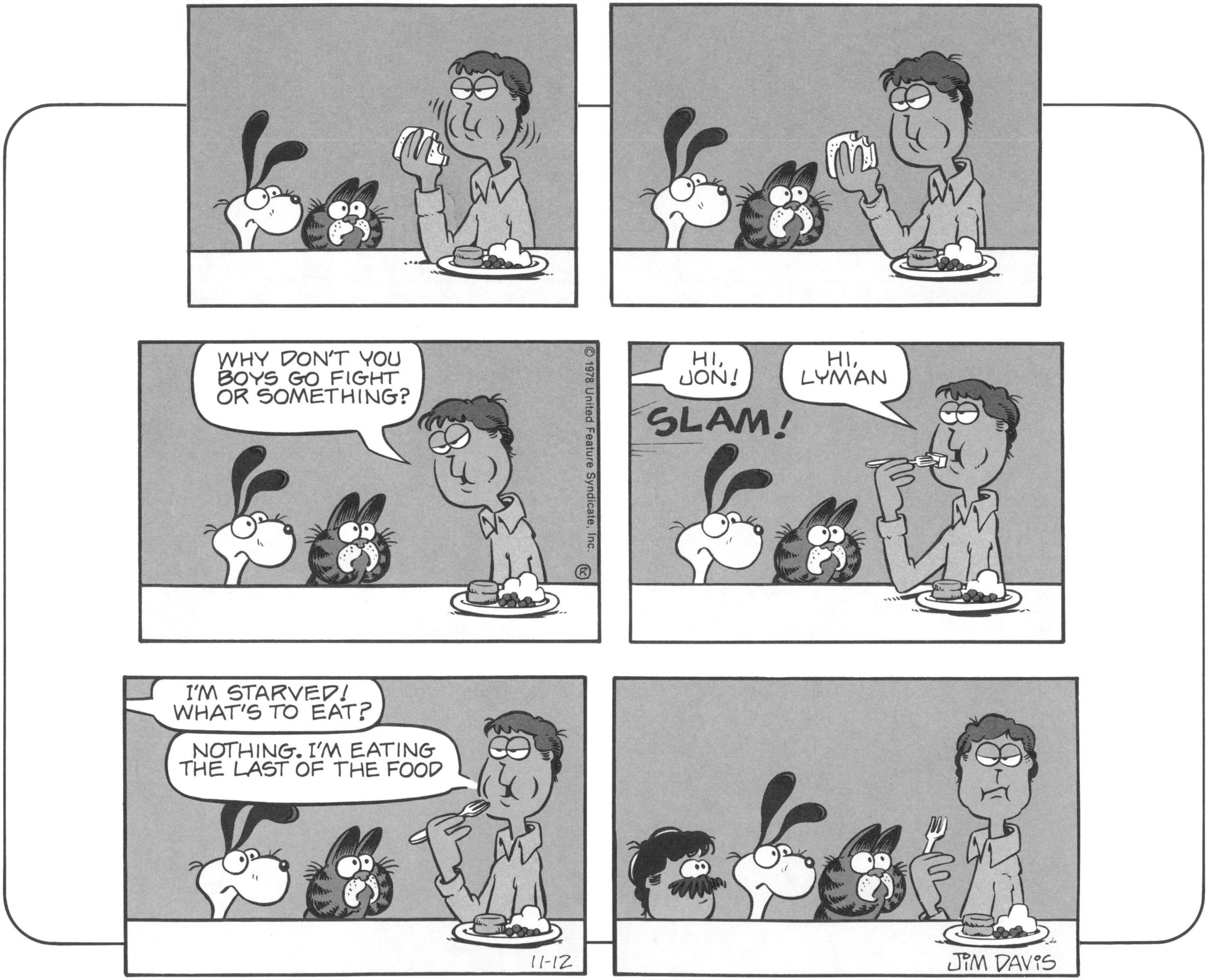
WHY DON'T YOU BOYS GO FIGHT OR SOMETHING?
© 1978 United Feature Syndicate, Inc.
HI, JON!
HI, LYMAN
SLAM!
I'M STARVED! WHAT'S TO EAT?
NOTHING. I'M EATING THE LAST OF THE FOOD
11-12
JIM DAVIS

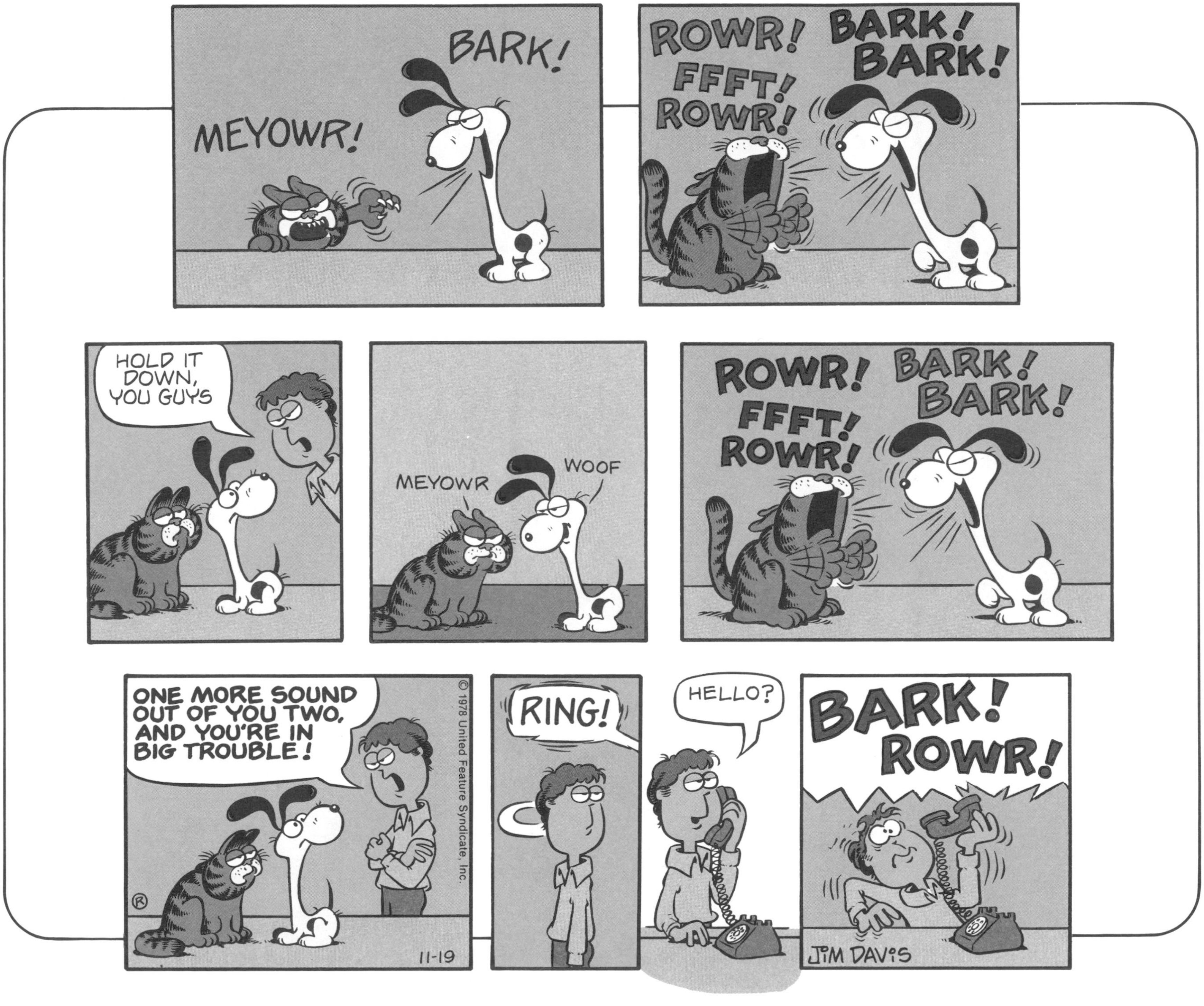
MEYOWR!
BARK!
ROWR! FFFT! ROWR!
BARK! BARK!
HOLD IT DOWN, YOU GUYS
MEYOWR
WOOF
ROWR! FFFT! ROWR!
BARK! BARK!
ONE MORE SOUND OUT OF YOU TWO, AND YOU'RE IN BIG TROUBLE!
© 1978 United Feature Syndicate, Inc.
11-19
RING!
HELLO?
BARK! ROWR!
JIM DAVIS

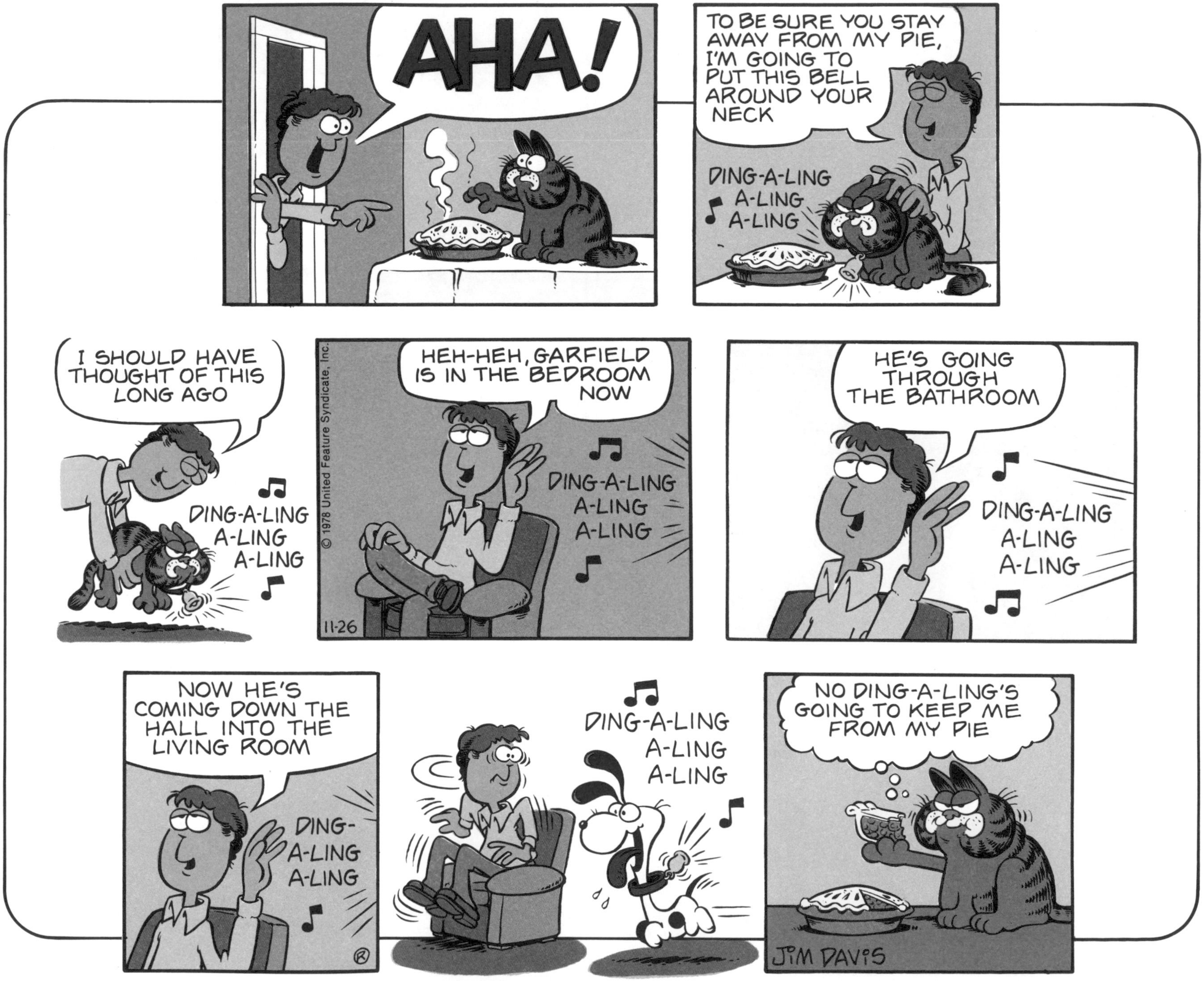
AHA!
TO BE SURE YOU STAY AWAY FROM MY PIE, I'M GOING TO PUT THIS BELL AROUND YOUR NECK
DING-A-LING A-LING A-LING
I SHOULD HAVE THOUGHT OF THIS LONG AGO
DING-A-LING A-LING A-LING
© 1978 United Feature Syndicate, Inc.
HEH-HEH, GARFIELD IS IN THE BEDROOM NOW
DING-A-LING A-LING A-LING
11-26
HE'S GOING THROUGH THE BATHROOM
DING-A-LING A-LING A-LING
NOW HE'S COMING DOWN THE HALL INTO THE LIVING ROOM
DING-A-LING A-LING
DING-A-LING A-LING A-LING
NO DING-A-LING'S GOING TO KEEP ME FROM MY PIE
JIM DAVIS

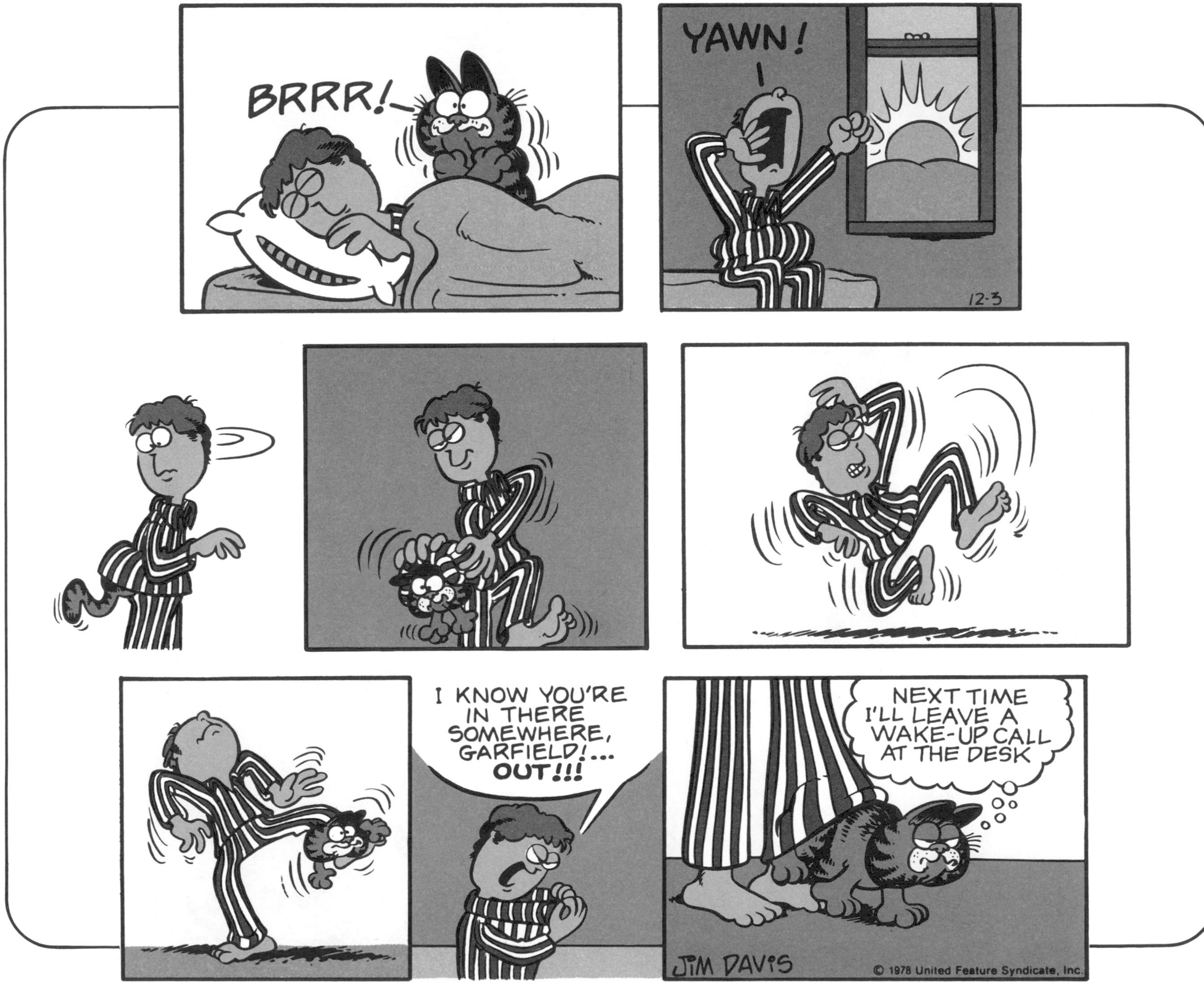
BRRR!
YAWN!
12-3
I KNOW YOU'RE IN THERE SOMEWHERE, GARFIELD!... **OUT!!!**
NEXT TIME I'LL LEAVE A WAKE-UP CALL AT THE DESK
JIM DAVIS
© 1978 United Feature Syndicate, Inc.

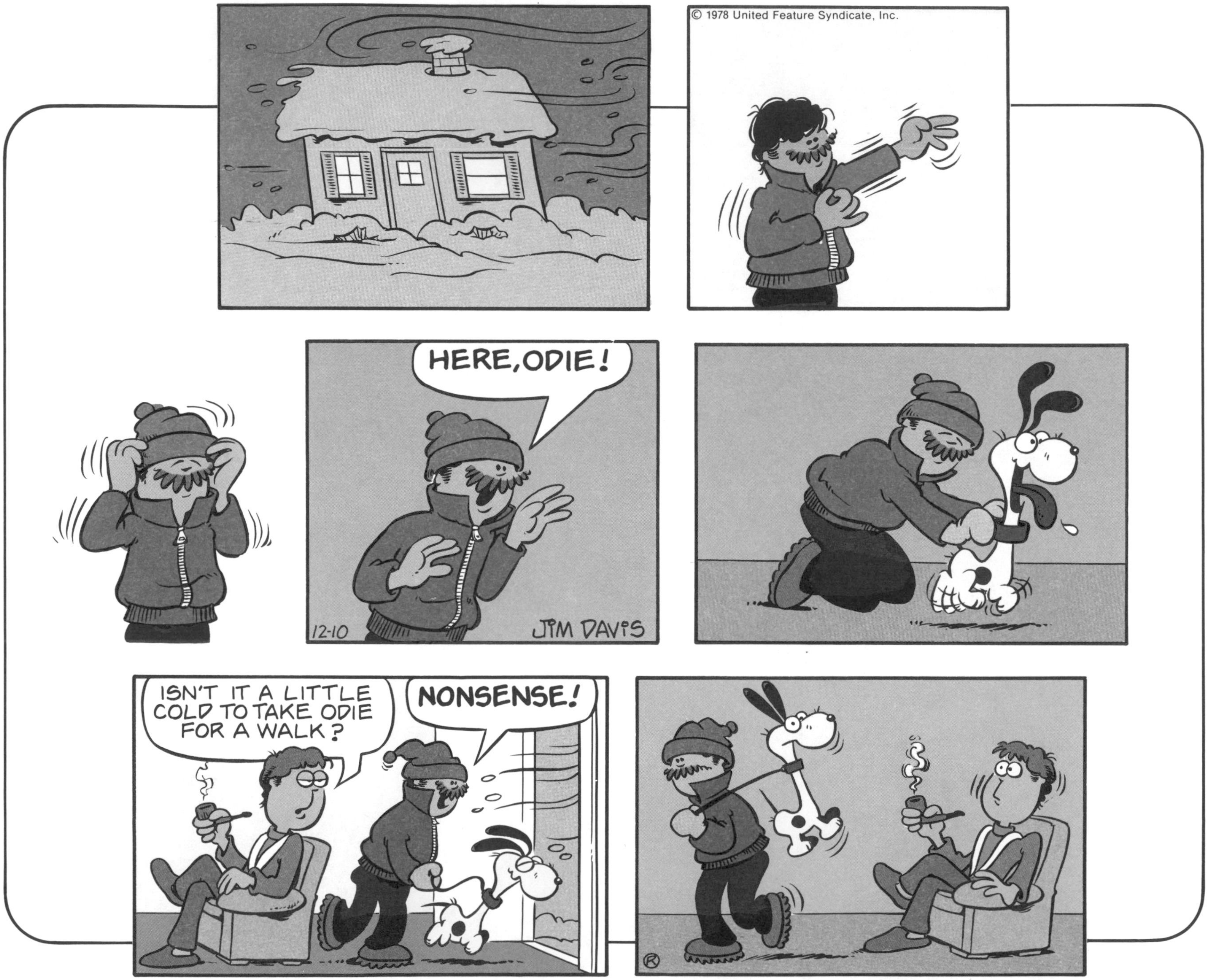
© 1978 United Feature Syndicate, Inc.
HERE, ODIE!
12-10
JIM DAVIS
ISN'T IT A LITTLE COLD TO TAKE ODIE FOR A WALK?
NONSENSE!

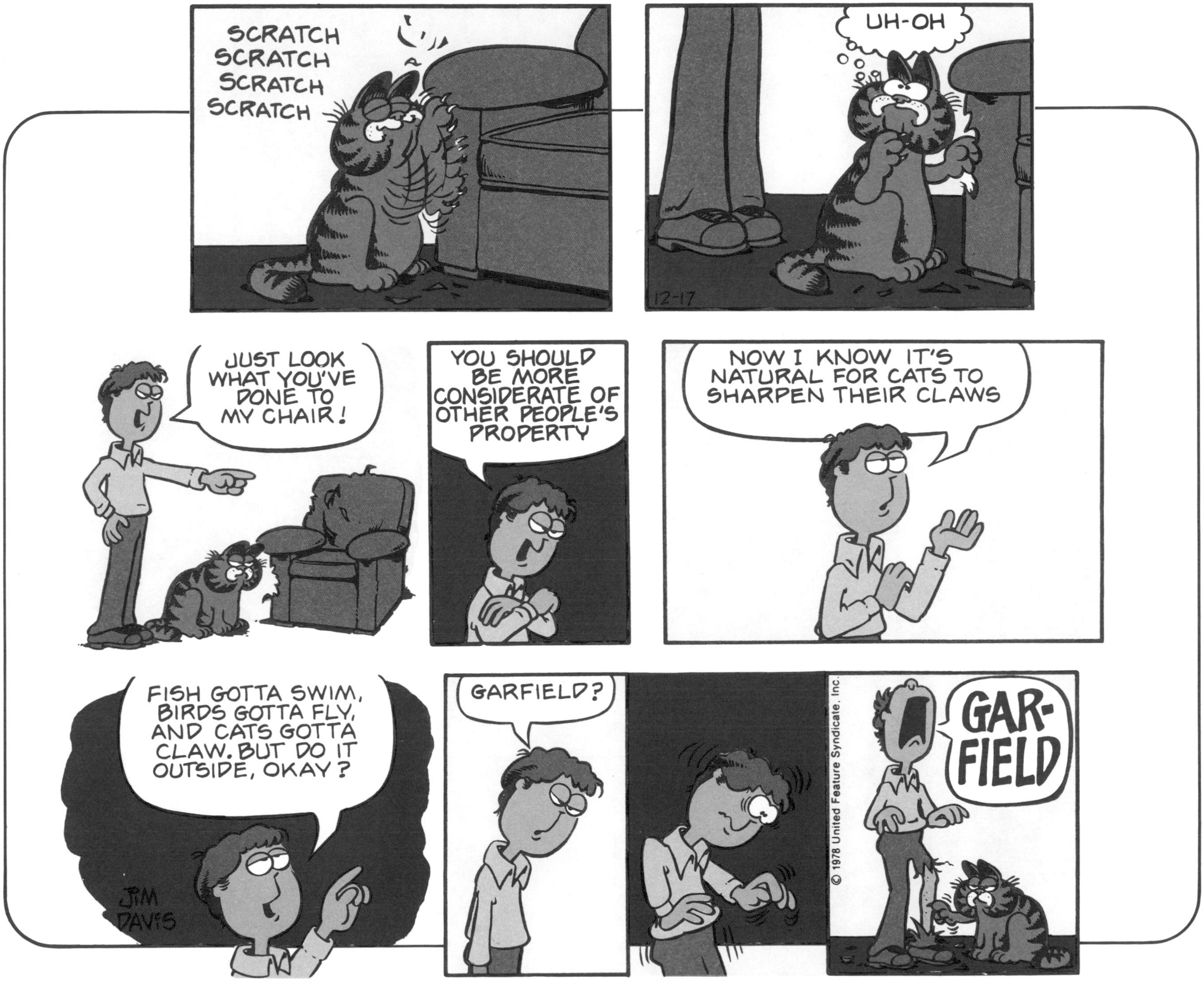
SCRATCH SCRATCH SCRATCH SCRATCH
UH-OH
12-17
JUST LOOK WHAT YOU'VE DONE TO MY CHAIR!
YOU SHOULD BE MORE CONSIDERATE OF OTHER PEOPLE'S PROPERTY
NOW I KNOW IT'S NATURAL FOR CATS TO SHARPEN THEIR CLAWS
FISH GOTTA SWIM, BIRDS GOTTA FLY, AND CATS GOTTA CLAW. BUT DO IT OUTSIDE, OKAY?
JIM DAVIS
GARFIELD?
© 1978 United Feature Syndicate, Inc.
GAR-FIELD

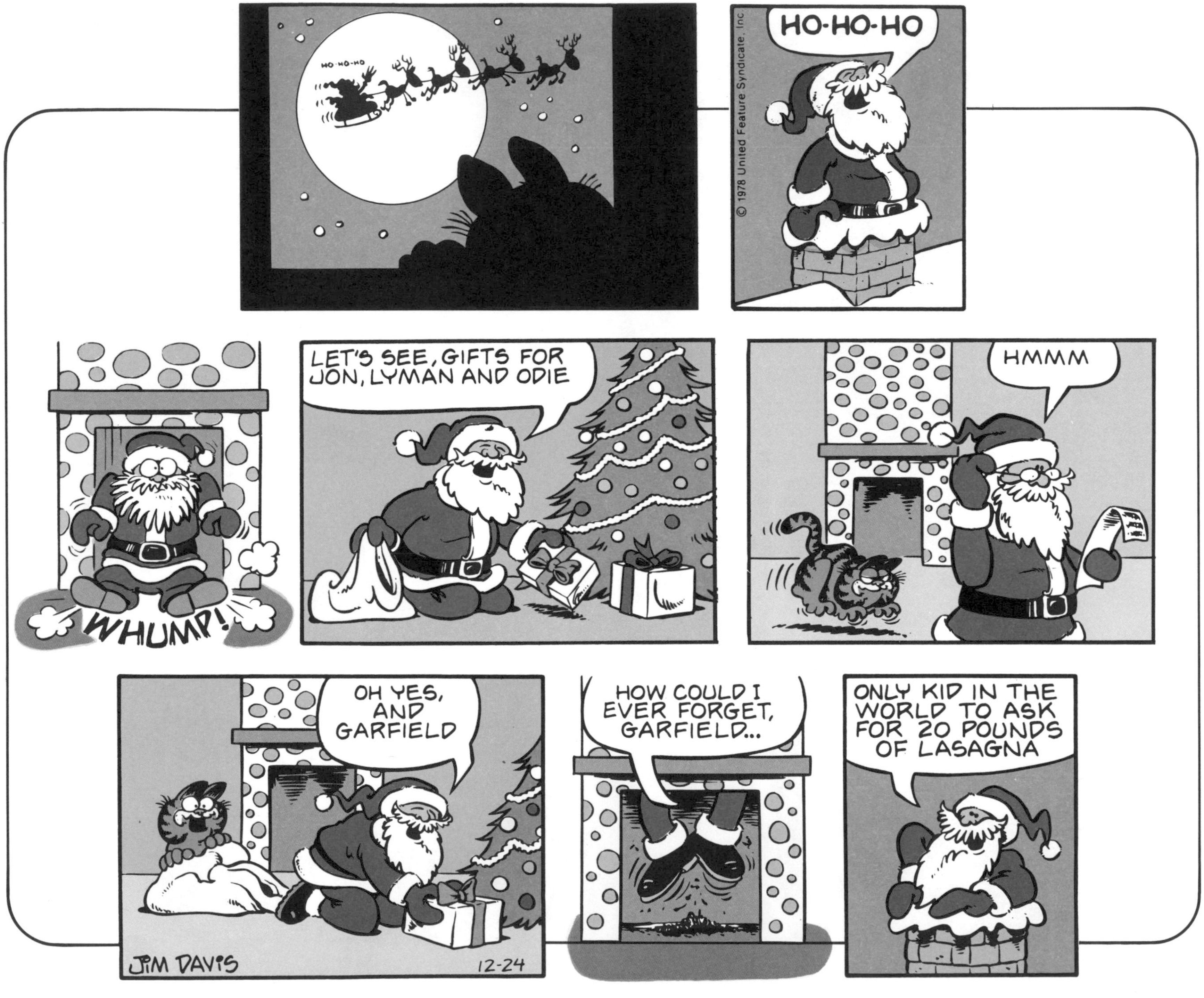
HO-HO-HO
© 1978 United Feature Syndicate, Inc.
HO-HO-HO
WHUMP!
LET'S SEE, GIFTS FOR JON, LYMAN AND ODIE
HMMM
OH YES, AND GARFIELD
JIM DAVIS
12-24
HOW COULD I EVER FORGET, GARFIELD...
ONLY KID IN THE WORLD TO ASK FOR 20 POUNDS OF LASAGNA

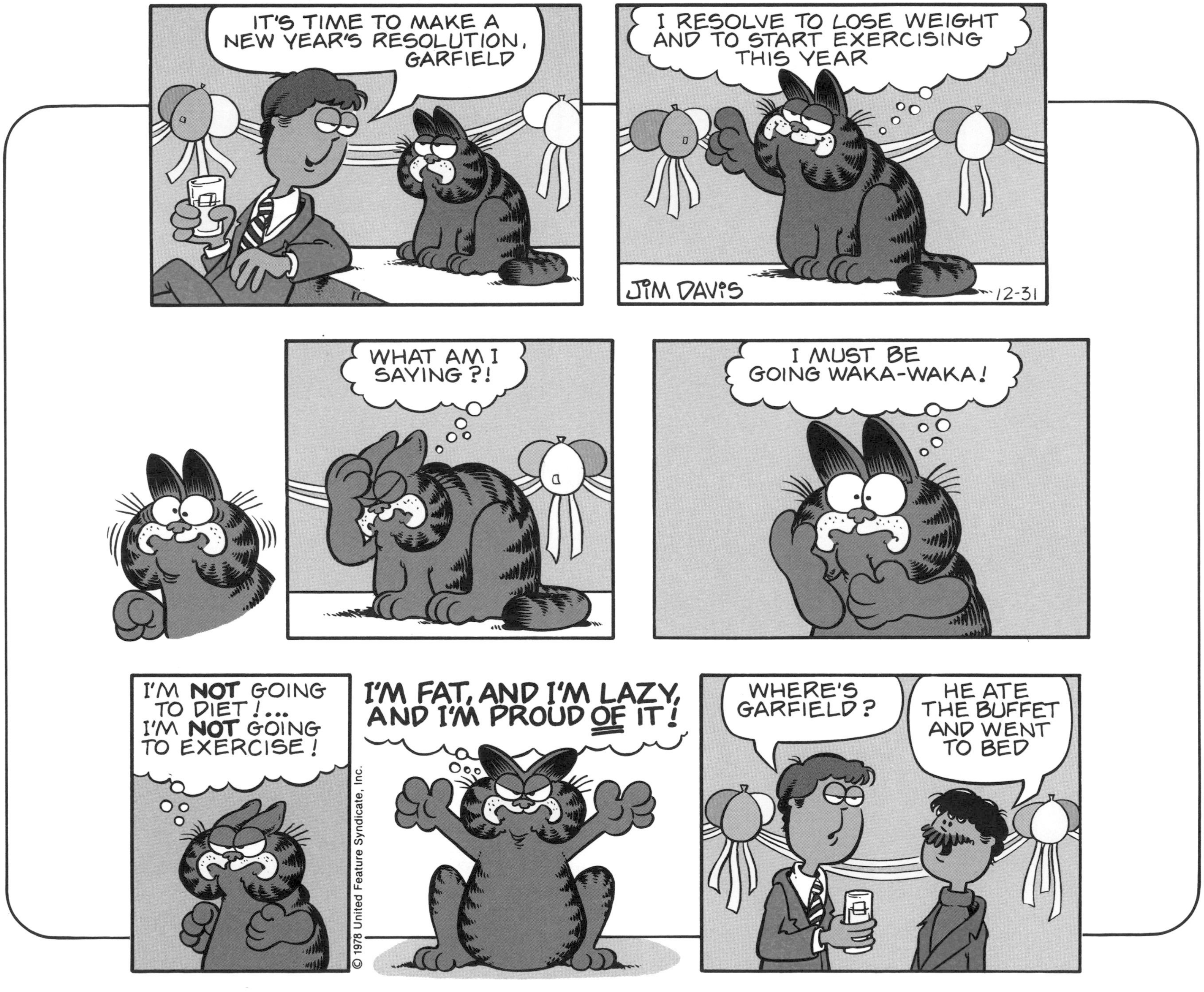
IT'S TIME TO MAKE A NEW YEAR'S RESOLUTION, GARFIELD
I RESOLVE TO LOSE WEIGHT AND TO START EXERCISING THIS YEAR
JIM DAVIS
12-31
WHAT AM I SAYING?!
I MUST BE GOING WAKA-WAKA!
I'M NOT GOING TO DIET!... I'M NOT GOING TO EXERCISE!
© 1978 United Feature Syndicate, Inc.
I'M FAT, AND I'M LAZY, AND I'M PROUD OF IT!
WHERE'S GARFIELD?
HE ATE THE BUFFET AND WENT TO BED

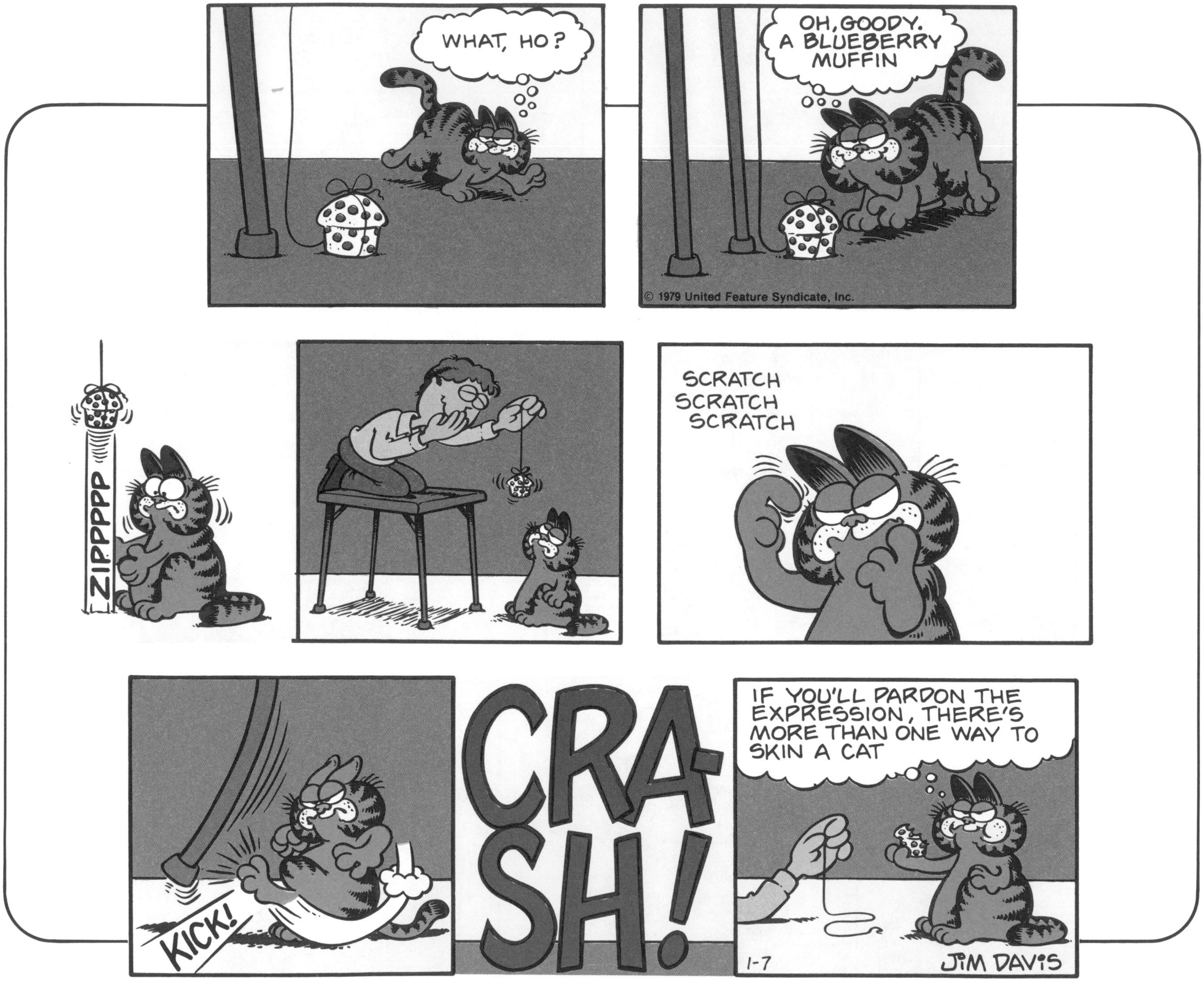
WHAT, HO?
OH, GOODY. A BLUEBERRY MUFFIN
© 1979 United Feature Syndicate, Inc.
ZIPPPPP
SCRATCH SCRATCH SCRATCH
KICK!
CRA-SH!
IF YOU'LL PARDON THE EXPRESSION, THERE'S MORE THAN ONE WAY TO SKIN A CAT
1-7
JIM DAVIS

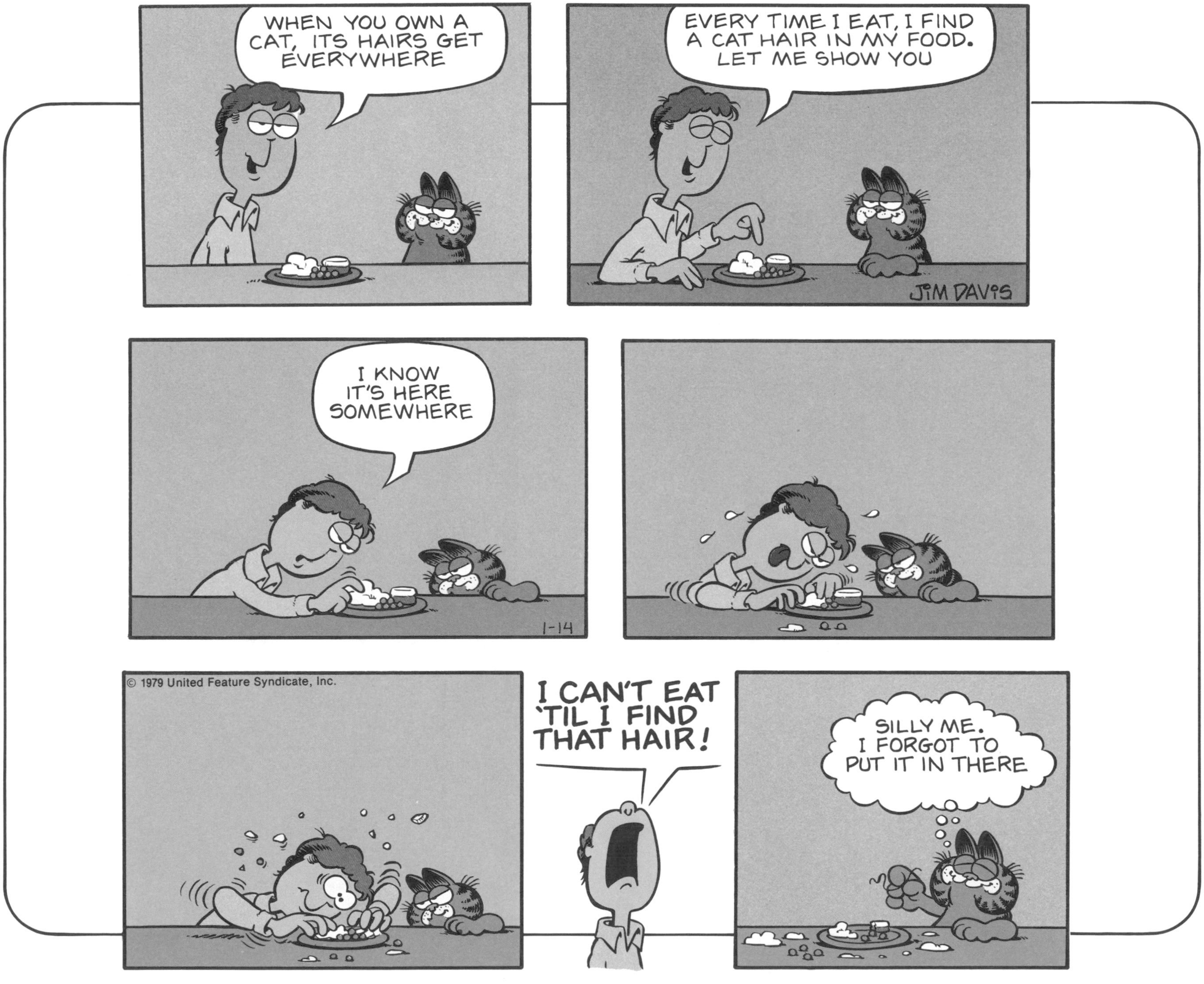
WHEN YOU OWN A CAT, ITS HAIRS GET EVERYWHERE
EVERY TIME I EAT, I FIND A CAT HAIR IN MY FOOD. LET ME SHOW YOU
JIM DAVIS
I KNOW IT'S HERE SOMEWHERE
1-14
© 1979 United Feature Syndicate, Inc.
I CAN'T EAT 'TIL I FIND THAT HAIR!
SILLY ME. I FORGOT TO PUT IT IN THERE

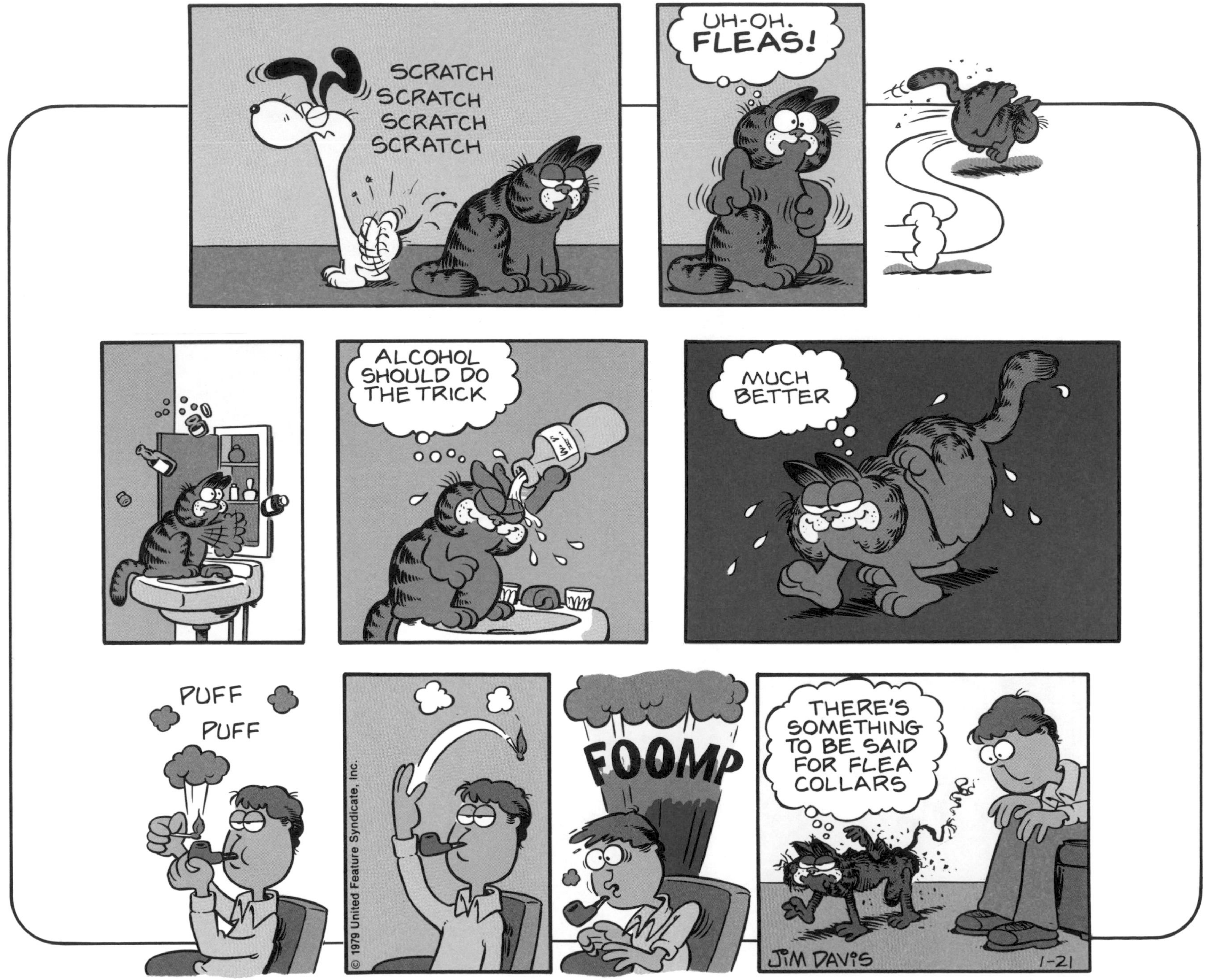
SCRATCH SCRATCH SCRATCH SCRATCH
UH-OH. FLEAS!
ALCOHOL SHOULD DO THE TRICK
MUCH BETTER
PUFF PUFF
FOOMP
THERE'S SOMETHING TO BE SAID FOR FLEA COLLARS
© 1979 United Feature Syndicate, Inc.
JIM DAVIS
1-21

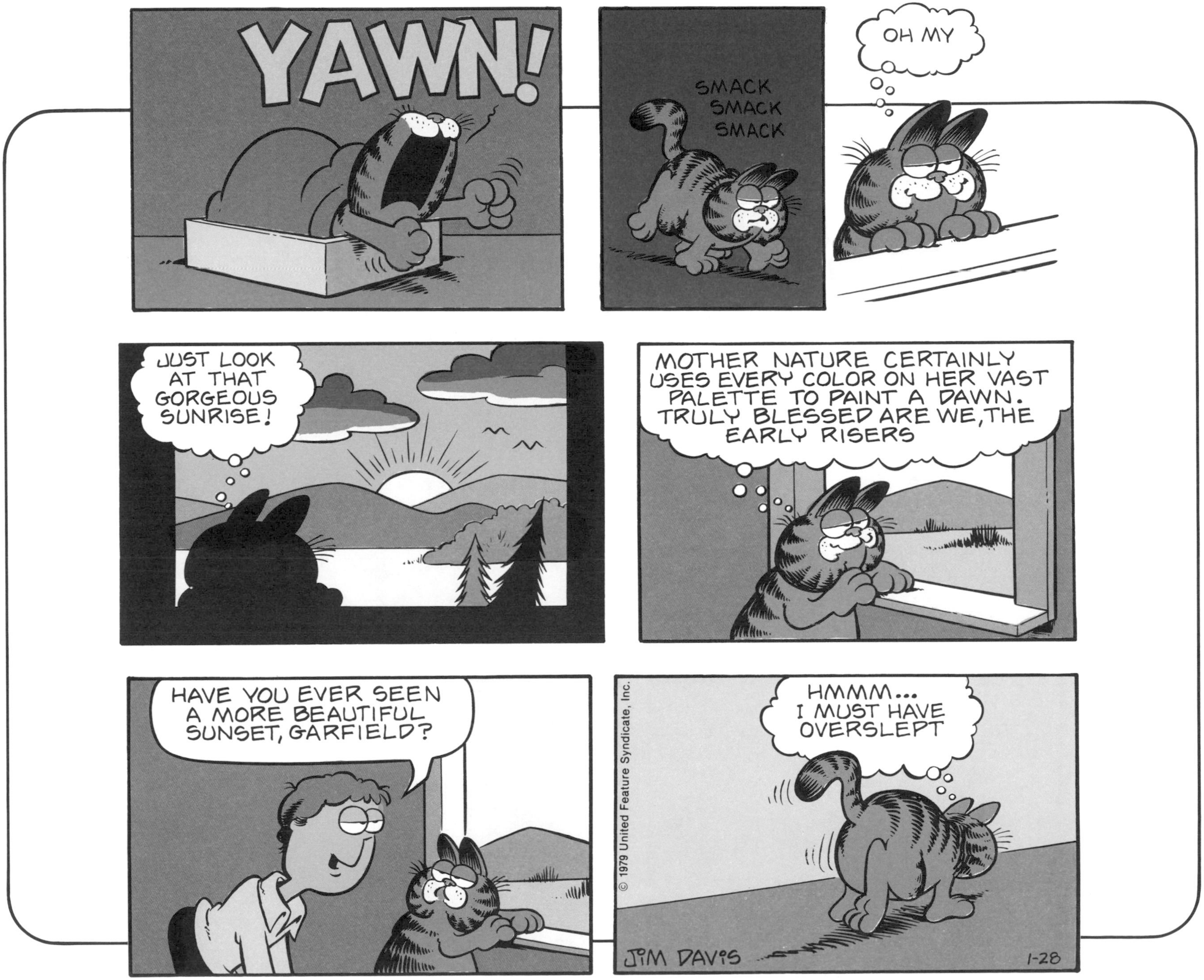
YAWN!
SMACK SMACK SMACK
OH MY
JUST LOOK AT THAT GORGEOUS SUNRISE!
MOTHER NATURE CERTAINLY USES EVERY COLOR ON HER VAST PALETTE TO PAINT A DAWN. TRULY BLESSED ARE WE, THE EARLY RISERS
HAVE YOU EVER SEEN A MORE BEAUTIFUL SUNSET, GARFIELD?
© 1979 United Feature Syndicate, Inc.
HMMM... I MUST HAVE OVERSLEPT
JIM DAVIS
1-28

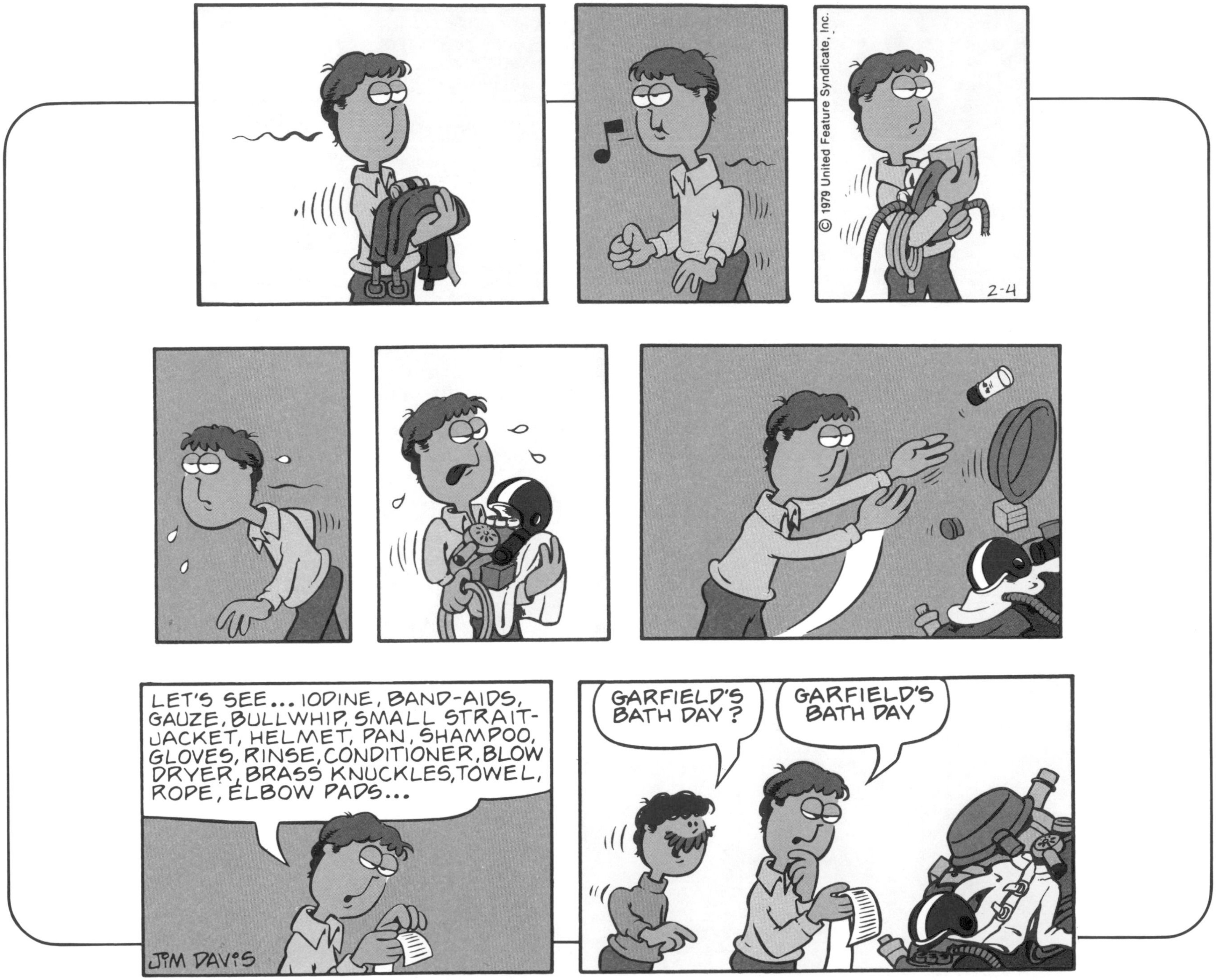
© 1979 United Feature Syndicate, Inc.
2-4
LET'S SEE... IODINE, BAND-AIDS, GAUZE, BULLWHIP, SMALL STRAIT-JACKET, HELMET, PAN, SHAMPOO, GLOVES, RINSE, CONDITIONER, BLOW DRYER, BRASS KNUCKLES, TOWEL, ROPE, ELBOW PADS...
JIM DAVIS
GARFIELD'S BATH DAY?
GARFIELD'S BATH DAY

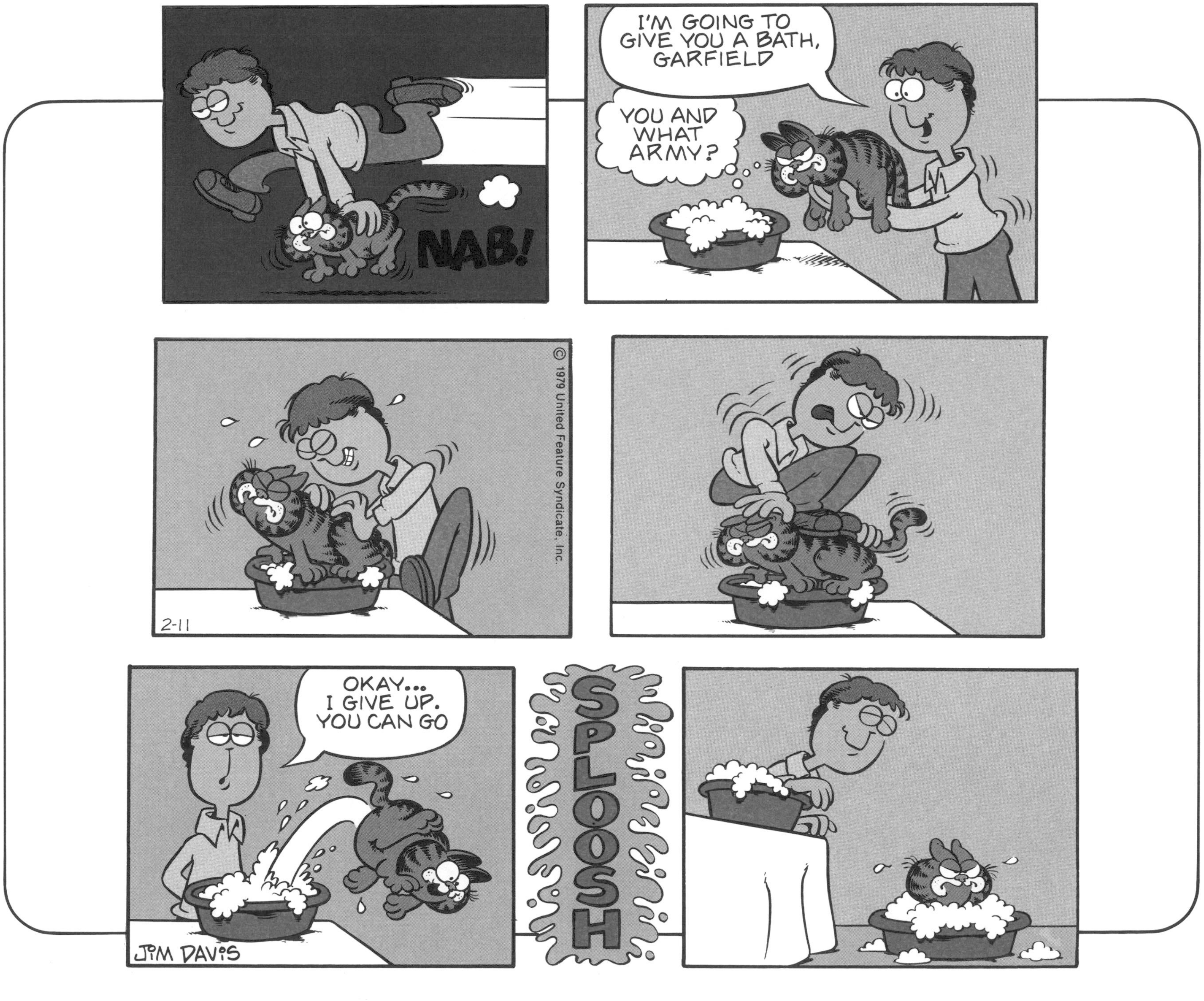
NAB!
I'M GOING TO GIVE YOU A BATH, GARFIELD
YOU AND WHAT ARMY?
© 1979 United Feature Syndicate, Inc.
2-11
OKAY... I GIVE UP. YOU CAN GO
JIM DAVIS
SPLOOSH

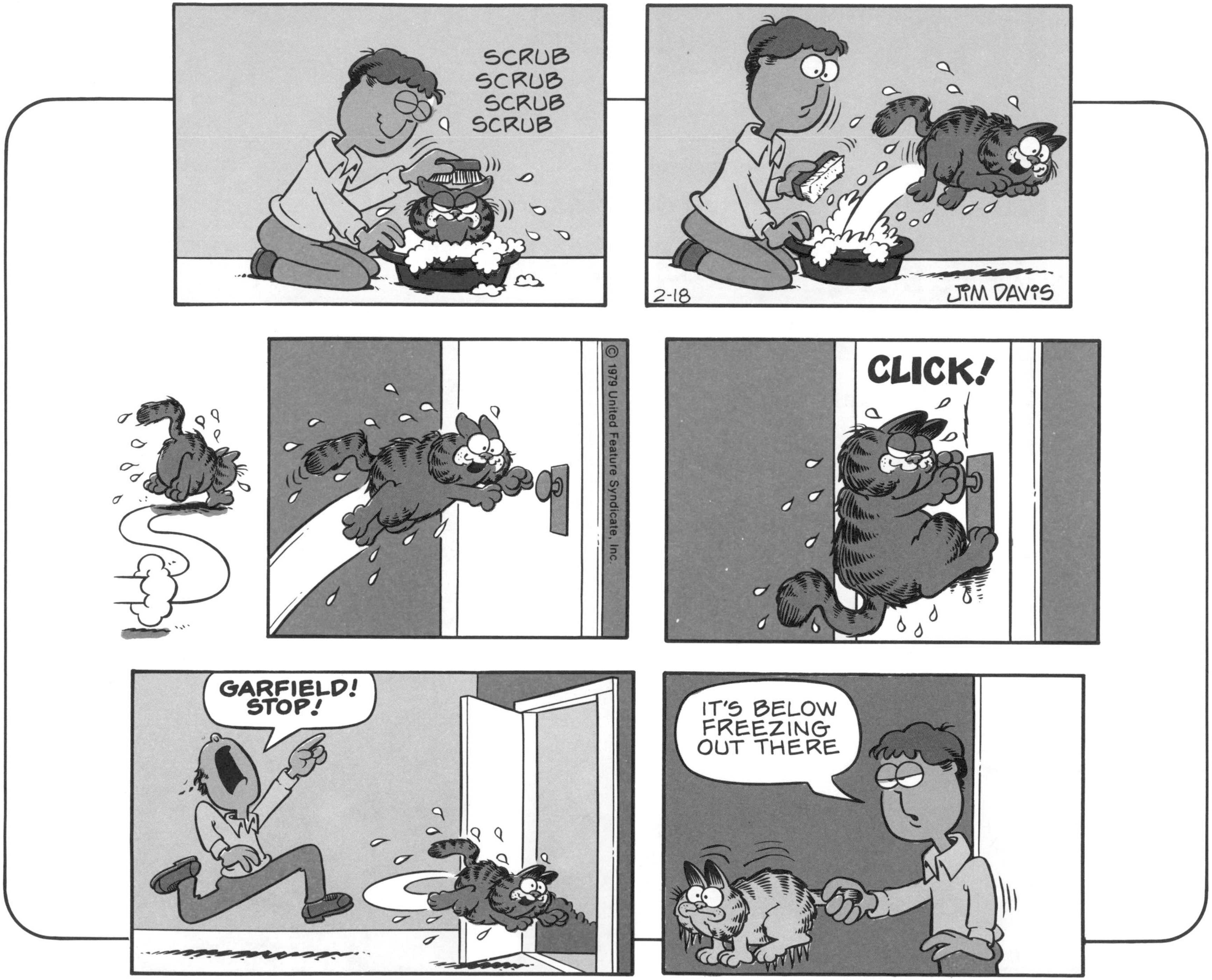
SCRUB
SCRUB
SCRUB
SCRUB
2-18
JIM DAVIS
© 1979 United Feature Syndicate, Inc.
CLICK!
GARFIELD! STOP!
IT'S BELOW FREEZING OUT THERE

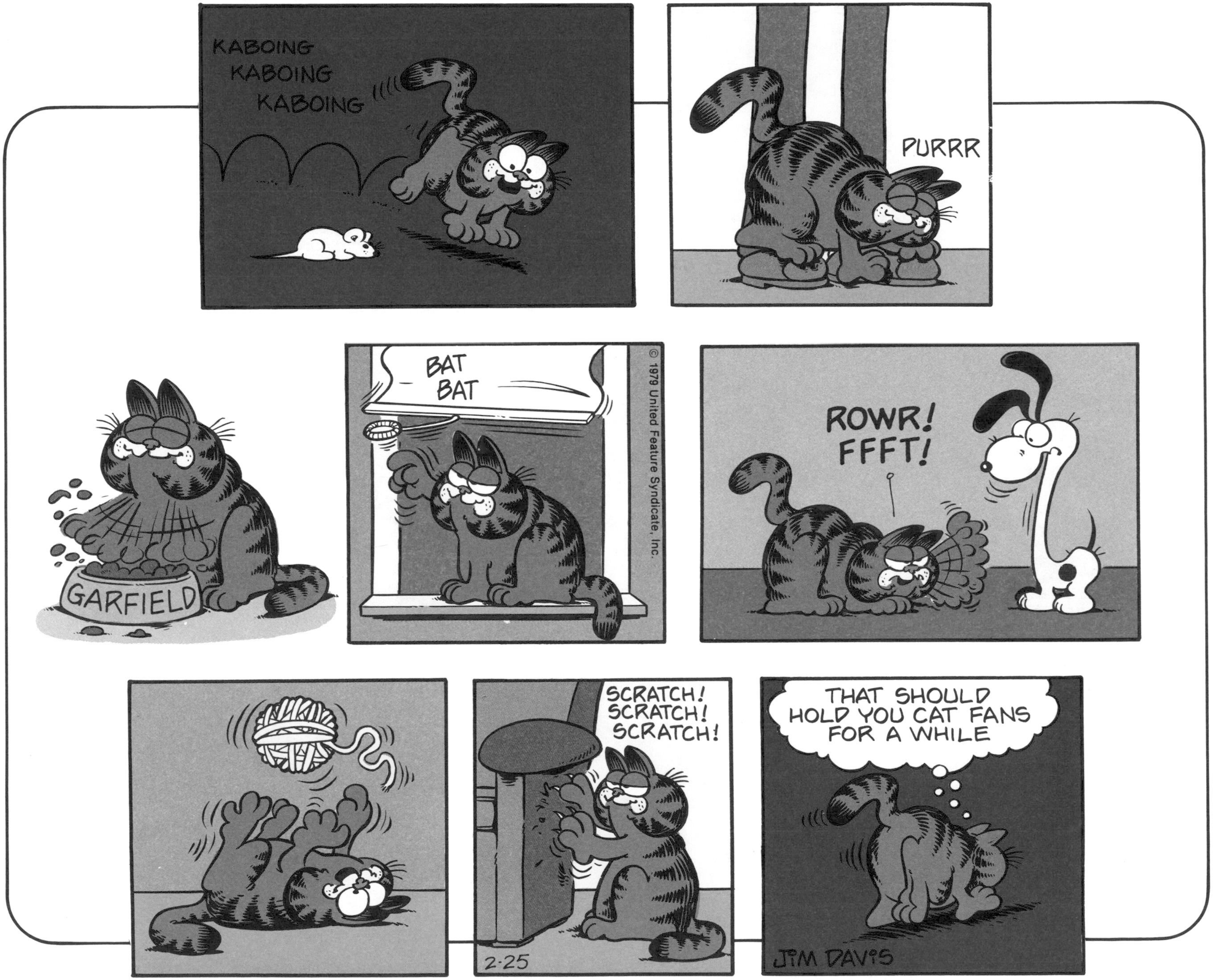
KABOING
KABOING
KABOING
PURRR
GARFIELD
BAT
BAT
© 1979 United Feature Syndicate, Inc.
ROWR!
FFFT!
SCRATCH!
SCRATCH!
SCRATCH!
2-25
THAT SHOULD HOLD YOU CAT FANS FOR A WHILE
JIM DAVIS

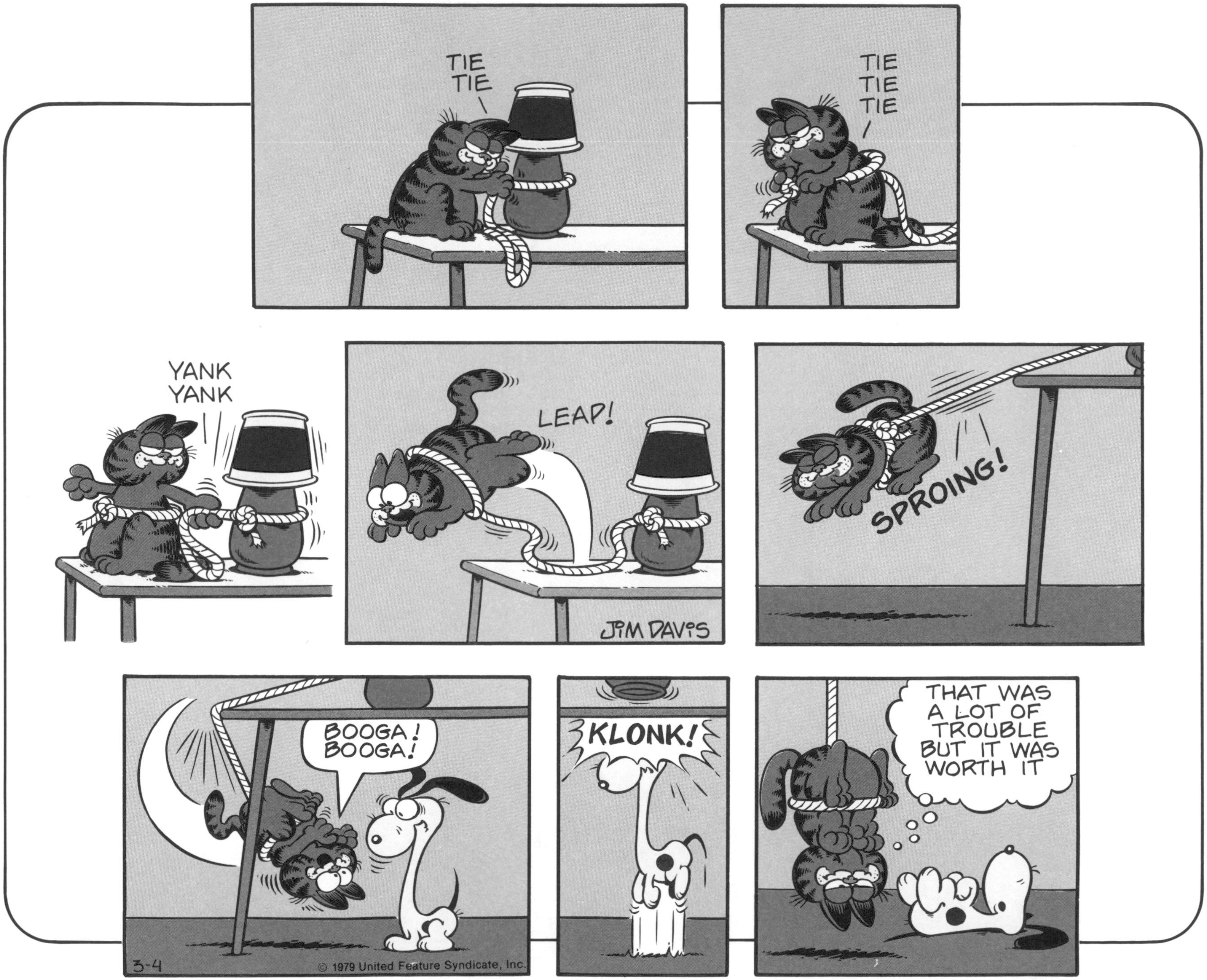

TIE TIE
TIE TIE TIE
YANK YANK
LEAP!
JIM DAVIS
SPROING!
BOOGA! BOOGA!
KLONK!
THAT WAS A LOT OF TROUBLE BUT IT WAS WORTH IT
3-4
© 1979 United Feature Syndicate, Inc.

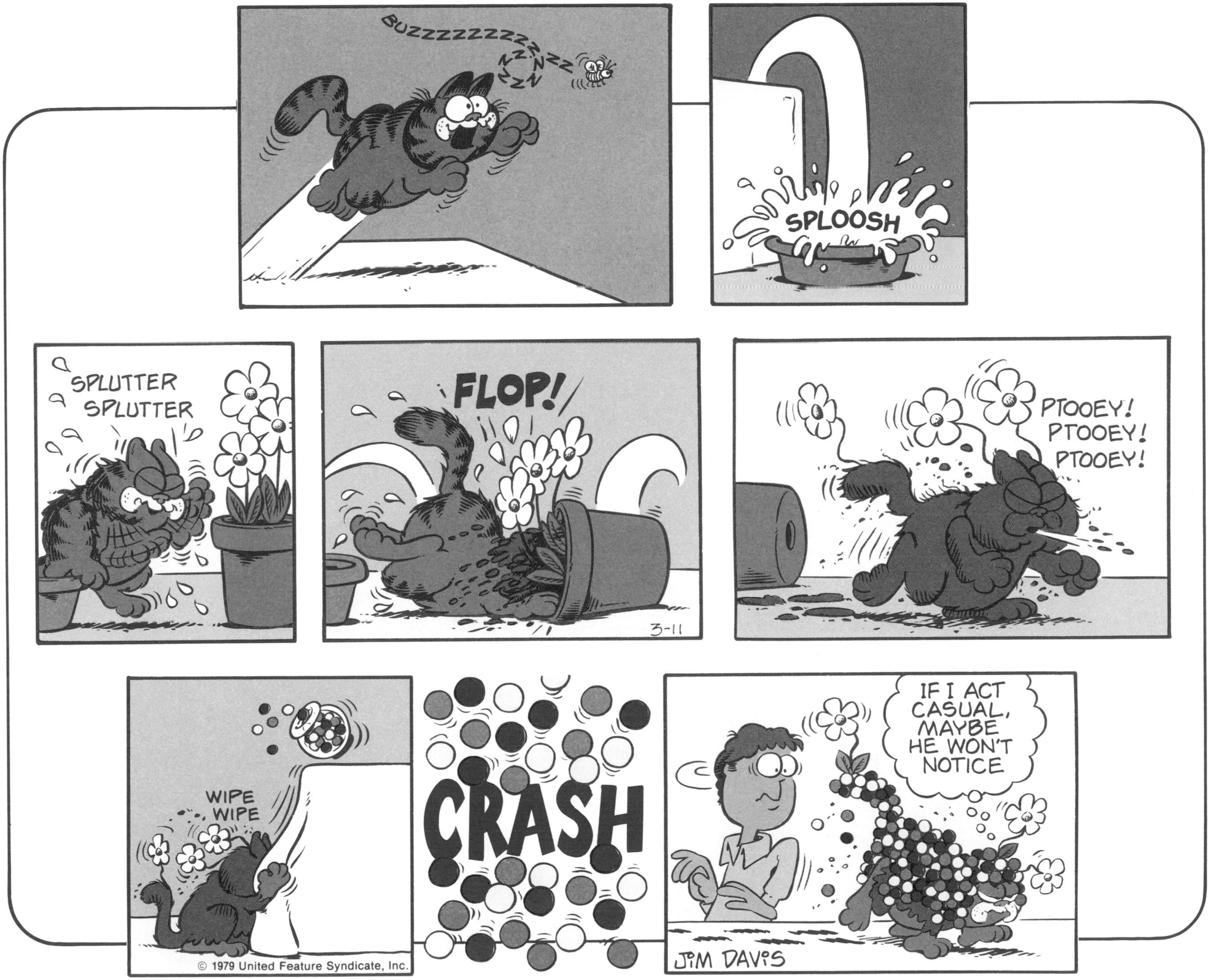
BUZZZZZZZZZZZZZZZZZZ
SPLOOSH
SPLUTTER
SPLUTTER
FLOP!
3-11
PTOOEY!
PTOOEY!
PTOOEY!
WIPE
WIPE
© 1979 United Feature Syndicate, Inc.
CRASH
IF I ACT CASUAL, MAYBE HE WON'T NOTICE
JIM DAVIS

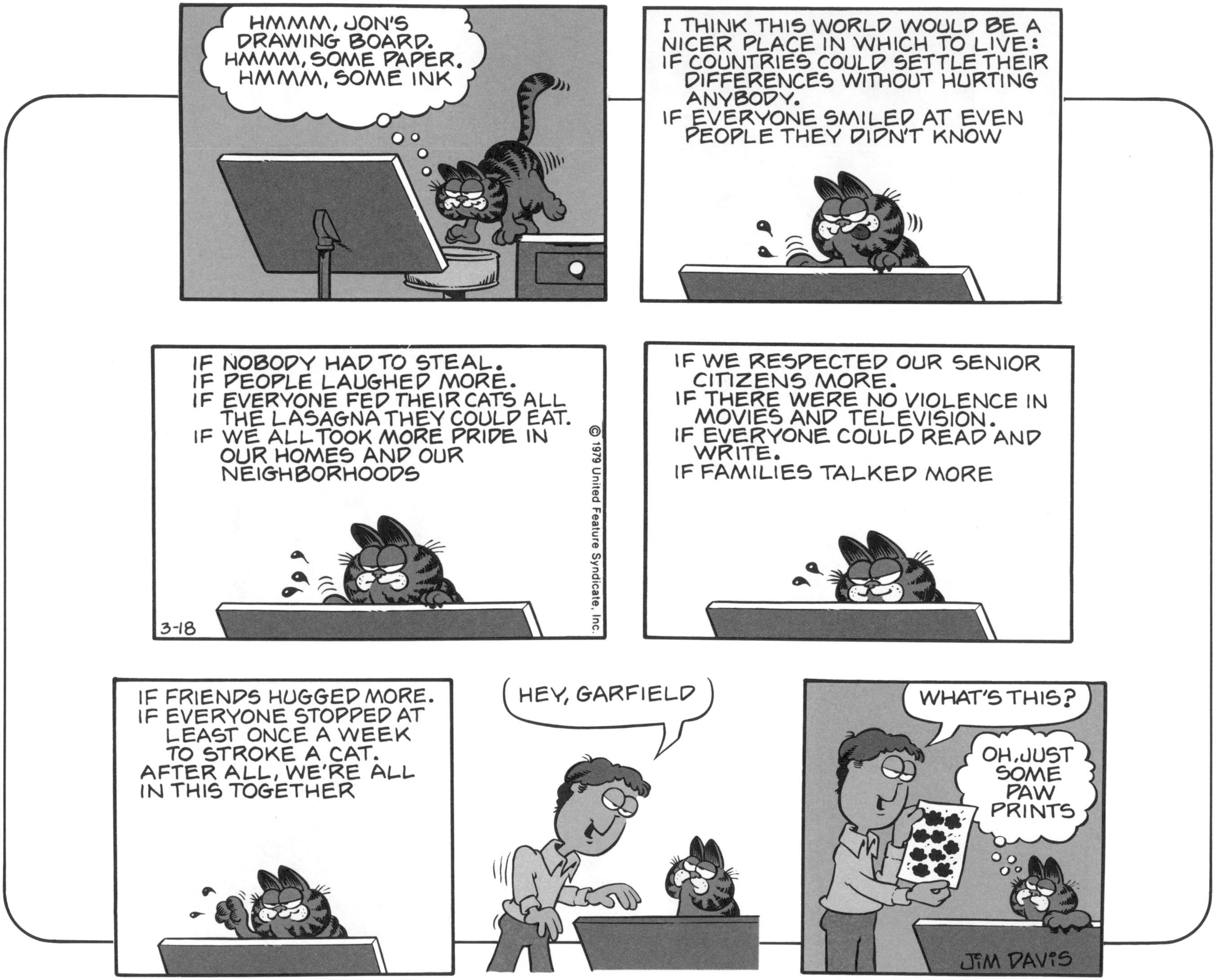
HMMM, JON'S DRAWING BOARD. HMMM, SOME PAPER. HMMM, SOME INK
I THINK THIS WORLD WOULD BE A NICER PLACE IN WHICH TO LIVE:
IF COUNTRIES COULD SETTLE THEIR DIFFERENCES WITHOUT HURTING ANYBODY.
IF EVERYONE SMILED AT EVEN PEOPLE THEY DIDN'T KNOW
IF NOBODY HAD TO STEAL.
IF PEOPLE LAUGHED MORE.
IF EVERYONE FED THEIR CATS ALL THE LASAGNA THEY COULD EAT.
IF WE ALL TOOK MORE PRIDE IN OUR HOMES AND OUR NEIGHBORHOODS
© 1979 United Feature Syndicate, Inc.
3-18
IF WE RESPECTED OUR SENIOR CITIZENS MORE.
IF THERE WERE NO VIOLENCE IN MOVIES AND TELEVISION.
IF EVERYONE COULD READ AND WRITE.
IF FAMILIES TALKED MORE
IF FRIENDS HUGGED MORE.
IF EVERYONE STOPPED AT LEAST ONCE A WEEK TO STROKE A CAT.
AFTER ALL, WE'RE ALL IN THIS TOGETHER
HEY, GARFIELD
WHAT'S THIS?
OH, JUST SOME PAW PRINTS
JIM DAVIS

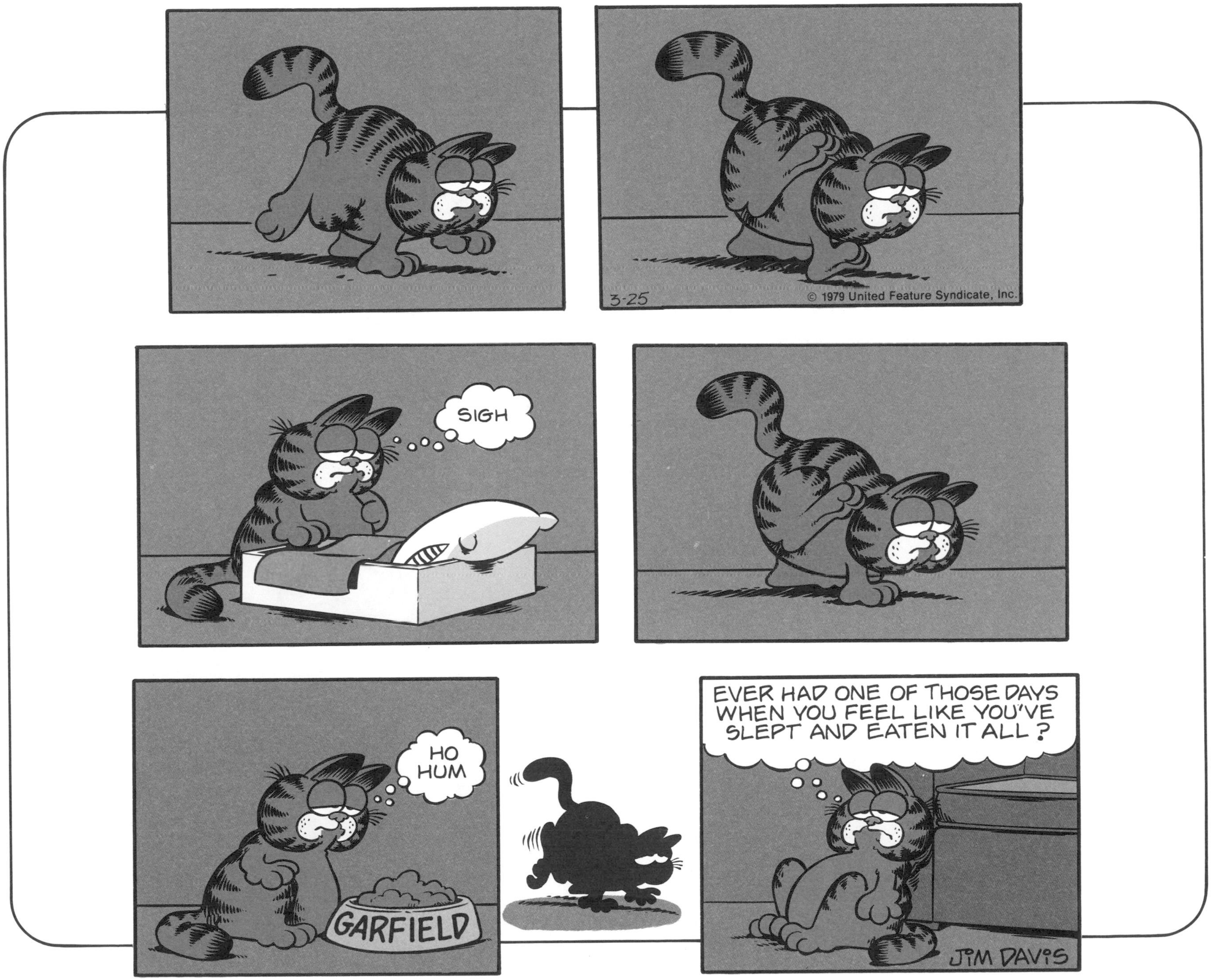
3-25
© 1979 United Feature Syndicate, Inc.
SIGH
HO HUM
GARFIELD
EVER HAD ONE OF THOSE DAYS WHEN YOU FEEL LIKE YOU'VE SLEPT AND EATEN IT ALL?
JIM DAVIS

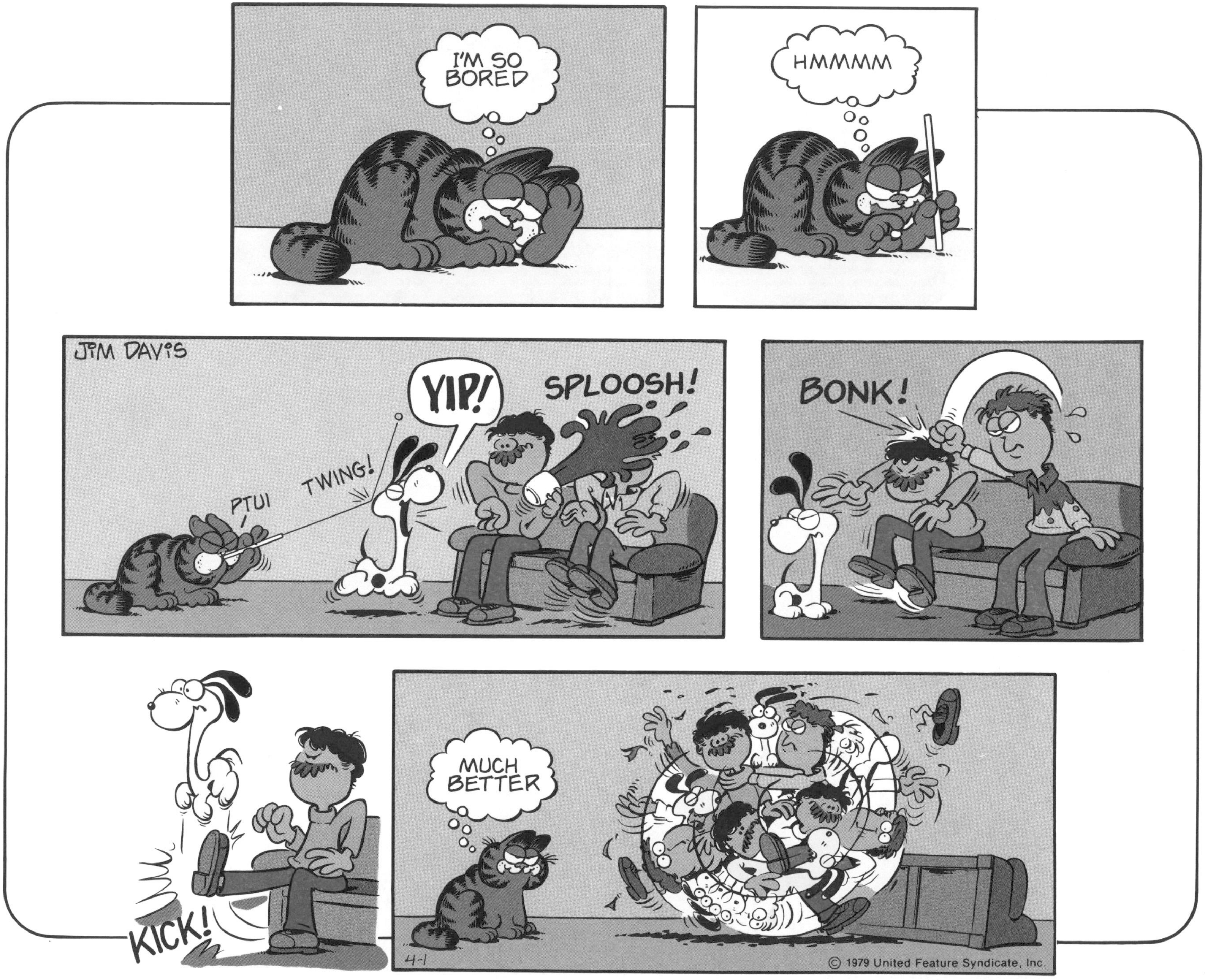
I'M SO BORED
HMMMM
JIM DAVIS
PTUI
TWING!
YIP!
SPLOOSH!
BONK!
KICK!
MUCH BETTER
4-1
© 1979 United Feature Syndicate, Inc.

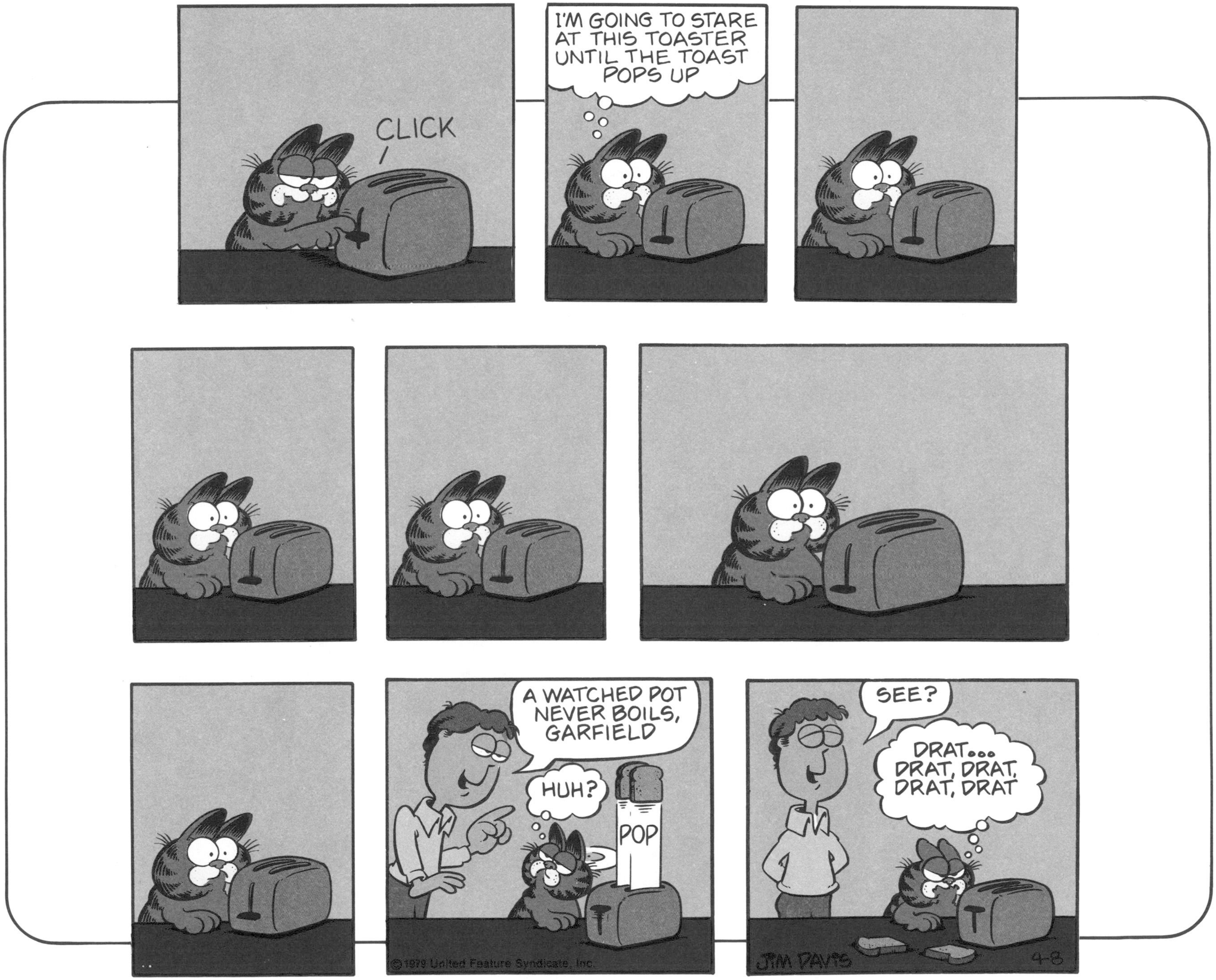
CLICK
I'M GOING TO STARE AT THIS TOASTER UNTIL THE TOAST POPS UP
A WATCHED POT NEVER BOILS, GARFIELD
HUH?
POP
SEE?
DRAT... DRAT, DRAT, DRAT, DRAT
© 1979 United Feature Syndicate, Inc.
JIM DAVIS
4-8

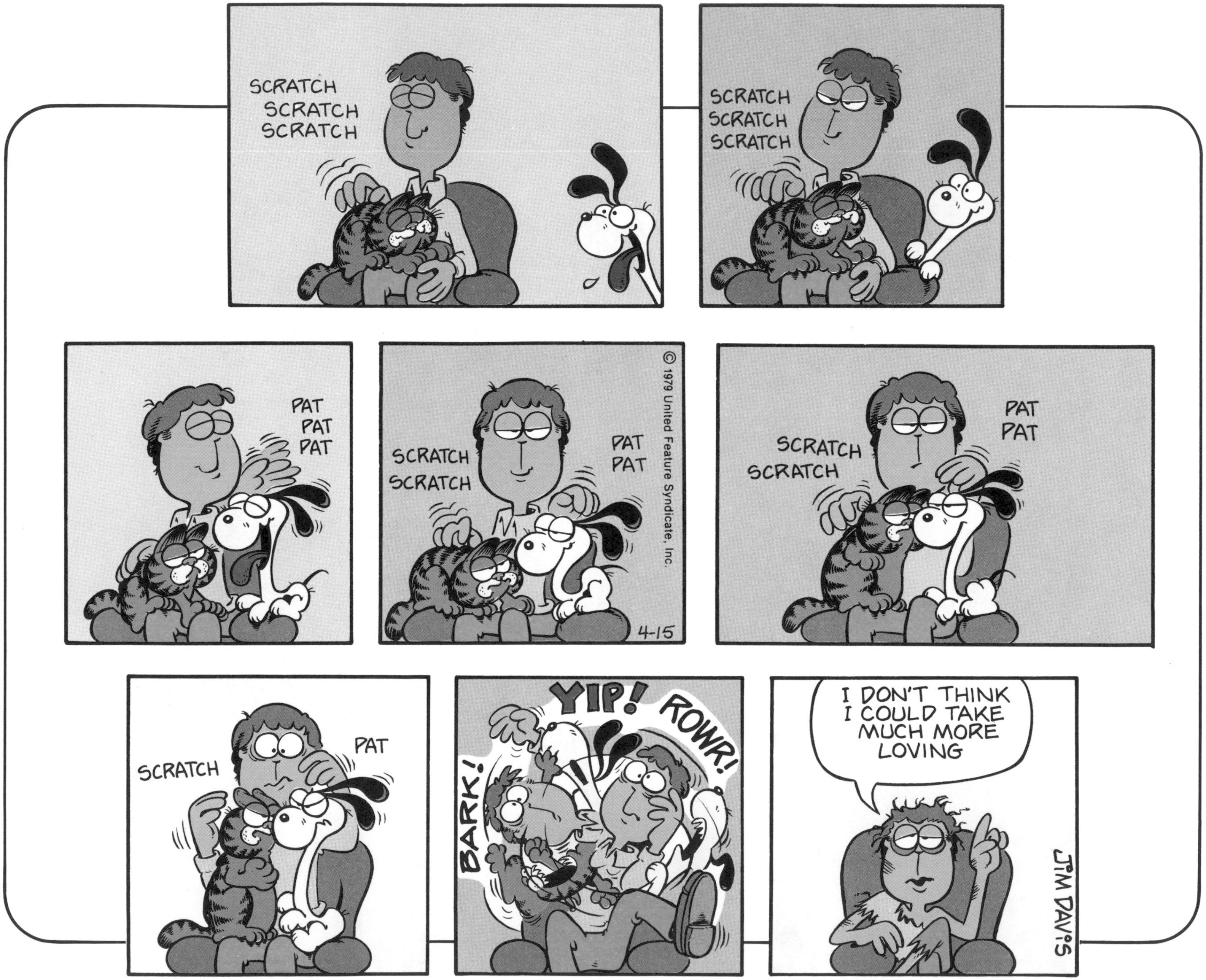
SCRATCH SCRATCH SCRATCH
SCRATCH SCRATCH SCRATCH
PAT PAT PAT
SCRATCH SCRATCH
PAT PAT
© 1979 United Feature Syndicate, Inc.
4-15
SCRATCH SCRATCH
PAT PAT
SCRATCH
PAT
BARK!
YIP!
ROWR!
I DON'T THINK I COULD TAKE MUCH MORE LOVING
JIM DAVIS

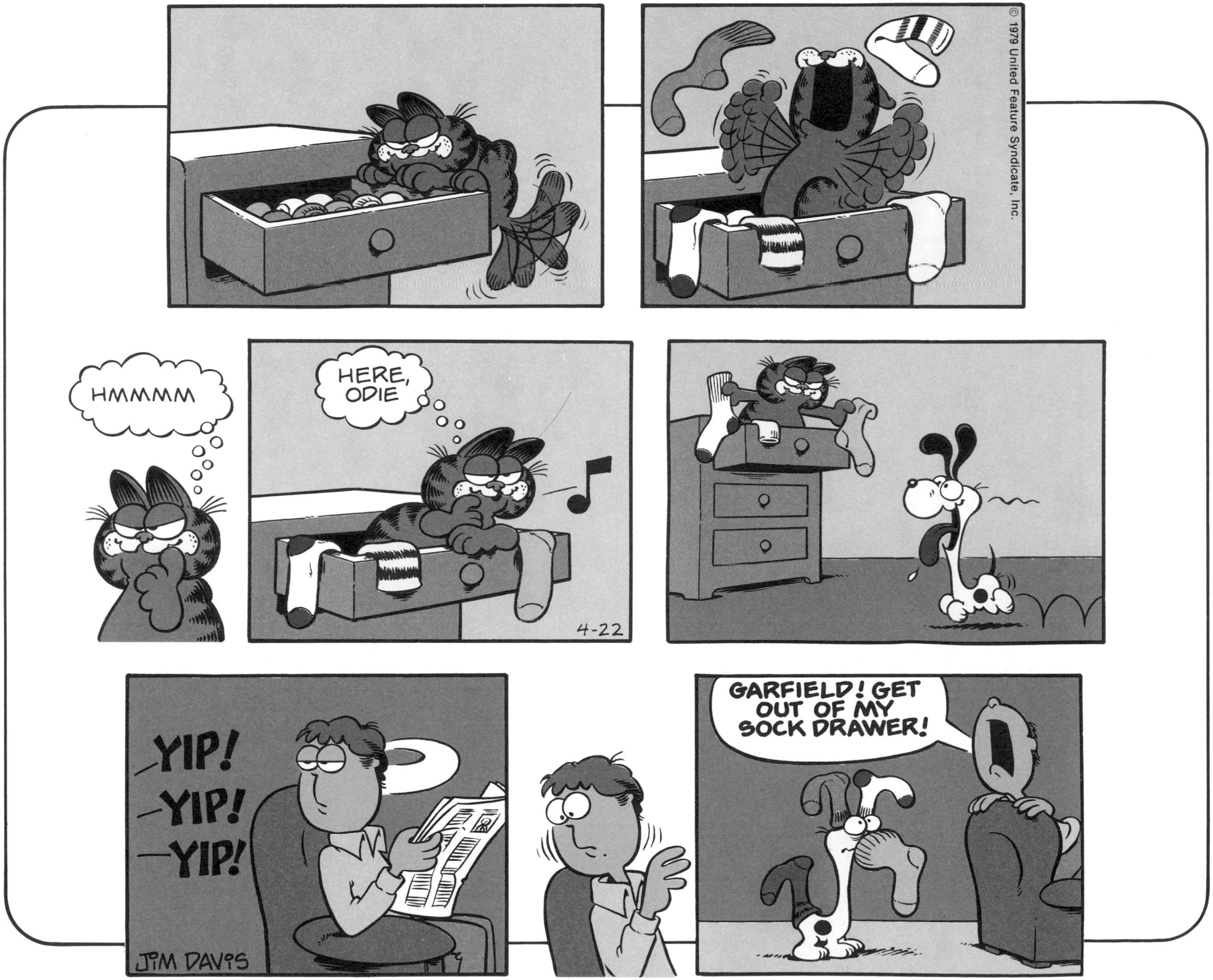
© 1979 United Feature Syndicate, Inc.
HMMMM
HERE, ODIE
4-22
YIP!
YIP!
YIP!
JIM DAVIS
GARFIELD! GET OUT OF MY SOCK DRAWER!

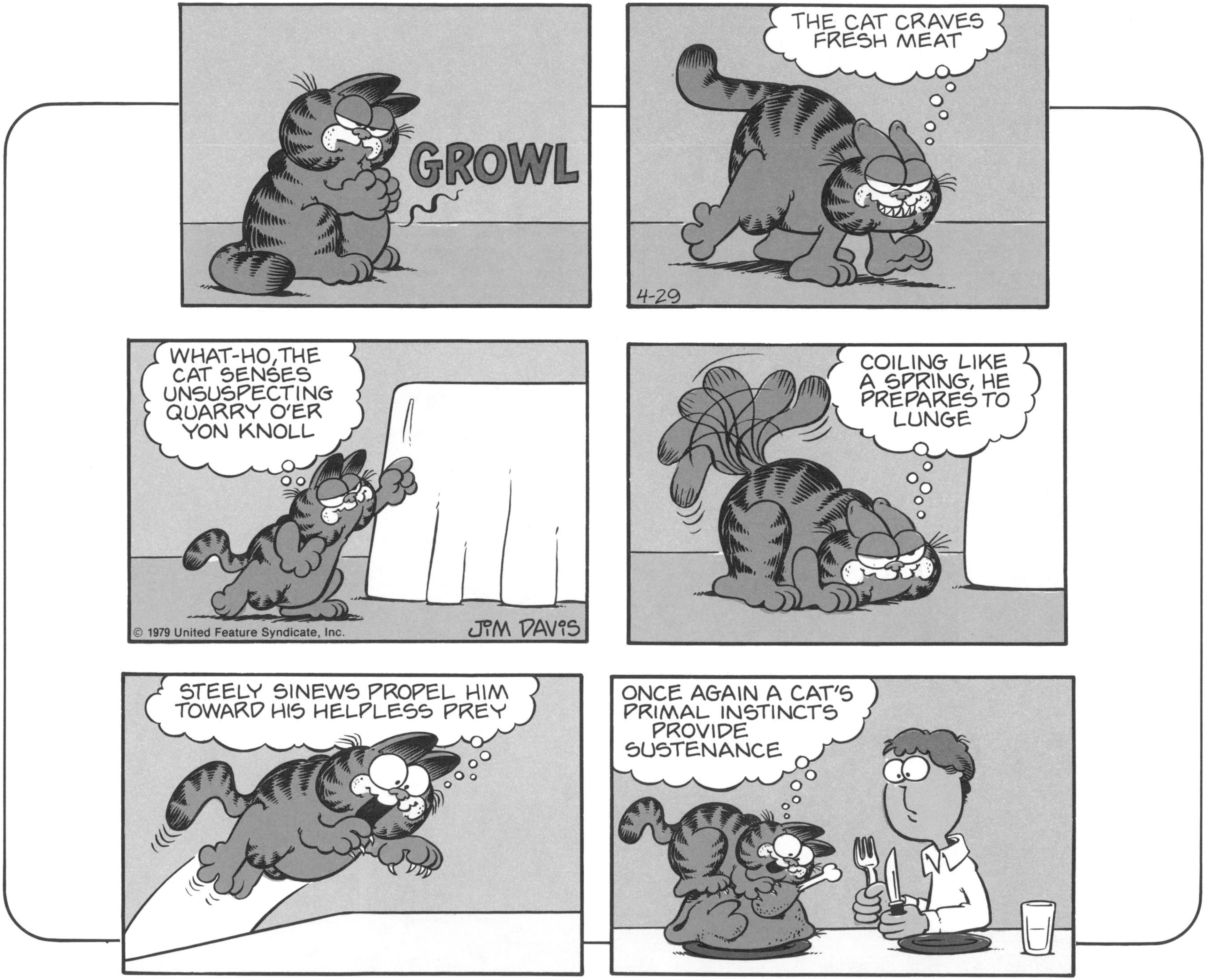
GROWL
THE CAT CRAVES FRESH MEAT
4-29
WHAT-HO, THE CAT SENSES UNSUSPECTING QUARRY O'ER YON KNOLL
© 1979 United Feature Syndicate, Inc.
JIM DAVIS
COILING LIKE A SPRING, HE PREPARES TO LUNGE
STEELY SINEWS PROPEL HIM TOWARD HIS HELPLESS PREY
ONCE AGAIN A CAT'S PRIMAL INSTINCTS PROVIDE SUSTENANCE

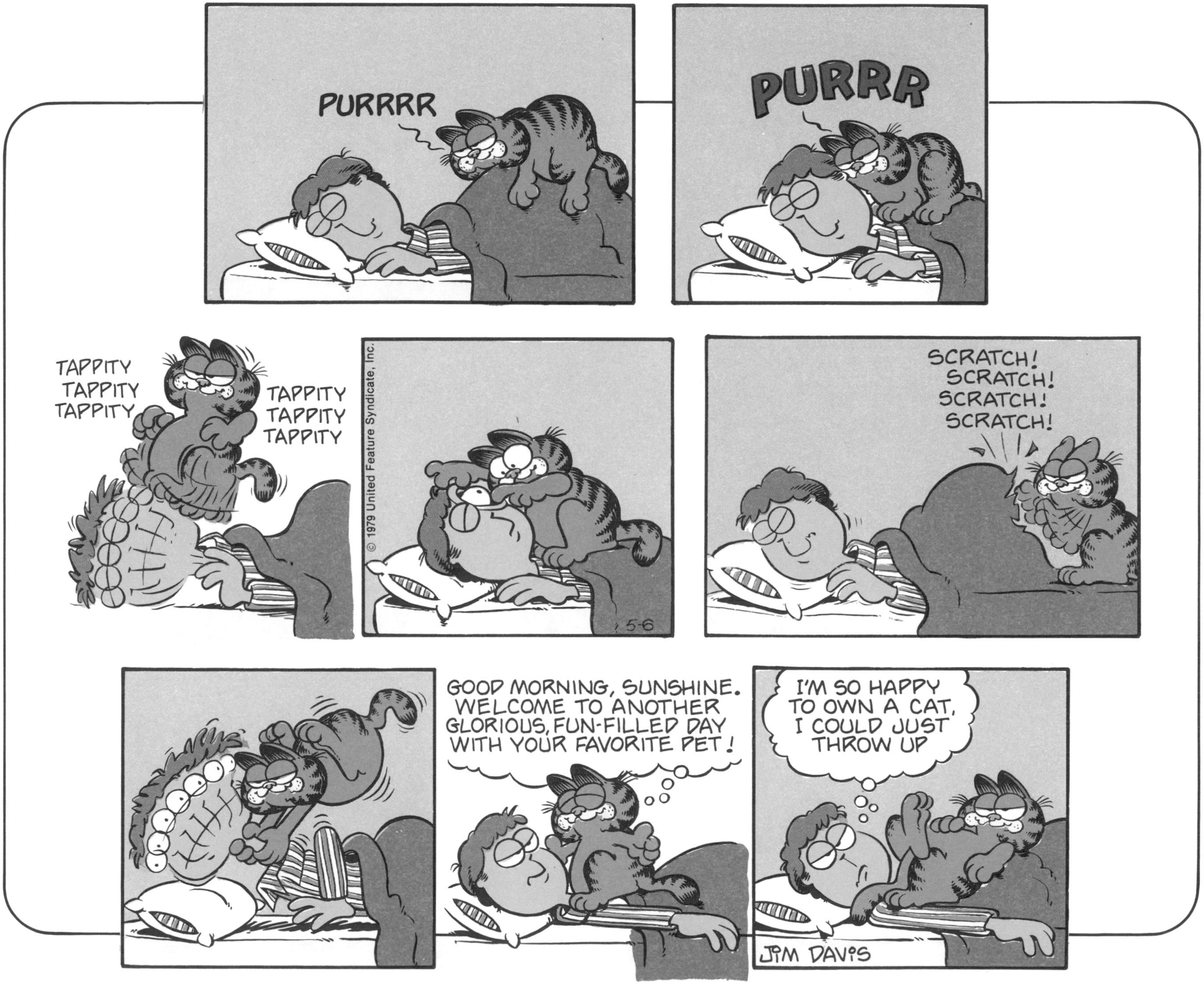
PURRRR
PURRR
TAPPITY TAPPITY TAPPITY
TAPPITY TAPPITY TAPPITY
© 1979 United Feature Syndicate, Inc.
5-6
SCRATCH! SCRATCH! SCRATCH! SCRATCH!
GOOD MORNING, SUNSHINE. WELCOME TO ANOTHER GLORIOUS, FUN-FILLED DAY WITH YOUR FAVORITE PET!
I'M SO HAPPY TO OWN A CAT, I COULD JUST THROW UP
JIM DAVIS

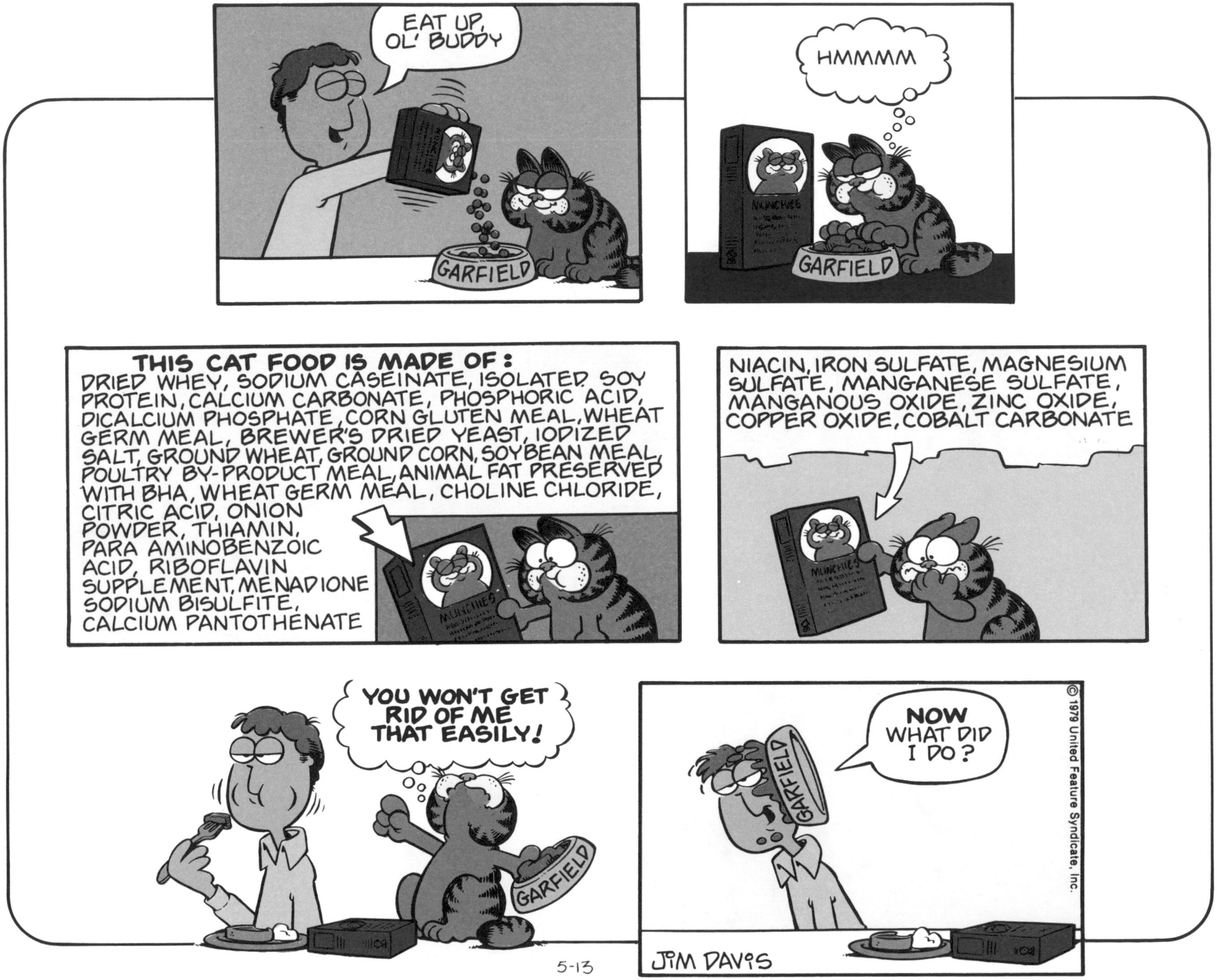
EAT UP, OL' BUDDY
GARFIELD
HMMMM
GARFIELD
THIS CAT FOOD IS MADE OF: DRIED WHEY, SODIUM CASEINATE, ISOLATED SOY PROTEIN, CALCIUM CARBONATE, PHOSPHORIC ACID, DICALCIUM PHOSPHATE, CORN GLUTEN MEAL, WHEAT GERM MEAL, BREWER'S DRIED YEAST, IODIZED SALT, GROUND WHEAT, GROUND CORN, SOYBEAN MEAL, POULTRY BY-PRODUCT MEAL, ANIMAL FAT PRESERVED WITH BHA, WHEAT GERM MEAL, CHOLINE CHLORIDE, CITRIC ACID, ONION POWDER, THIAMIN, PARA AMINOBENZOIC ACID, RIBOFLAVIN SUPPLEMENT, MENADIONE SODIUM BISULFITE, CALCIUM PANTOTHENATE
NIACIN, IRON SULFATE, MAGNESIUM SULFATE, MANGANESE SULFATE, MANGANOUS OXIDE, ZINC OXIDE, COPPER OXIDE, COBALT CARBONATE
YOU WON'T GET RID OF ME THAT EASILY!
GARFIELD
NOW WHAT DID I DO?
GARFIELD
© 1979 United Feature Syndicate, Inc.
JIM DAVIS
5-13

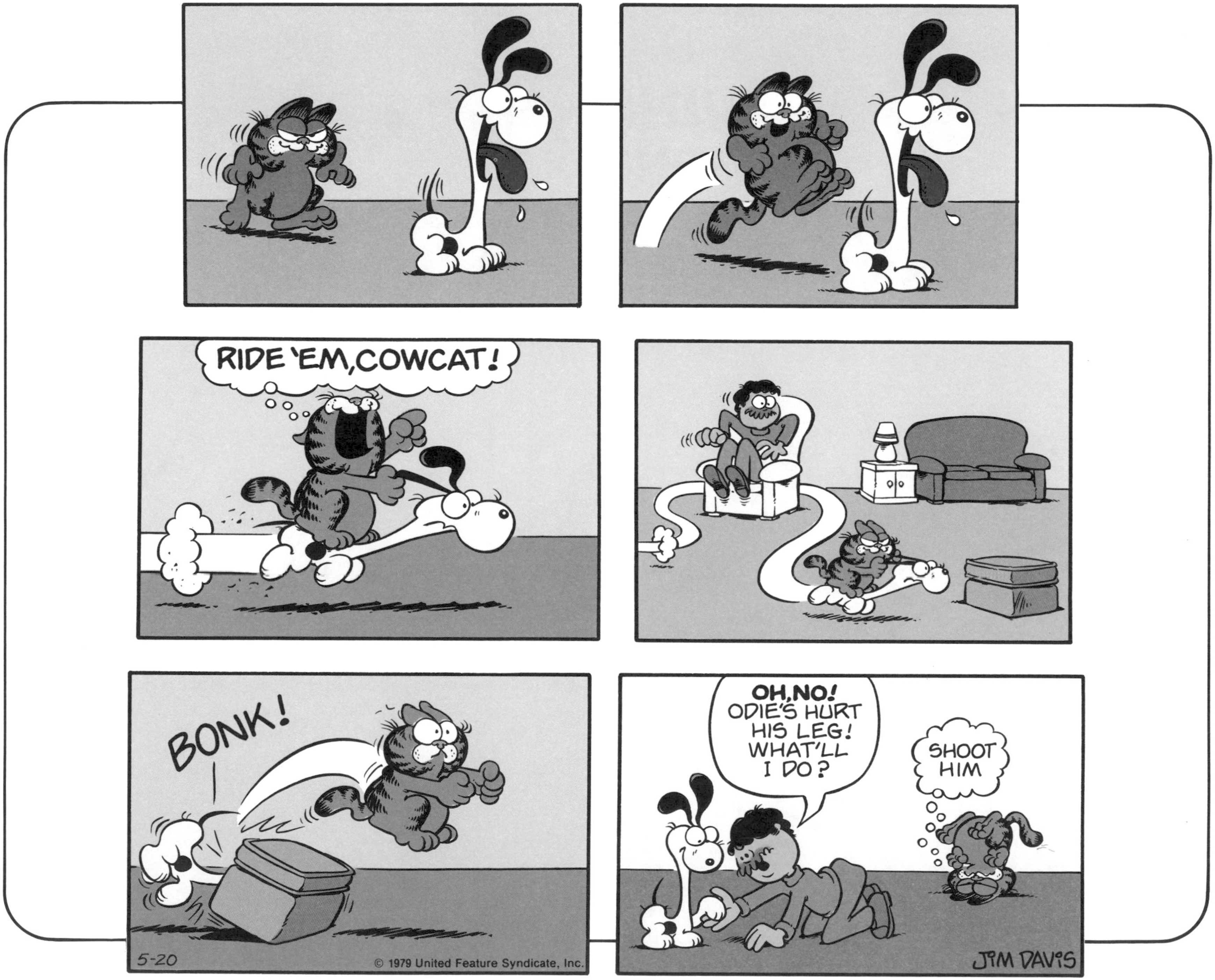
RIDE 'EM, COWCAT!
BONK!
OH, NO! ODIE'S HURT HIS LEG! WHAT'LL I DO?
SHOOT HIM
5-20
© 1979 United Feature Syndicate, Inc.
JIM DAVIS

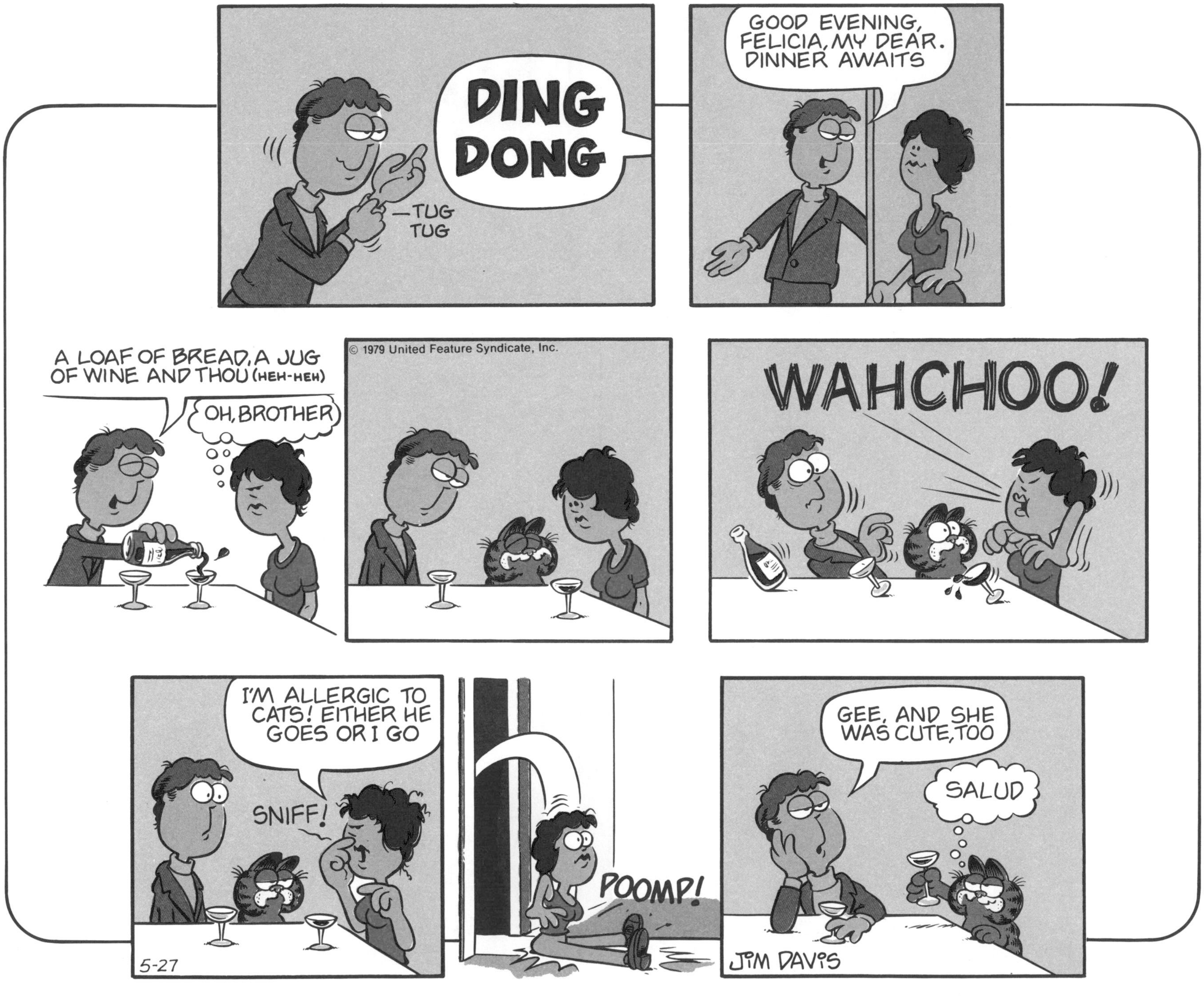
DING DONG
—TUG TUG
GOOD EVENING, FELICIA, MY DEAR. DINNER AWAITS
A LOAF OF BREAD, A JUG OF WINE AND THOU (HEH-HEH)
OH, BROTHER
© 1979 United Feature Syndicate, Inc.
WAHCHOO!
I'M ALLERGIC TO CATS! EITHER HE GOES OR I GO
SNIFF!
5-27
POOMP!
GEE, AND SHE WAS CUTE, TOO
SALUD
JIM DAVIS

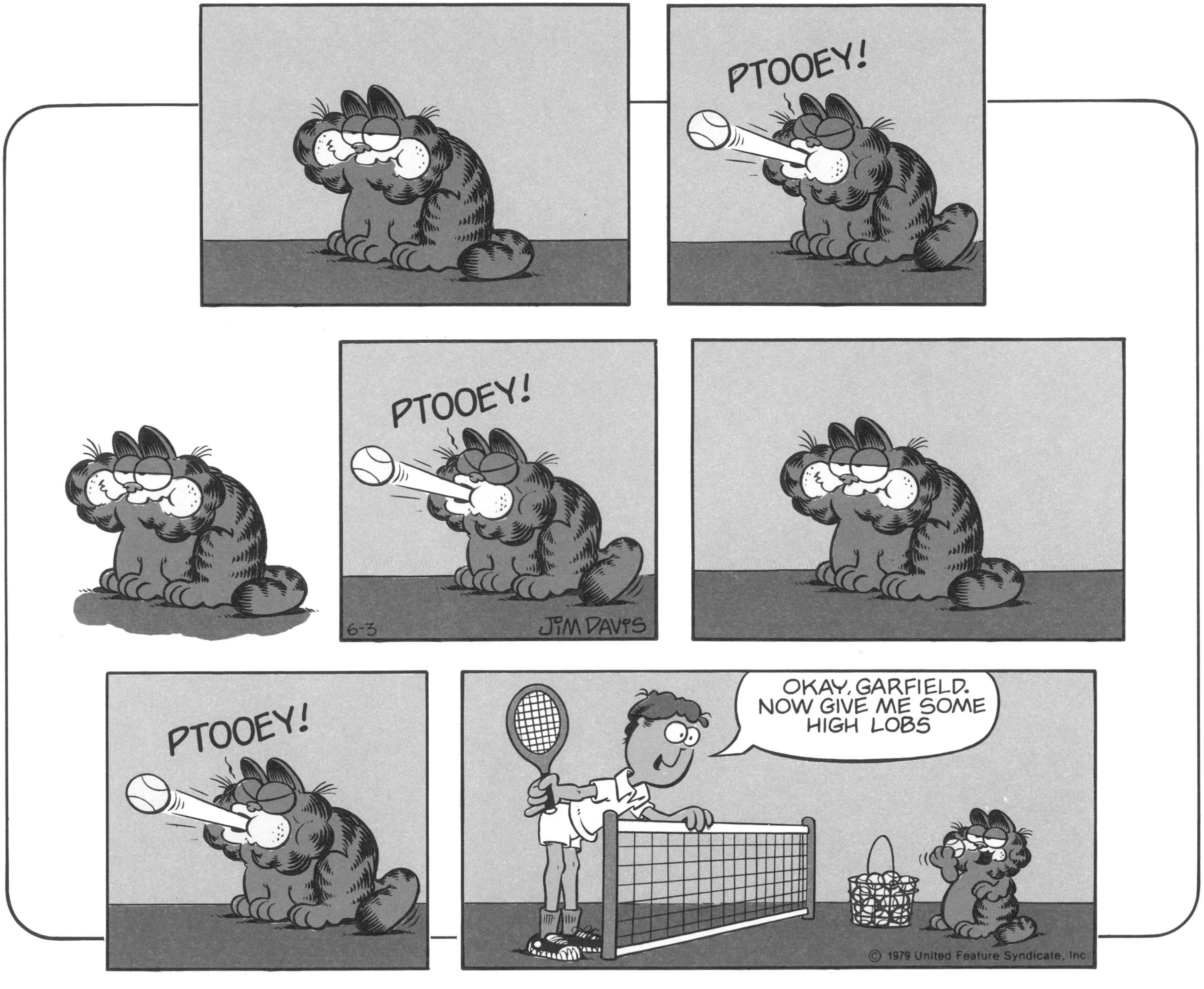
PTOOEY!
PTOOEY!
6-3
JIM DAVIS
PTOOEY!
OKAY, GARFIELD. NOW GIVE ME SOME HIGH LOBS
© 1979 United Feature Syndicate, Inc.

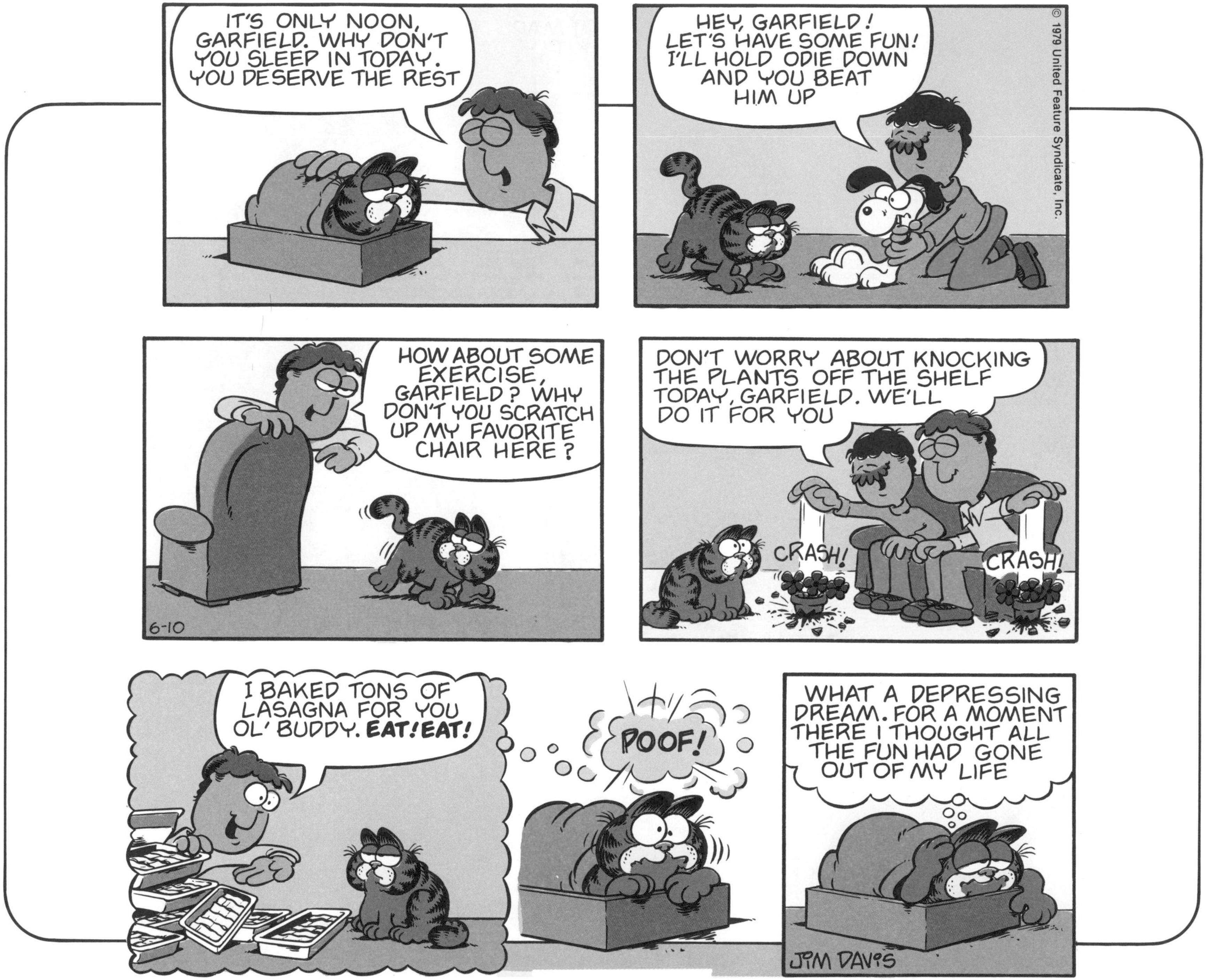
IT'S ONLY NOON, GARFIELD. WHY DON'T YOU SLEEP IN TODAY. YOU DESERVE THE REST
HEY, GARFIELD! LET'S HAVE SOME FUN! I'LL HOLD ODIE DOWN AND YOU BEAT HIM UP
© 1979 United Feature Syndicate, Inc.
HOW ABOUT SOME EXERCISE, GARFIELD? WHY DON'T YOU SCRATCH UP MY FAVORITE CHAIR HERE?
6-10
DON'T WORRY ABOUT KNOCKING THE PLANTS OFF THE SHELF TODAY, GARFIELD. WE'LL DO IT FOR YOU
CRASH!
CRASH!
I BAKED TONS OF LASAGNA FOR YOU OL' BUDDY. EAT! EAT!
POOF!
WHAT A DEPRESSING DREAM. FOR A MOMENT THERE I THOUGHT ALL THE FUN HAD GONE OUT OF MY LIFE
JIM DAVIS

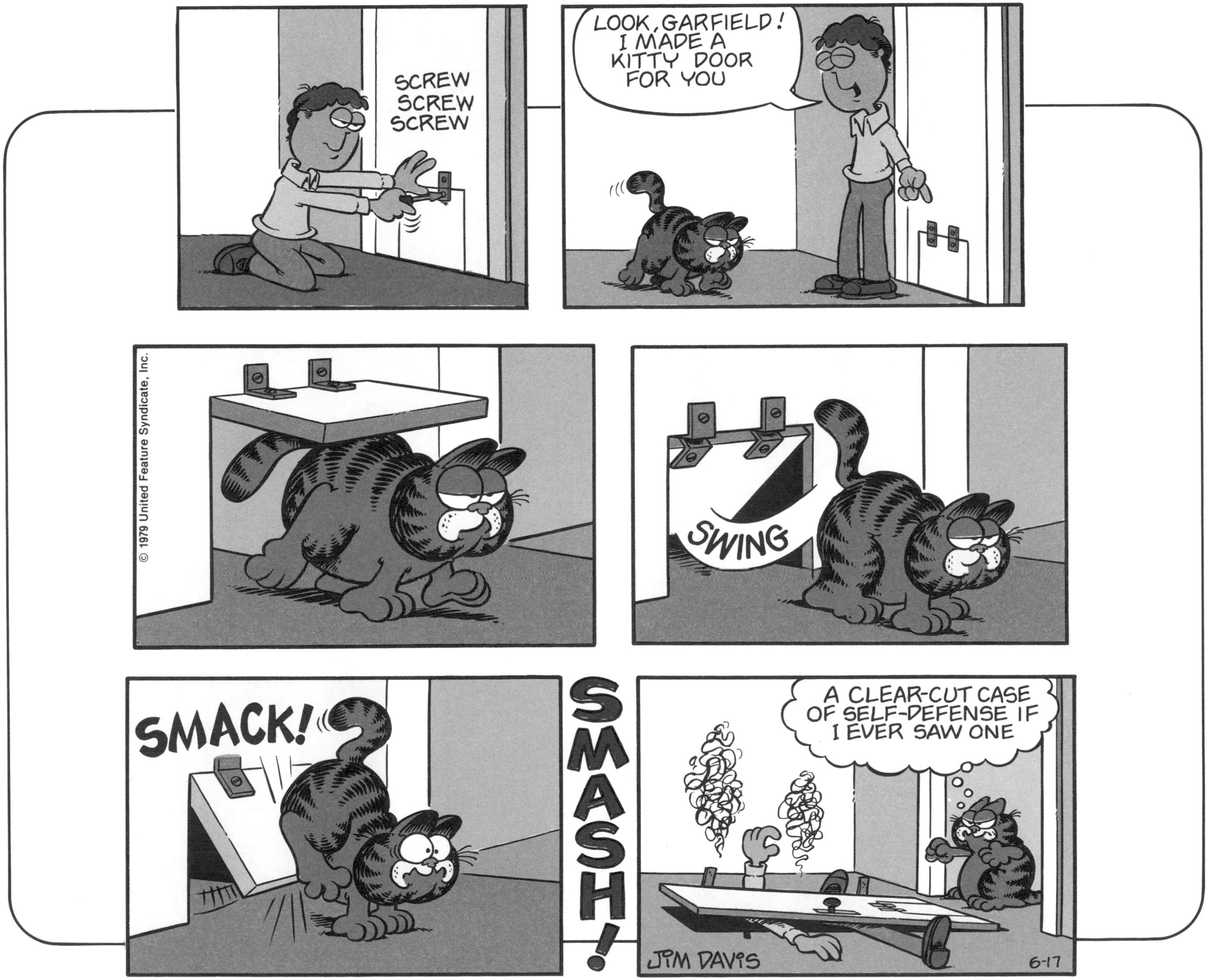
SCREW SCREW SCREW
LOOK, GARFIELD! I MADE A KITTY DOOR FOR YOU
© 1979 United Feature Syndicate, Inc.
SWING
SMACK!
SMASH!
A CLEAR-CUT CASE OF SELF-DEFENSE IF I EVER SAW ONE
JIM DAVIS
6-17

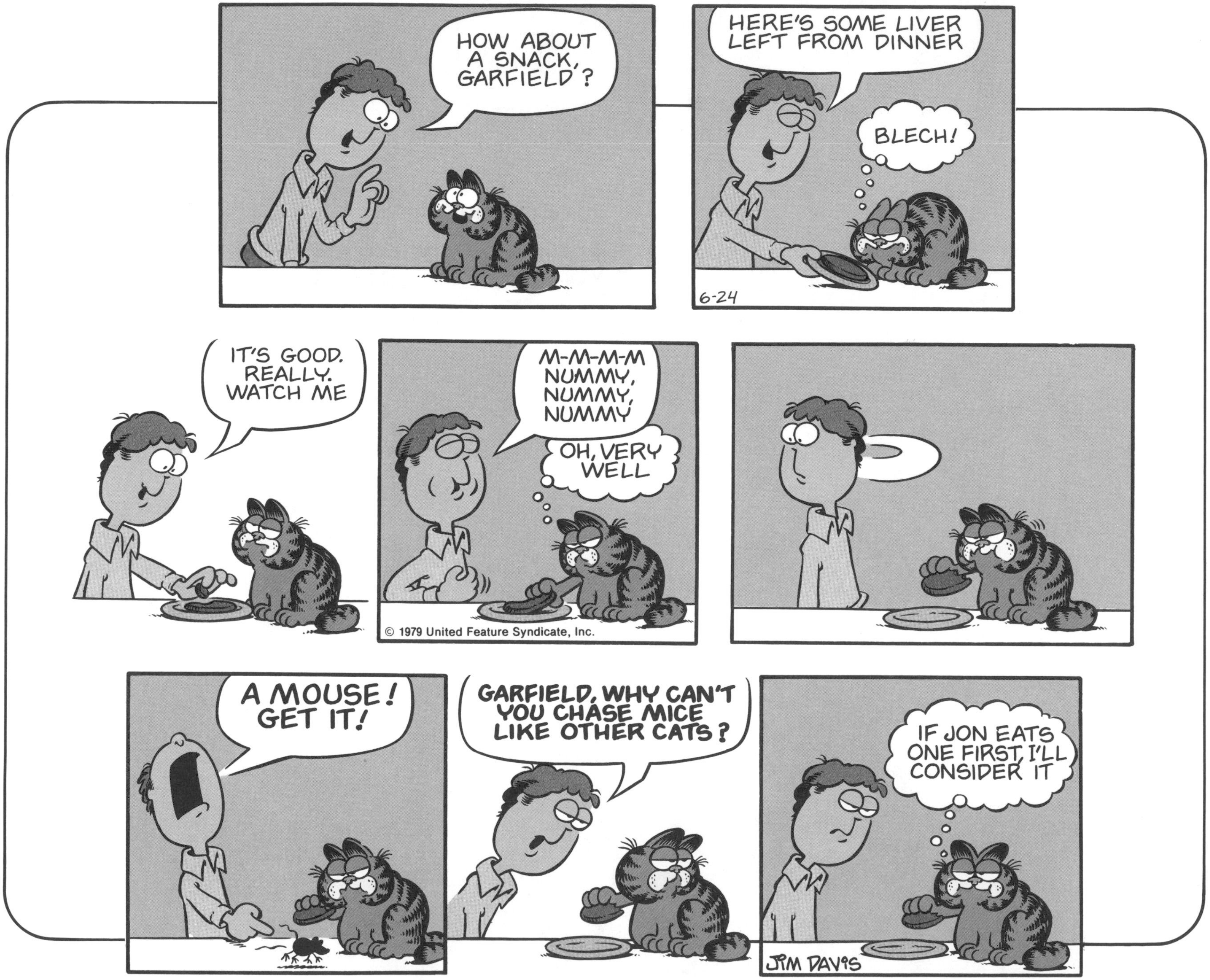
HOW ABOUT A SNACK, GARFIELD?
HERE'S SOME LIVER LEFT FROM DINNER
BLECH!
6-24
IT'S GOOD. REALLY. WATCH ME
M-M-M-M NUMMY, NUMMY, NUMMY
OH, VERY WELL
© 1979 United Feature Syndicate, Inc.
A MOUSE! GET IT!
GARFIELD, WHY CAN'T YOU CHASE MICE LIKE OTHER CATS?
IF JON EATS ONE FIRST, I'LL CONSIDER IT
JIM DAVIS

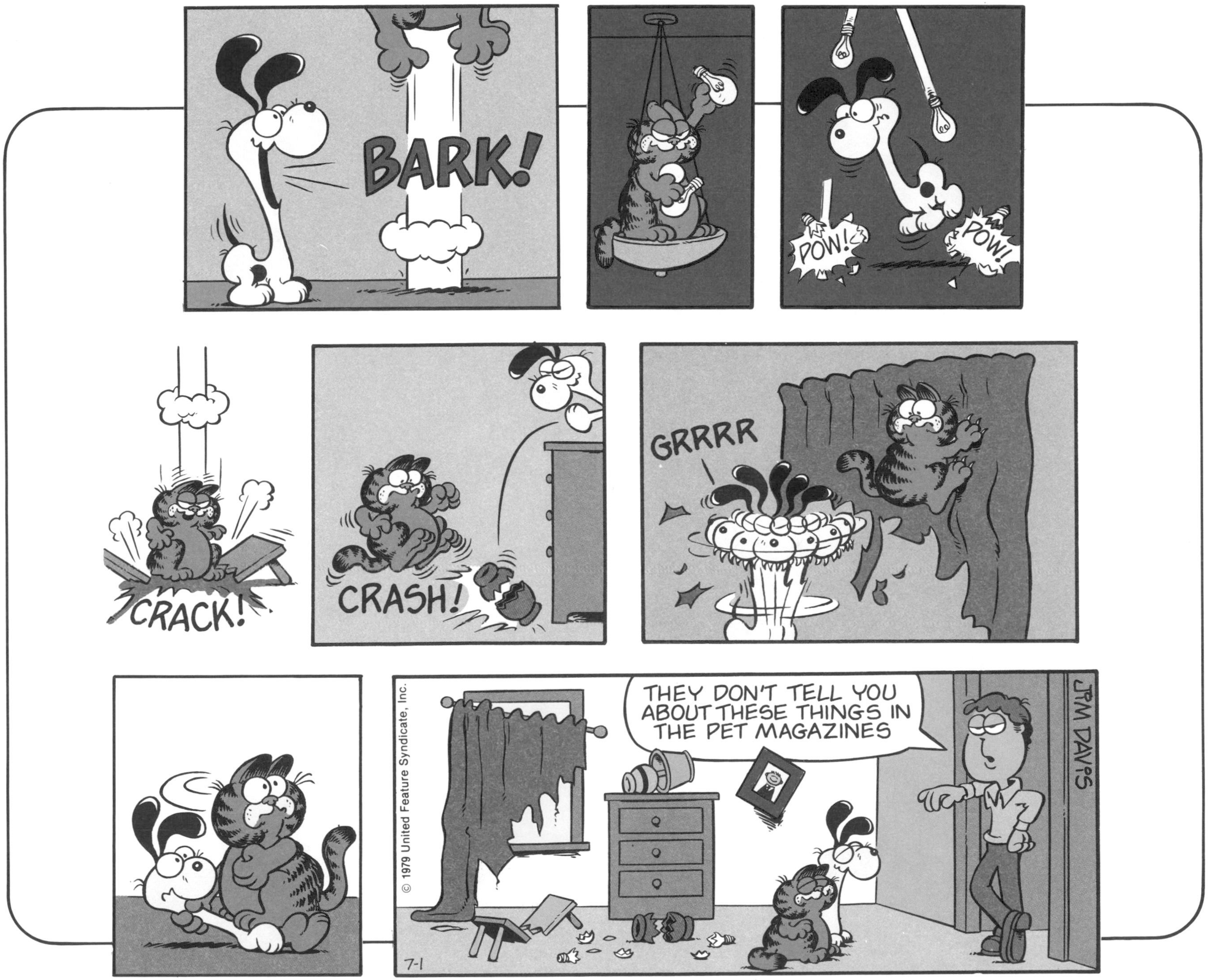
BARK!
POW!
POW!
CRACK!
CRASH!
GRRRR
THEY DON'T TELL YOU ABOUT THESE THINGS IN THE PET MAGAZINES
JIM DAVIS
© 1979 United Feature Syndicate, Inc.
7-1

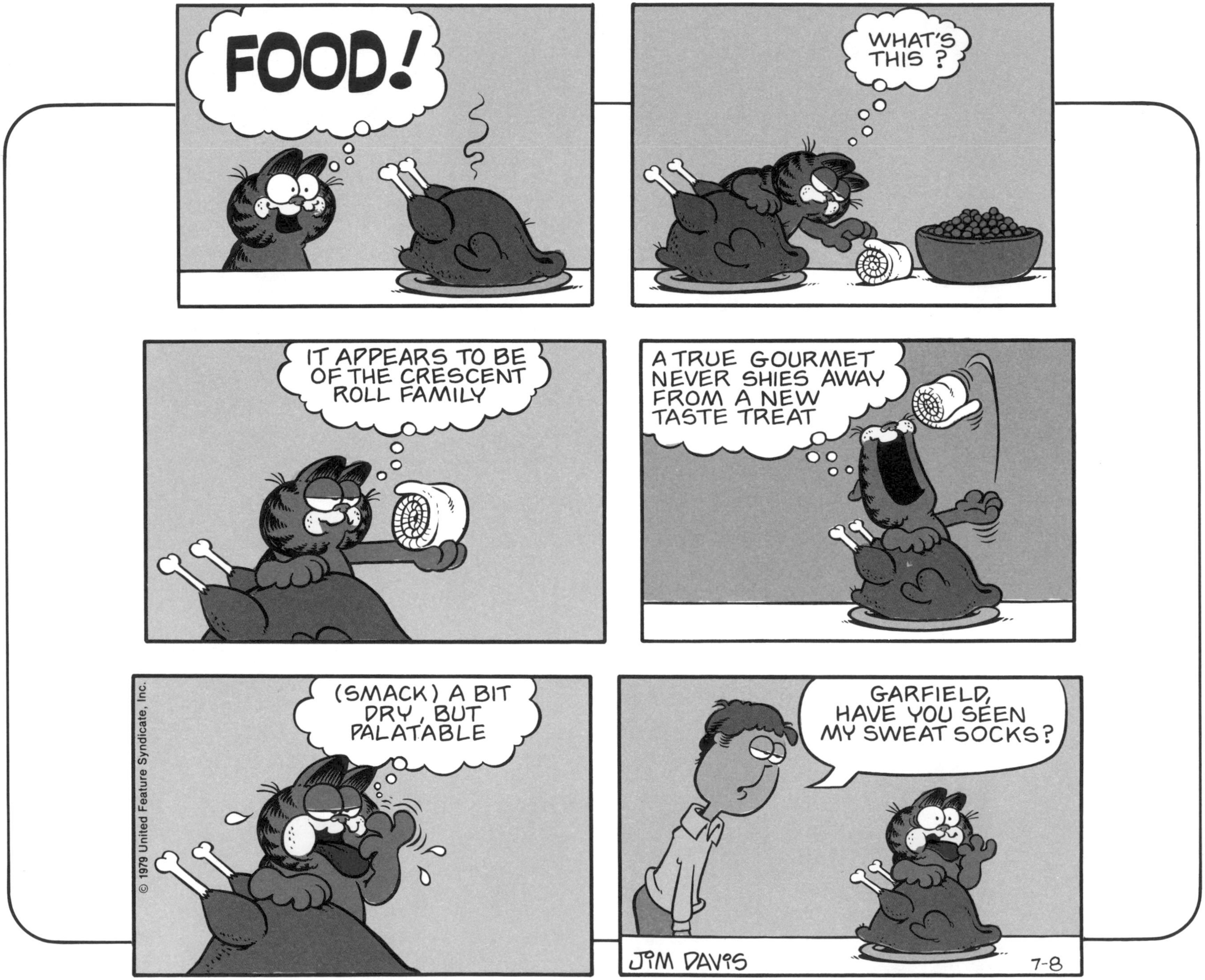
FOOD!
WHAT'S THIS ?
IT APPEARS TO BE OF THE CRESCENT ROLL FAMILY
A TRUE GOURMET NEVER SHIES AWAY FROM A NEW TASTE TREAT
(SMACK) A BIT DRY , BUT PALATABLE
© 1979 United Feature Syndicate, Inc.
GARFIELD, HAVE YOU SEEN MY SWEAT SOCKS?
JIM DAVIS
7-8

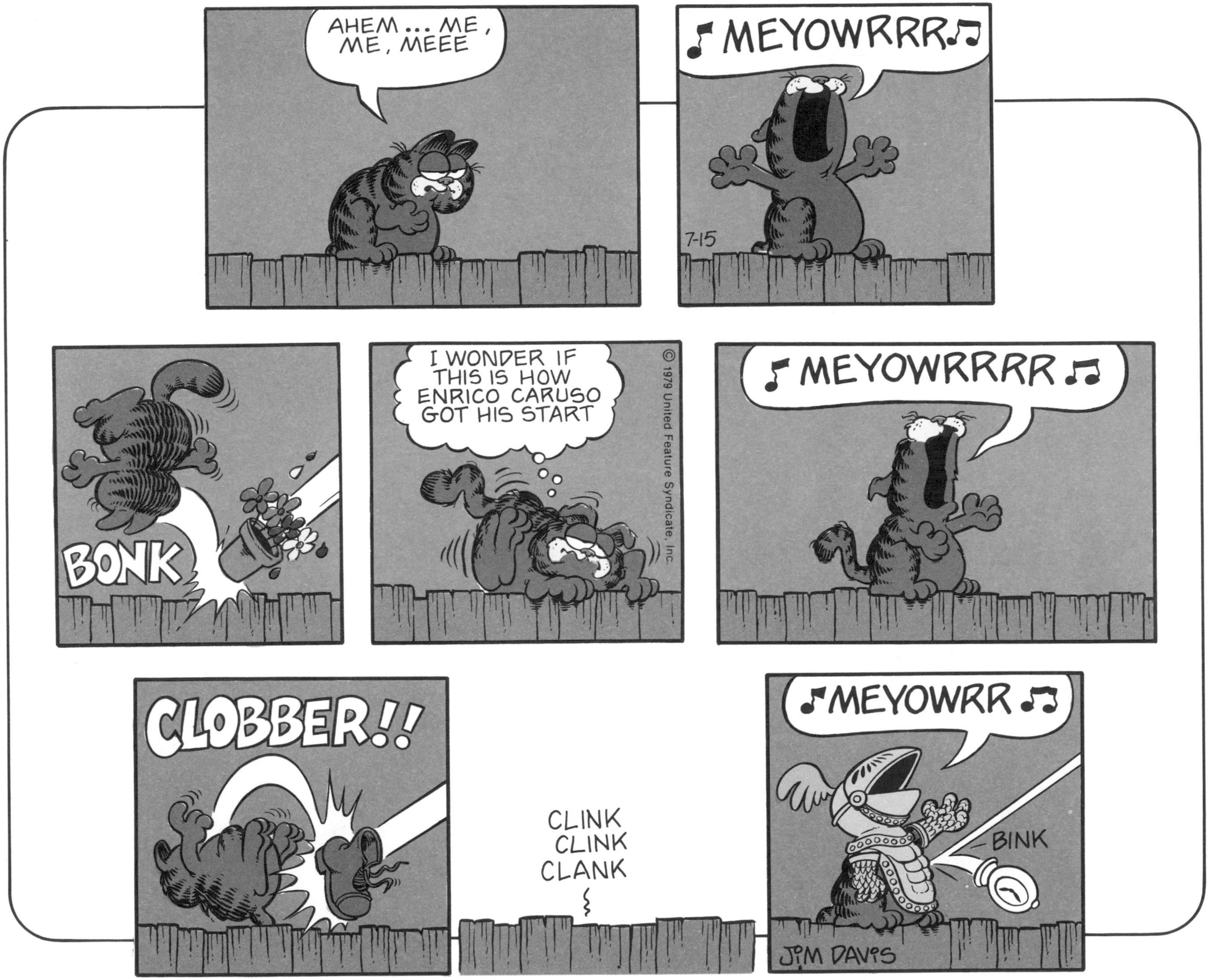
AHEM... ME, ME, MEEE
MEYOWRRR
7-15
BONK
I WONDER IF THIS IS HOW ENRICO CARUSO GOT HIS START
© 1979 United Feature Syndicate, Inc.
MEYOWRRRR
CLOBBER!!
CLINK CLINK CLANK
MEYOWRR
BINK
JIM DAVIS

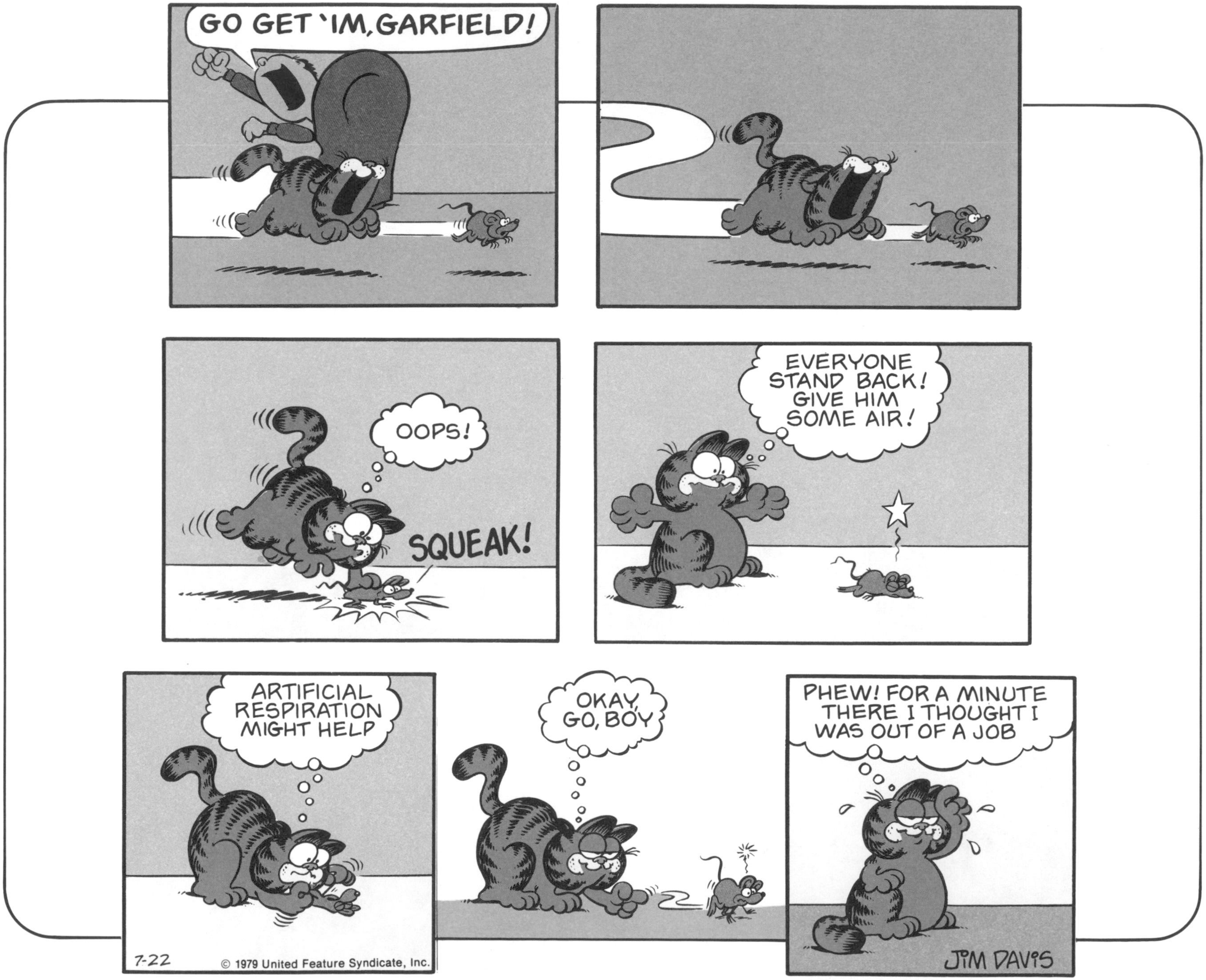
GO GET 'IM, GARFIELD!
OOPS!
SQUEAK!
EVERYONE STAND BACK! GIVE HIM SOME AIR!
ARTIFICIAL RESPIRATION MIGHT HELP
OKAY, GO, BOY
PHEW! FOR A MINUTE THERE I THOUGHT I WAS OUT OF A JOB
7-22
© 1979 United Feature Syndicate, Inc.
JIM DAVIS

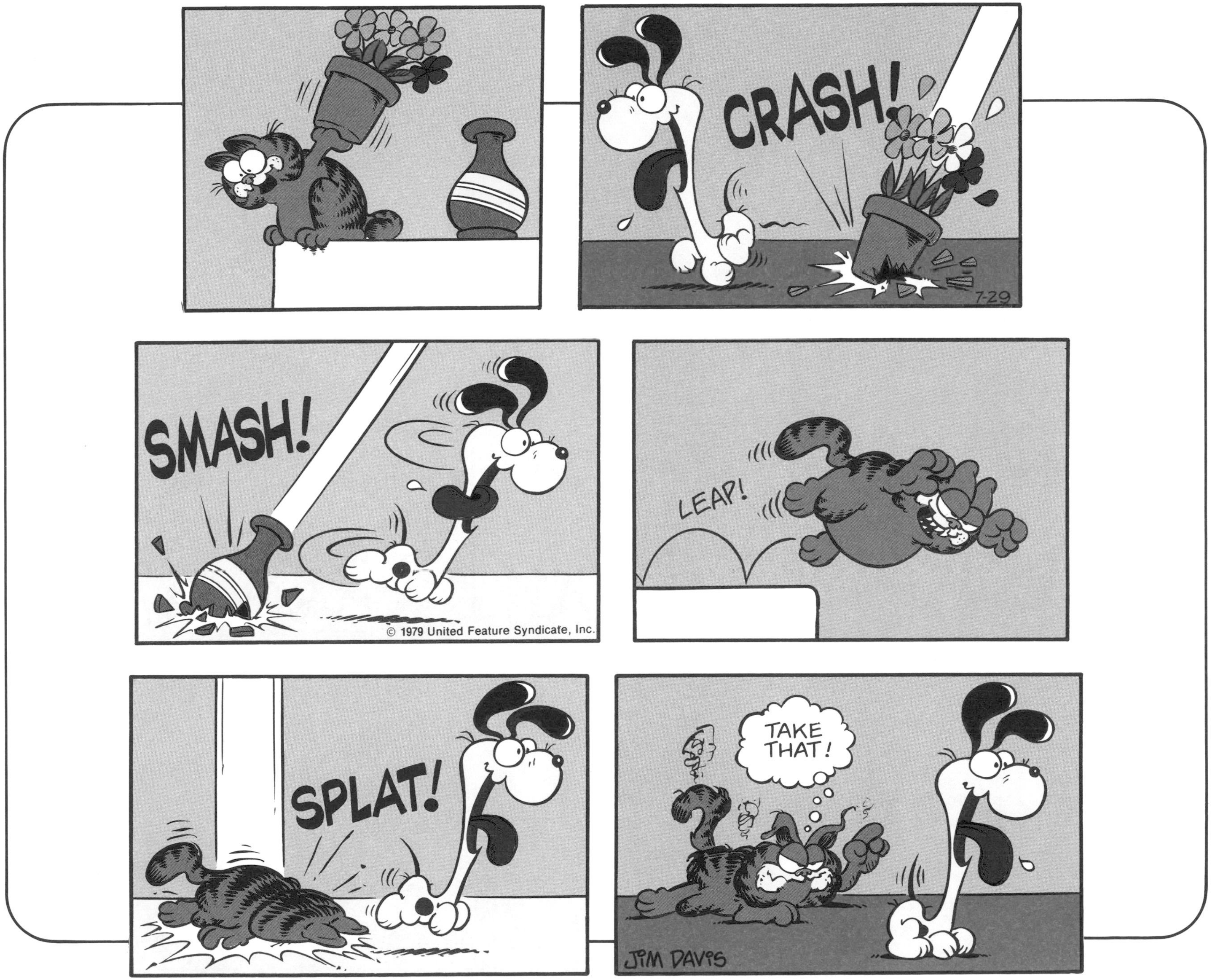
CRASH!
7-29
SMASH!
© 1979 United Feature Syndicate, Inc.
LEAP!
SPLAT!
TAKE THAT!
JIM DAVIS

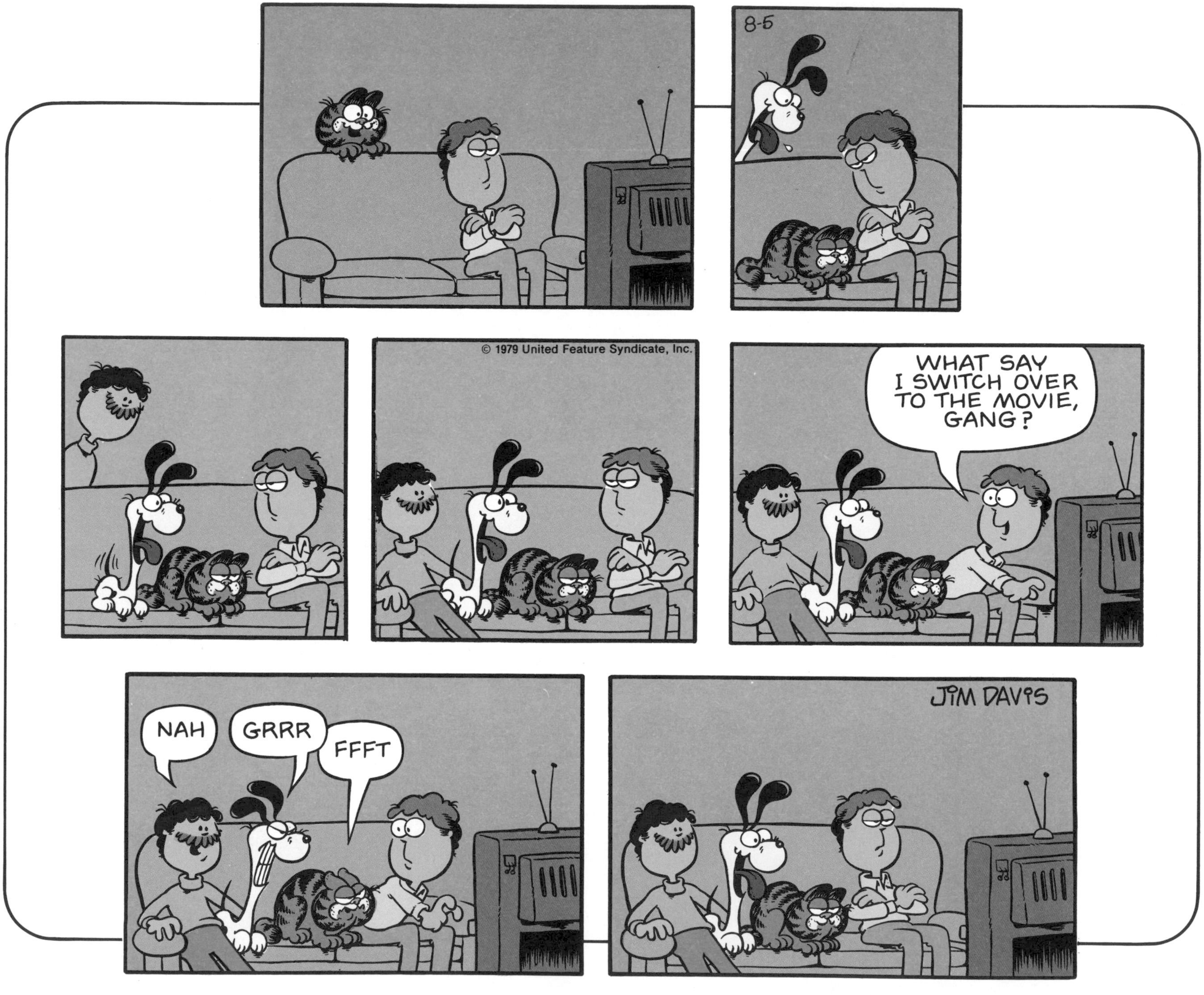
8-5
© 1979 United Feature Syndicate, Inc.
WHAT SAY I SWITCH OVER TO THE MOVIE, GANG?
NAH
GRRR
FFFT
JIM DAVIS

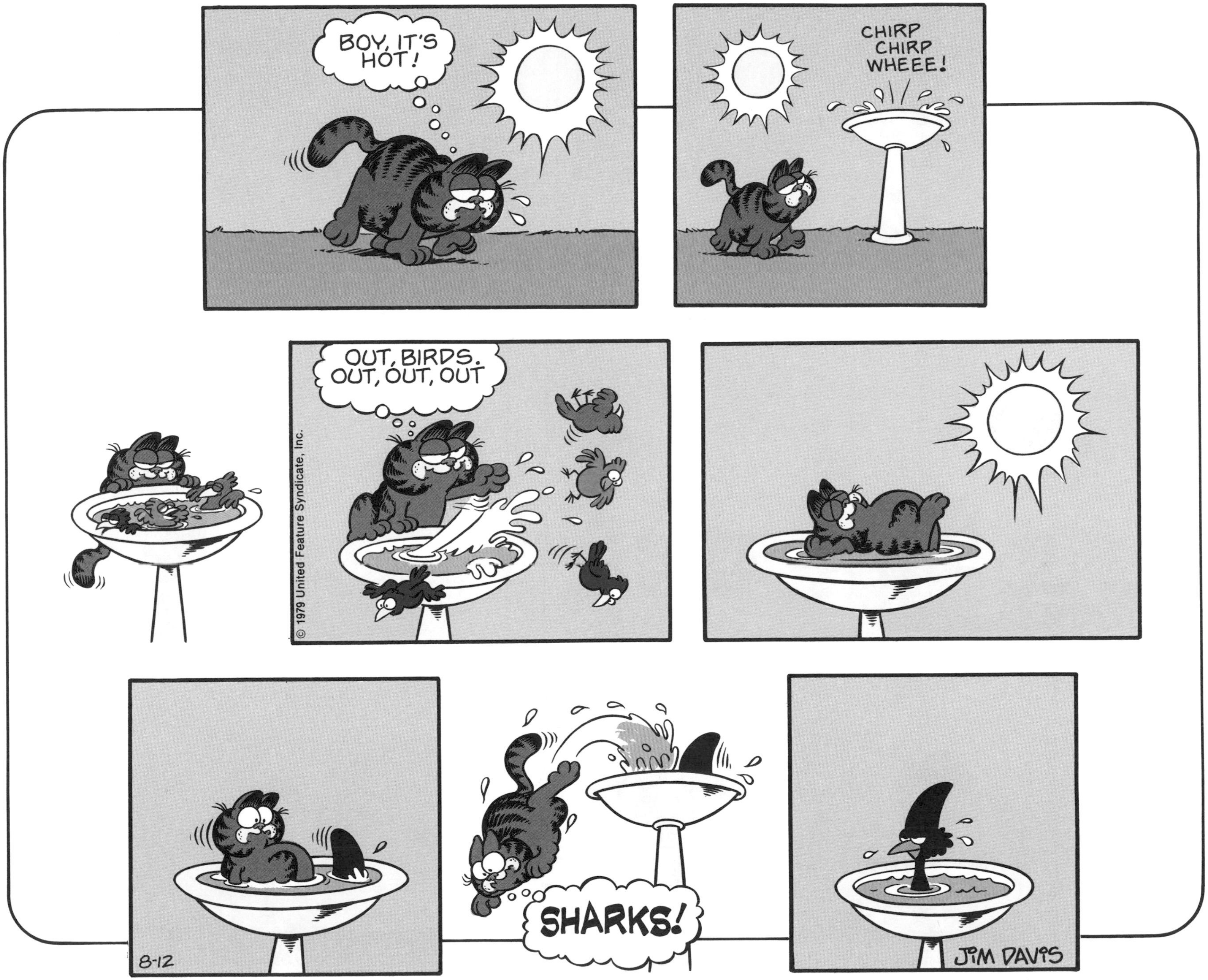
BOY, IT'S HOT!
CHIRP CHIRP WHEEE!
OUT, BIRDS. OUT, OUT, OUT
© 1979 United Feature Syndicate, Inc.
SHARKS!
8-12
JIM DAVIS

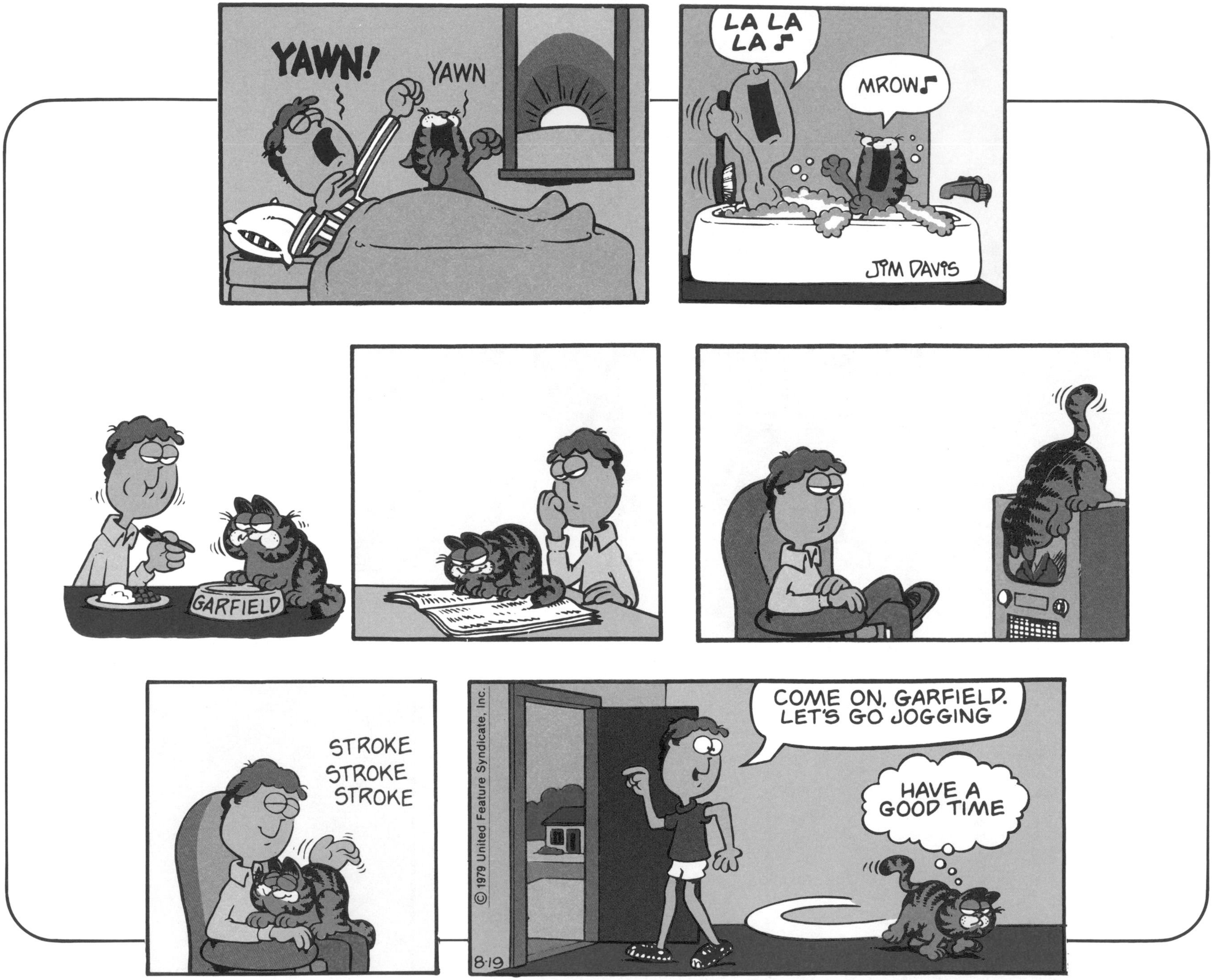
YAWN!
YAWN
LA LA LA
MROW
JIM DAVIS
GARFIELD
STROKE STROKE STROKE
© 1979 United Feature Syndicate, Inc.
8·19
COME ON, GARFIELD. LET'S GO JOGGING
HAVE A GOOD TIME

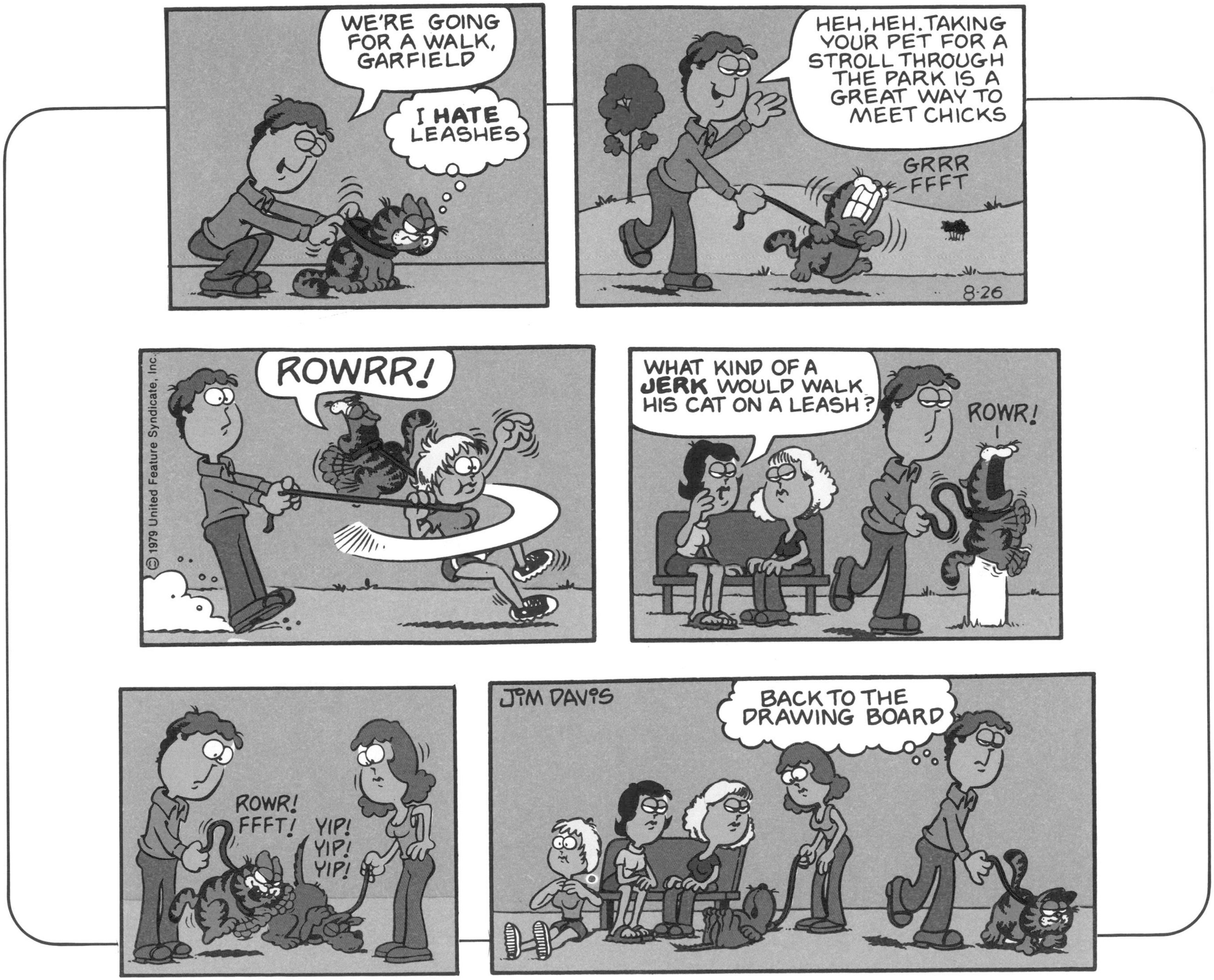
WE'RE GOING FOR A WALK, GARFIELD
I HATE LEASHES
HEH, HEH. TAKING YOUR PET FOR A STROLL THROUGH THE PARK IS A GREAT WAY TO MEET CHICKS
GRRR FFFT
8·26
© 1979 United Feature Syndicate, Inc.
ROWRR!
WHAT KIND OF A JERK WOULD WALK HIS CAT ON A LEASH?
ROWR!
ROWR! FFFT!
YIP! YIP! YIP!
JIM DAVIS
BACK TO THE DRAWING BOARD

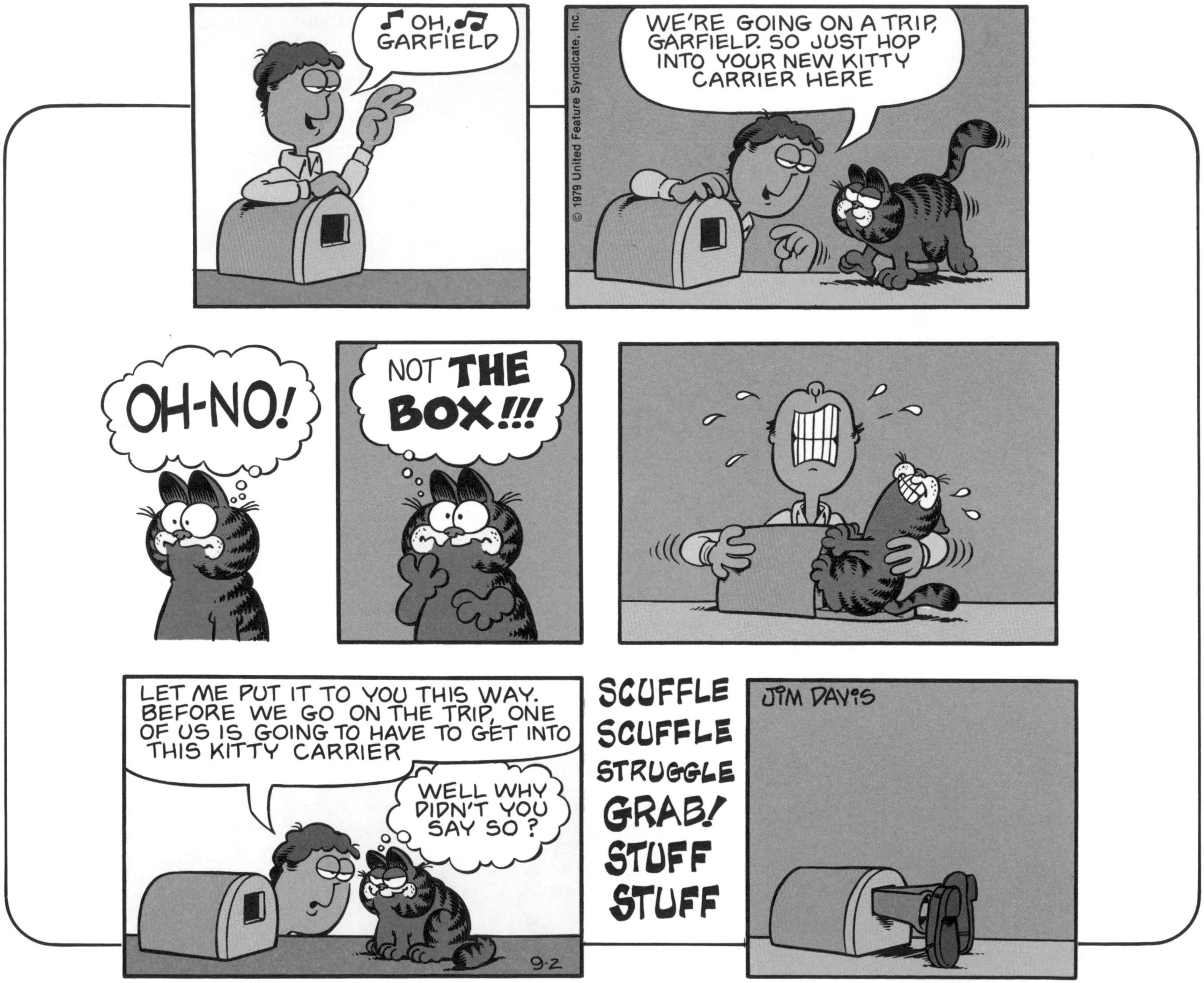

♪ OH, ♫ GARFIELD
© 1979 United Feature Syndicate, Inc.
WE'RE GOING ON A TRIP, GARFIELD. SO JUST HOP INTO YOUR NEW KITTY CARRIER HERE
OH-NO!
NOT THE BOX!!!
LET ME PUT IT TO YOU THIS WAY. BEFORE WE GO ON THE TRIP, ONE OF US IS GOING TO HAVE TO GET INTO THIS KITTY CARRIER
WELL WHY DIDN'T YOU SAY SO?
9-2
SCUFFLE
SCUFFLE
STRUGGLE
GRAB!
STUFF
STUFF
JIM DAVIS

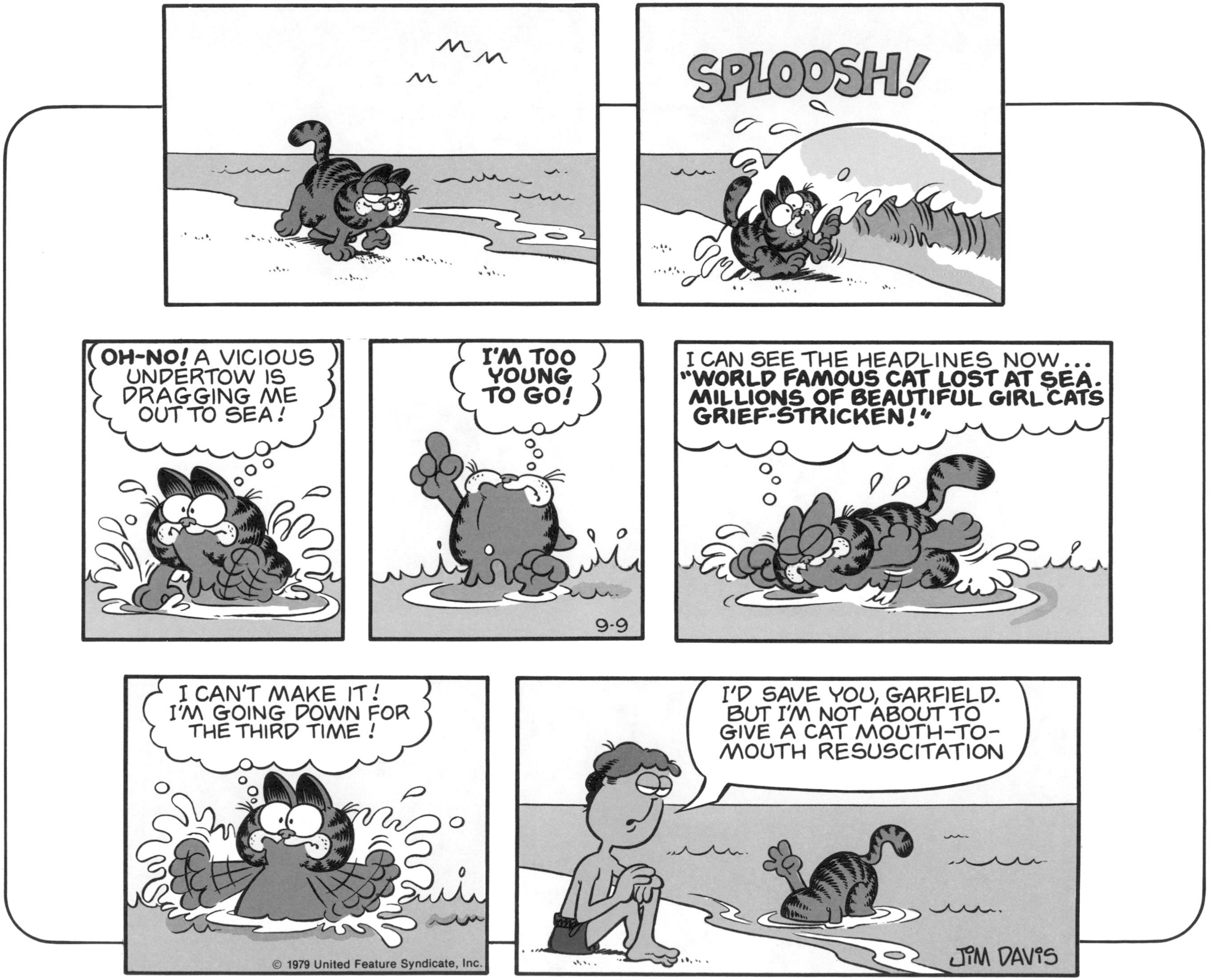
SPLOOSH!
OH-NO! A VICIOUS UNDERTOW IS DRAGGING ME OUT TO SEA!
I'M TOO YOUNG TO GO!
9-9
I CAN SEE THE HEADLINES NOW... "WORLD FAMOUS CAT LOST AT SEA. MILLIONS OF BEAUTIFUL GIRL CATS GRIEF-STRICKEN!"
I CAN'T MAKE IT! I'M GOING DOWN FOR THE THIRD TIME!
© 1979 United Feature Syndicate, Inc.
I'D SAVE YOU, GARFIELD. BUT I'M NOT ABOUT TO GIVE A CAT MOUTH-TO-MOUTH RESUSCITATION
JIM DAVIS

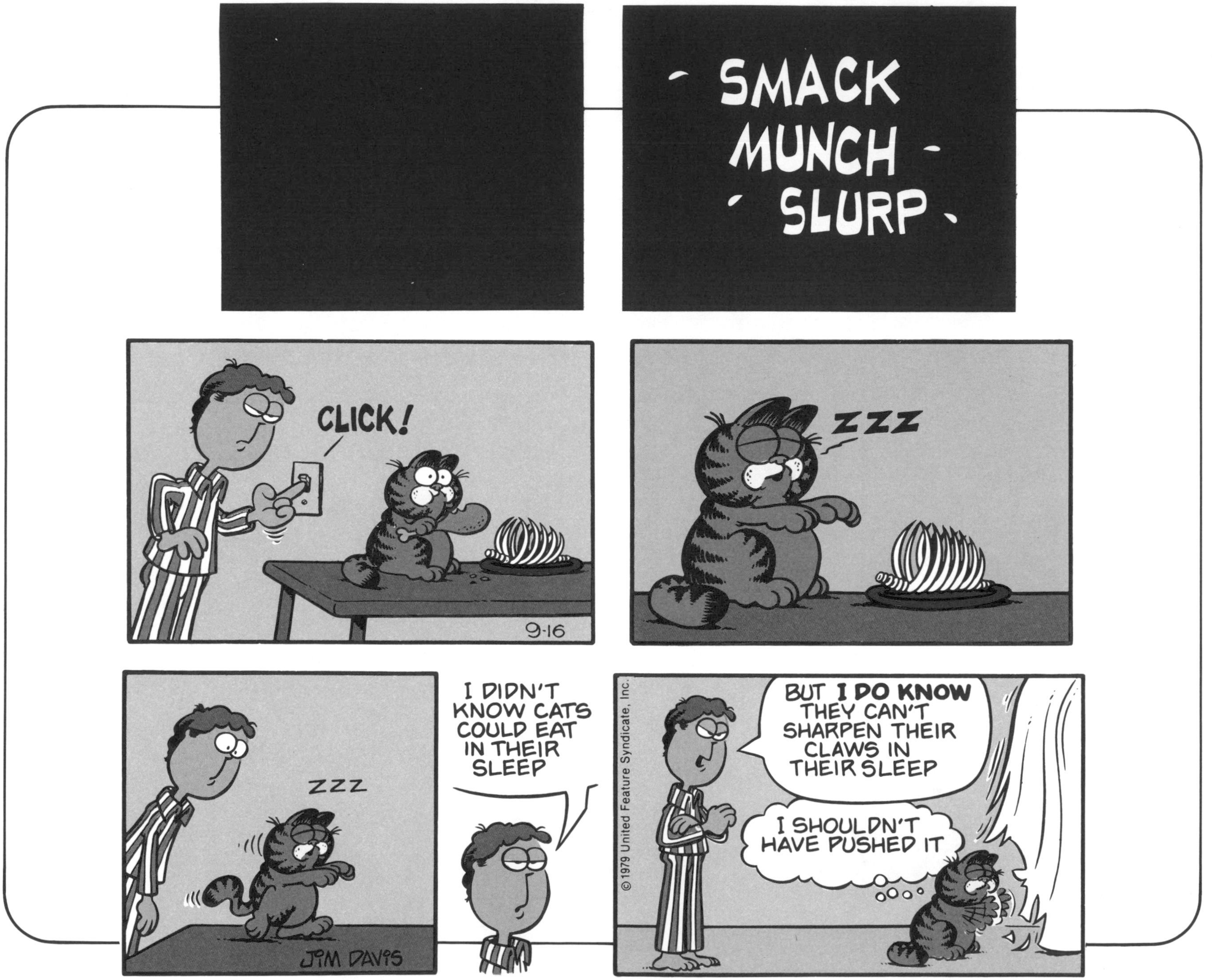
SMACK
MUNCH
SLURP
CLICK!
9·16
ZZZ
ZZZ
JIM DAVIS
I DIDN'T KNOW CATS COULD EAT IN THEIR SLEEP
© 1979 United Feature Syndicate, Inc.
BUT I DO KNOW THEY CAN'T SHARPEN THEIR CLAWS IN THEIR SLEEP
I SHOULDN'T HAVE PUSHED IT

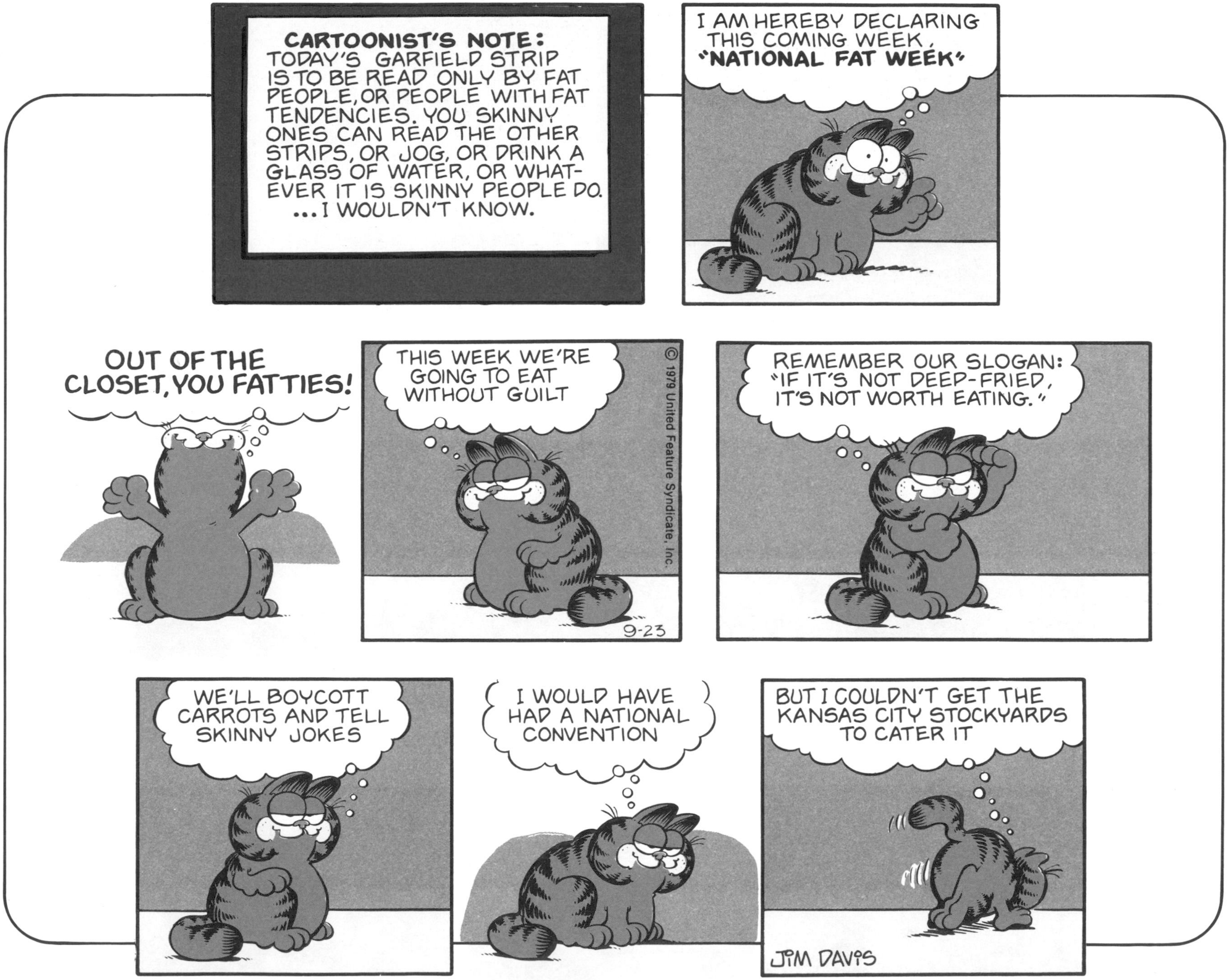
CARTOONIST'S NOTE:
TODAY'S GARFIELD STRIP IS TO BE READ ONLY BY FAT PEOPLE, OR PEOPLE WITH FAT TENDENCIES. YOU SKINNY ONES CAN READ THE OTHER STRIPS, OR JOG, OR DRINK A GLASS OF WATER, OR WHATEVER IT IS SKINNY PEOPLE DO. ...I WOULDN'T KNOW.
I AM HEREBY DECLARING THIS COMING WEEK, "NATIONAL FAT WEEK"
OUT OF THE CLOSET, YOU FATTIES!
THIS WEEK WE'RE GOING TO EAT WITHOUT GUILT
© 1979 United Feature Syndicate, Inc.
9-23
REMEMBER OUR SLOGAN: "IF IT'S NOT DEEP-FRIED, IT'S NOT WORTH EATING."
WE'LL BOYCOTT CARROTS AND TELL SKINNY JOKES
I WOULD HAVE HAD A NATIONAL CONVENTION
BUT I COULDN'T GET THE KANSAS CITY STOCKYARDS TO CATER IT
JIM DAVIS

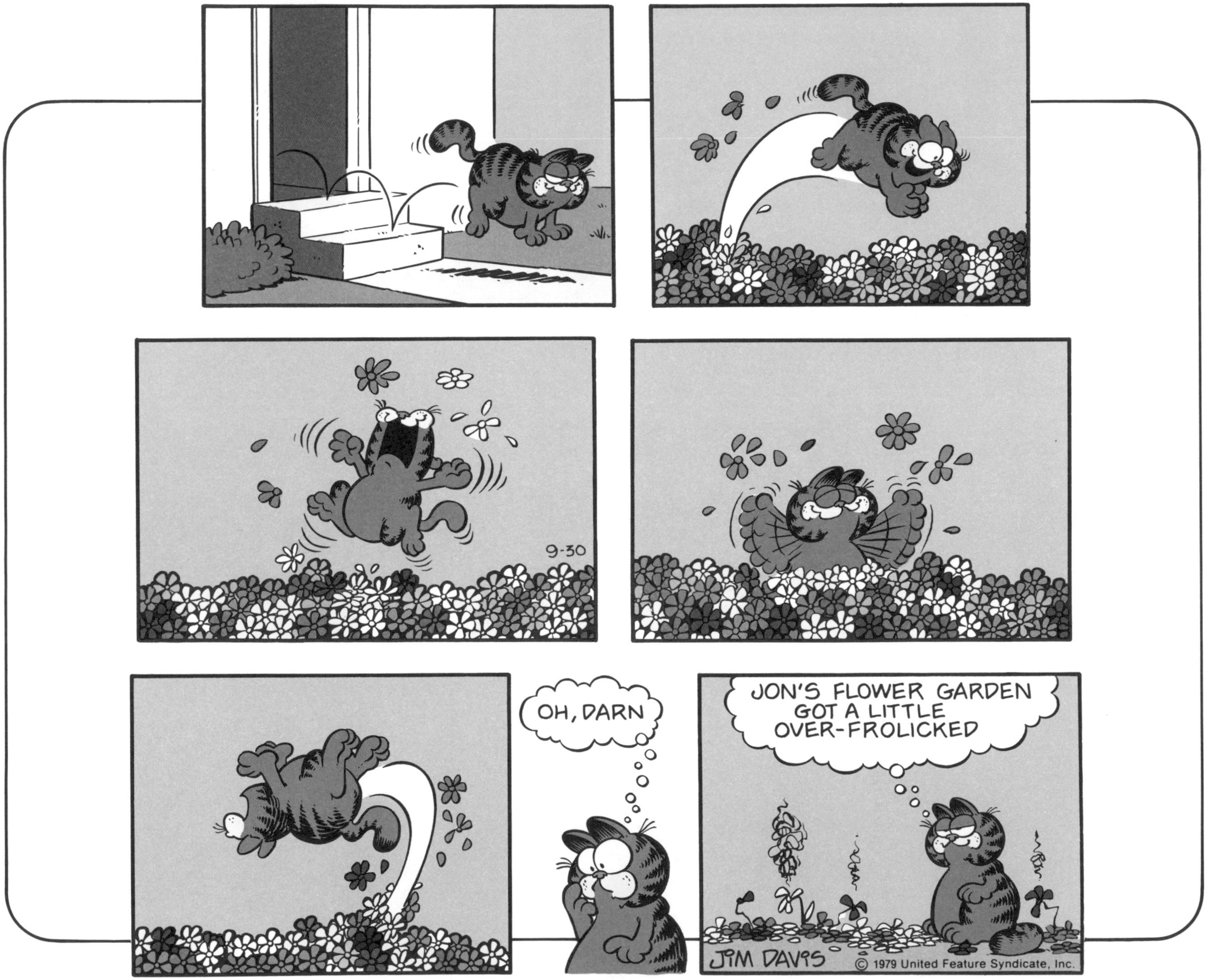
9-30
OH, DARN
JON'S FLOWER GARDEN GOT A LITTLE OVER-FROLICKED
JIM DAVIS
© 1979 United Feature Syndicate, Inc.

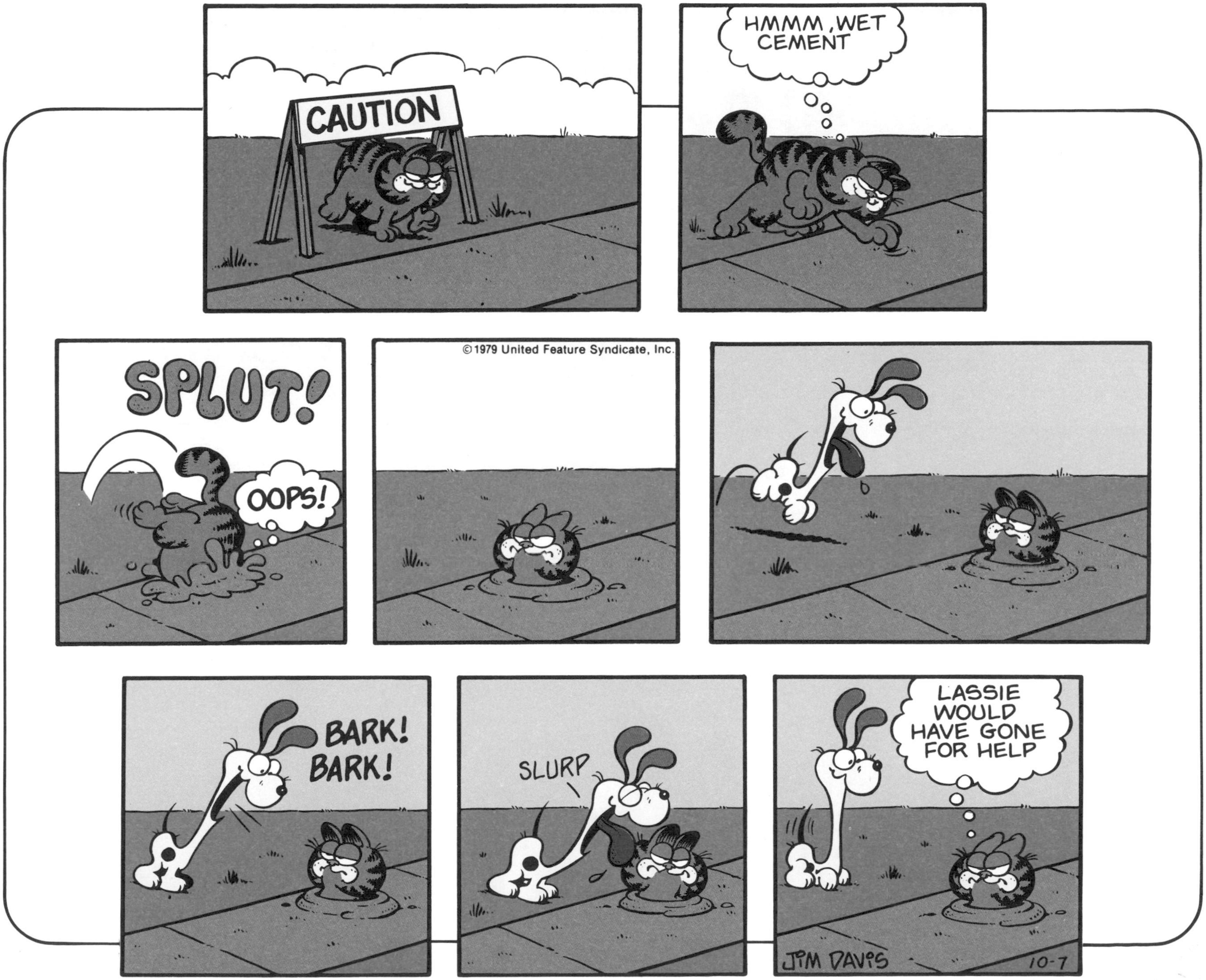
CAUTION
HMMM, WET CEMENT
SPLUT!
OOPS!
©1979 United Feature Syndicate, Inc.
BARK! BARK!
SLURP
LASSIE WOULD HAVE GONE FOR HELP
JIM DAVIS
10-7

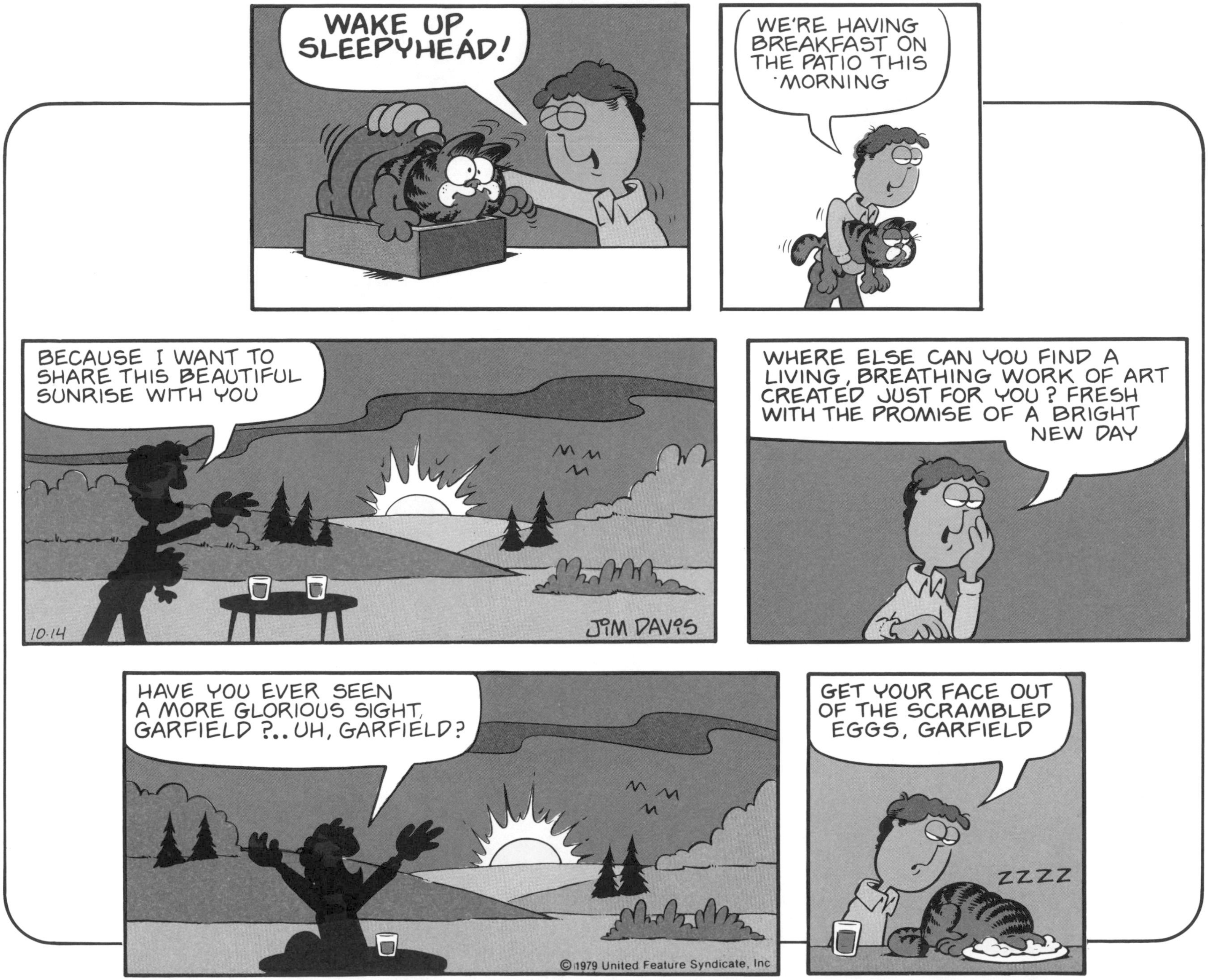
WAKE UP, SLEEPYHEAD!
WE'RE HAVING BREAKFAST ON THE PATIO THIS MORNING
BECAUSE I WANT TO SHARE THIS BEAUTIFUL SUNRISE WITH YOU
WHERE ELSE CAN YOU FIND A LIVING, BREATHING WORK OF ART CREATED JUST FOR YOU? FRESH WITH THE PROMISE OF A BRIGHT NEW DAY
10·14
JIM DAVIS
HAVE YOU EVER SEEN A MORE GLORIOUS SIGHT, GARFIELD?.. UH, GARFIELD?
© 1979 United Feature Syndicate, Inc
GET YOUR FACE OUT OF THE SCRAMBLED EGGS, GARFIELD
ZZZZ

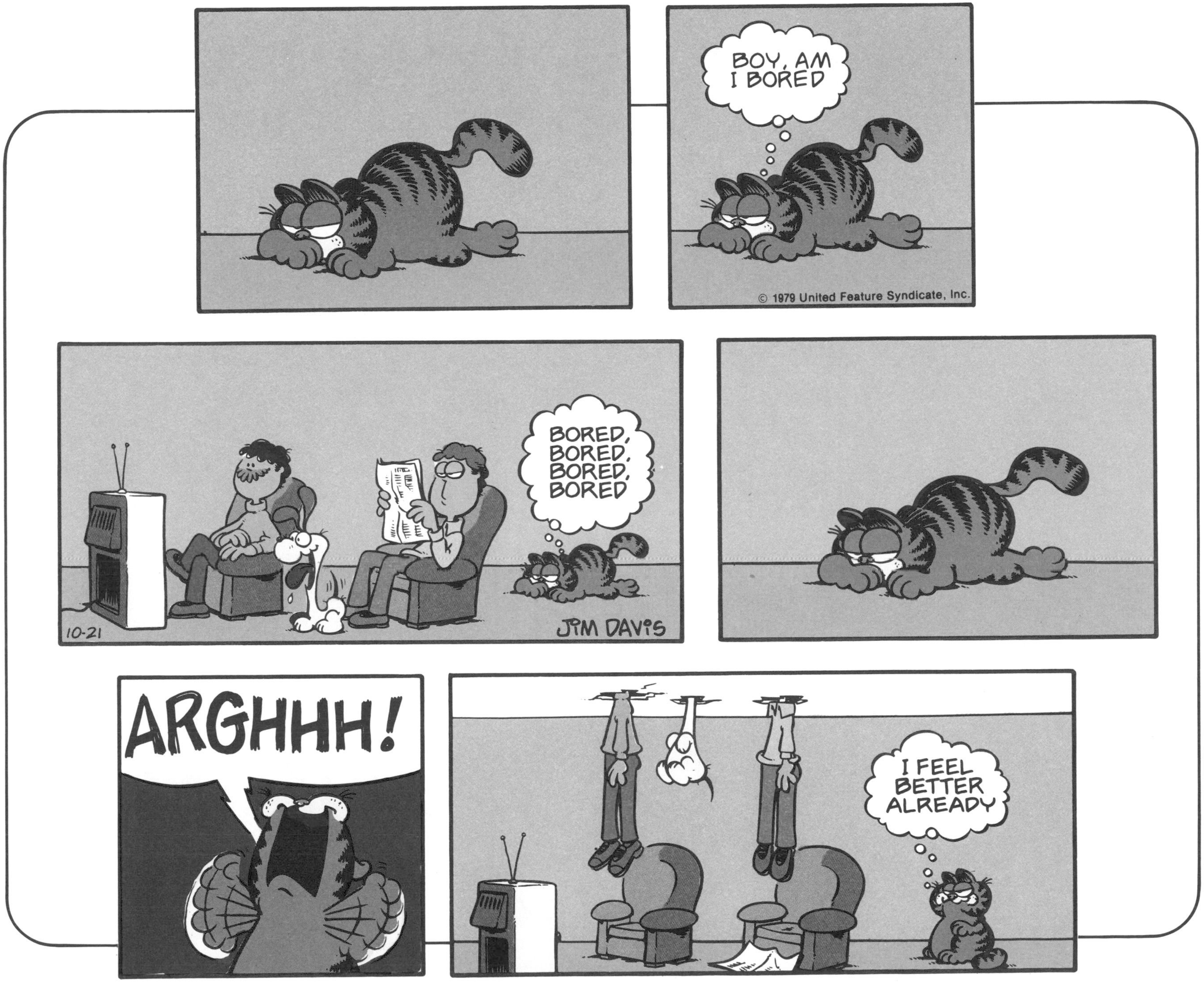

BOY, AM I BORED
© 1979 United Feature Syndicate, Inc.
BORED, BORED, BORED, BORED
10-21
JIM DAVIS
ARGHHH!
I FEEL BETTER ALREADY

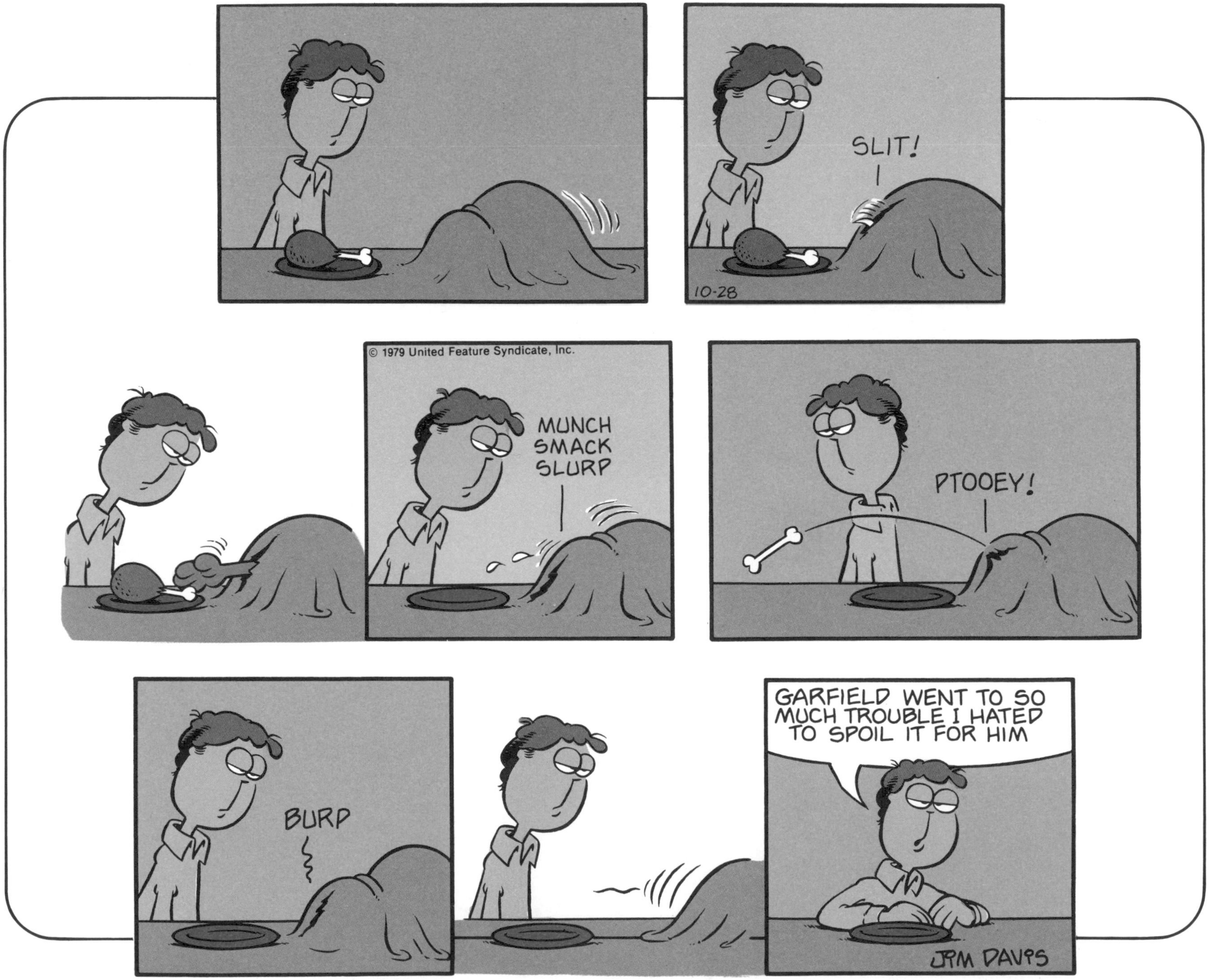
SLIT!
10-28
© 1979 United Feature Syndicate, Inc.
MUNCH SMACK SLURP
PTOOEY!
BURP
GARFIELD WENT TO SO MUCH TROUBLE I HATED TO SPOIL IT FOR HIM
JIM DAVIS

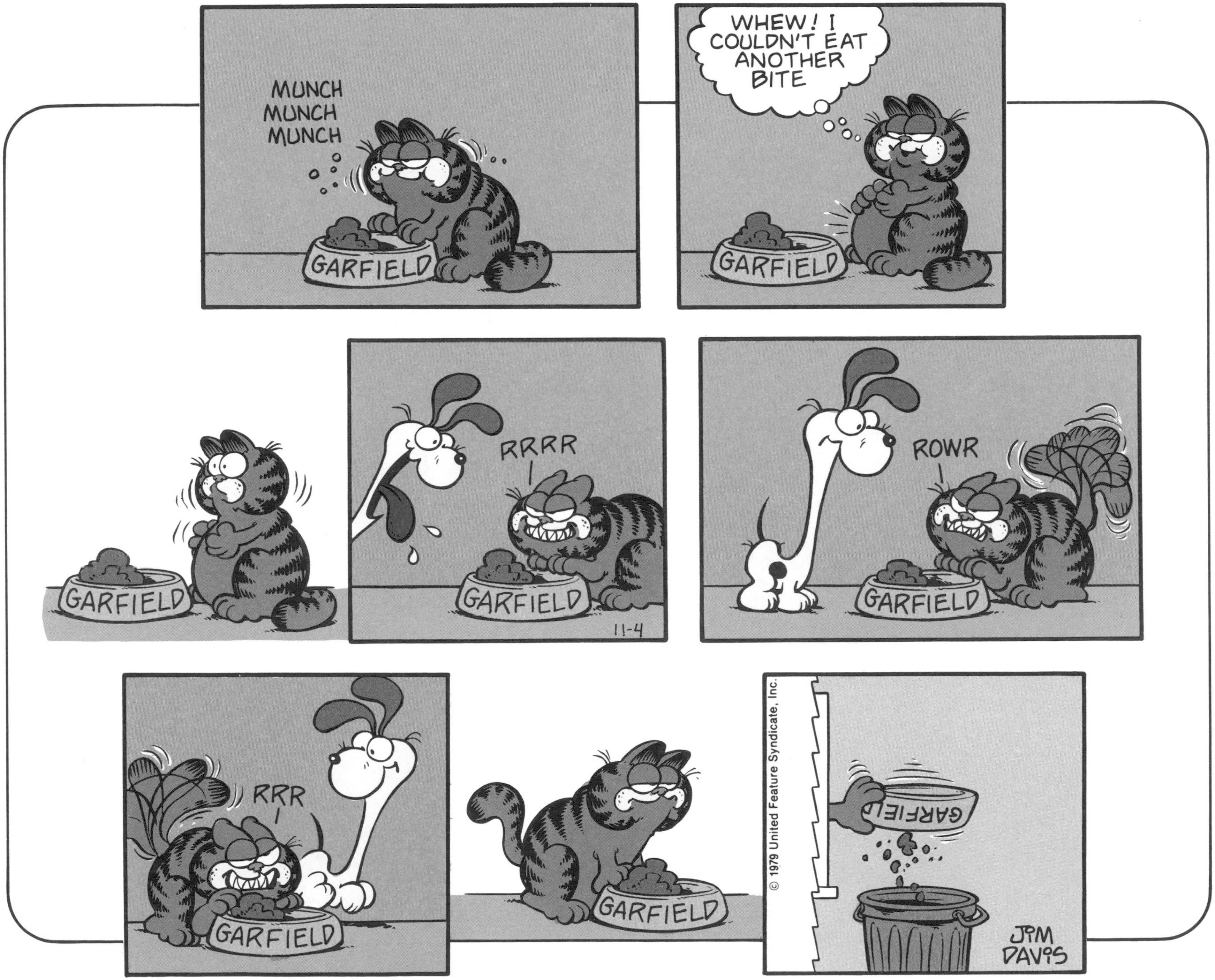
MUNCH
MUNCH
MUNCH
GARFIELD
WHEW! I COULDN'T EAT ANOTHER BITE
GARFIELD
GARFIELD
RRRR
GARFIELD
11-4
ROWR
GARFIELD
RRR
GARFIELD
GARFIELD
© 1979 United Feature Syndicate, Inc.
GARFIELD
JIM DAVIS

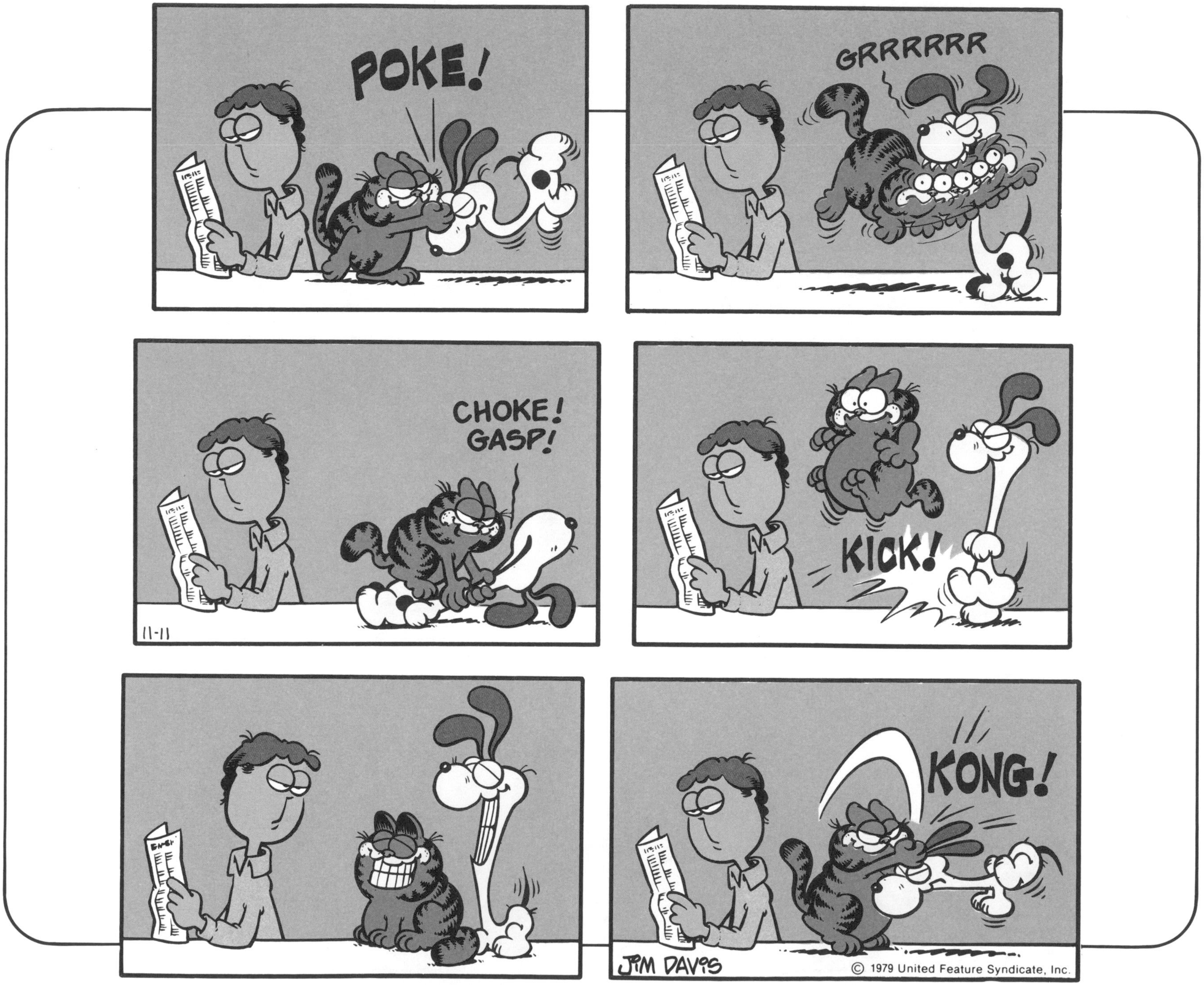
POKE!
GRRRRRR
CHOKE!
GASP!
11-11
KICK!
KONG!
JIM DAVIS
© 1979 United Feature Syndicate, Inc.

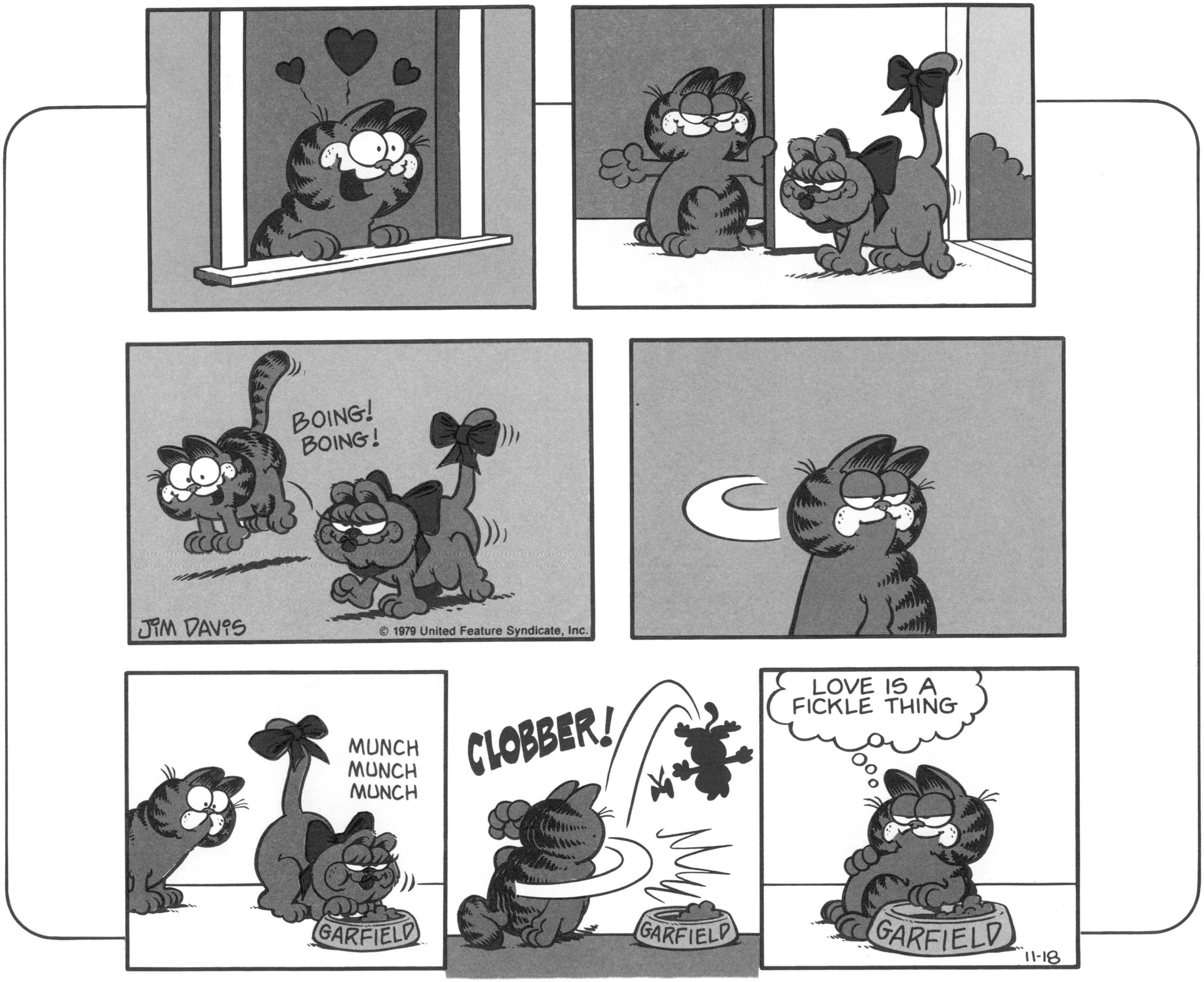
BOING!
BOING!
JIM DAVIS
© 1979 United Feature Syndicate, Inc.
MUNCH
MUNCH
MUNCH
GARFIELD
CLOBBER!
GARFIELD
LOVE IS A
FICKLE THING
GARFIELD
11-18

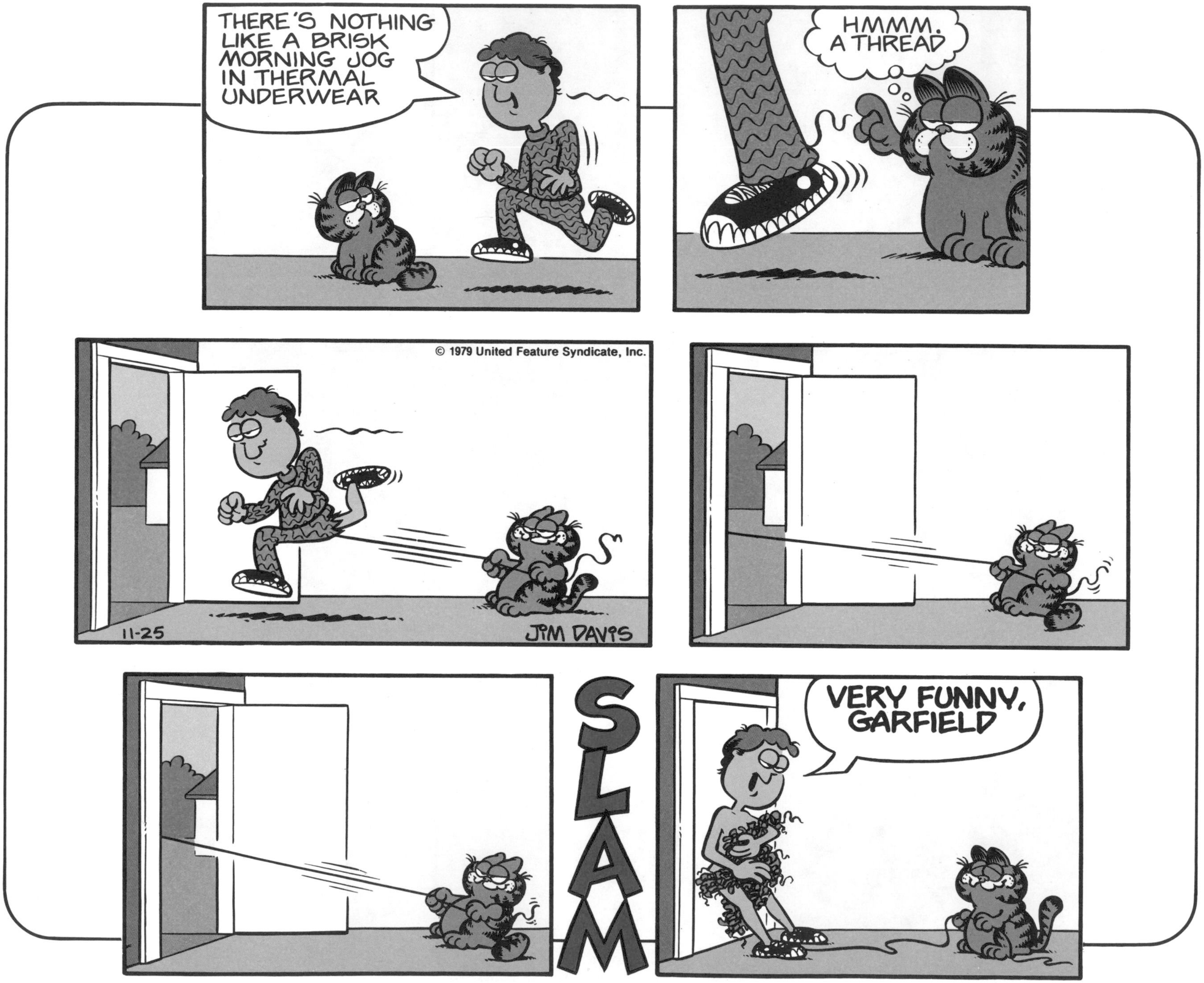
THERE'S NOTHING LIKE A BRISK MORNING JOG IN THERMAL UNDERWEAR
HMMM. A THREAD
© 1979 United Feature Syndicate, Inc.
11-25
JIM DAVIS
SLAM
VERY FUNNY, GARFIELD

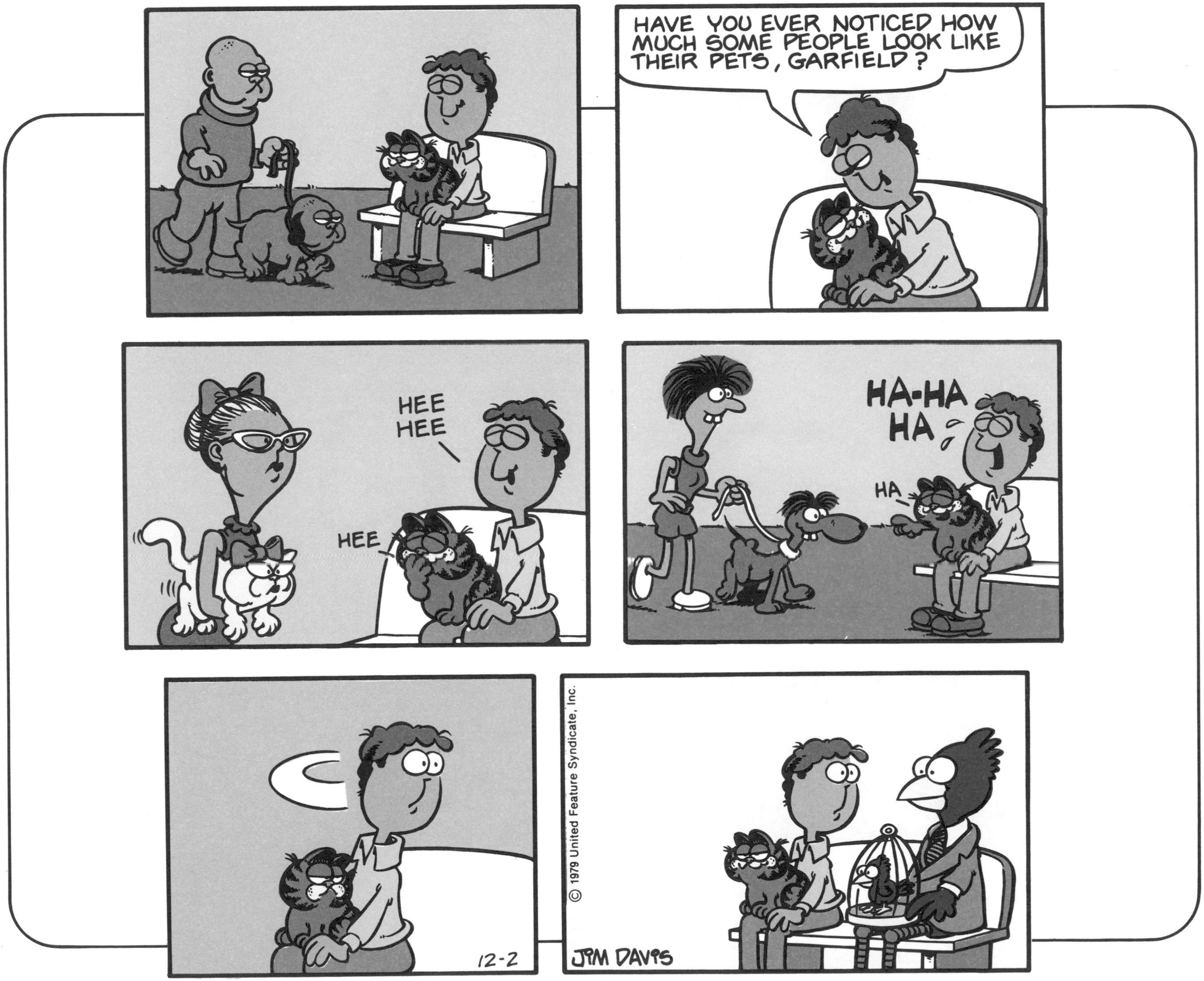
HAVE YOU EVER NOTICED HOW MUCH SOME PEOPLE LOOK LIKE THEIR PETS, GARFIELD?
HEE HEE
HEE
HA-HA HA
HA
12-2
JIM DAVIS
© 1979 United Feature Syndicate, Inc.

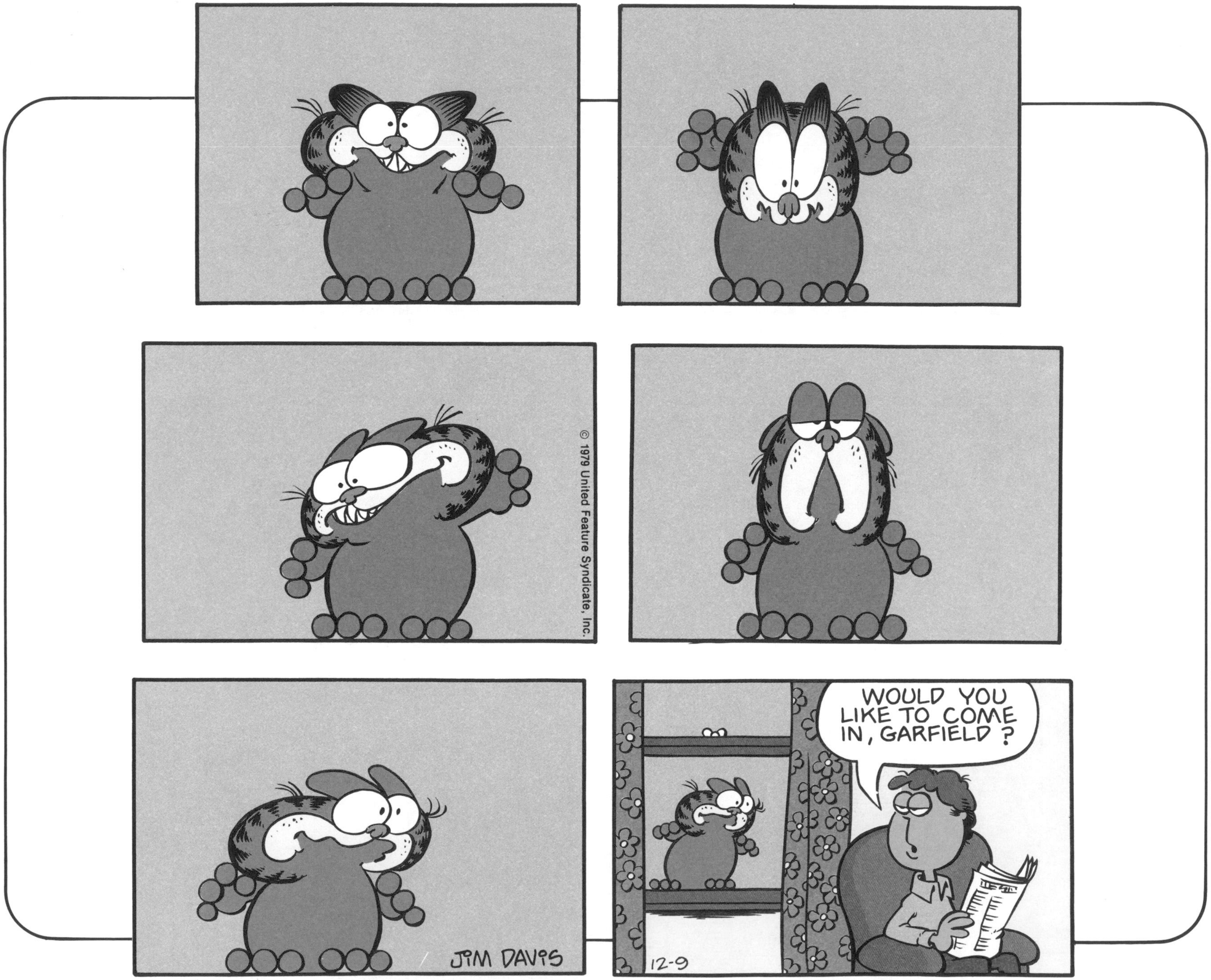
WOULD YOU LIKE TO COME IN, GARFIELD ?
JIM DAVIS
12-9
© 1979 United Feature Syndicate, Inc.

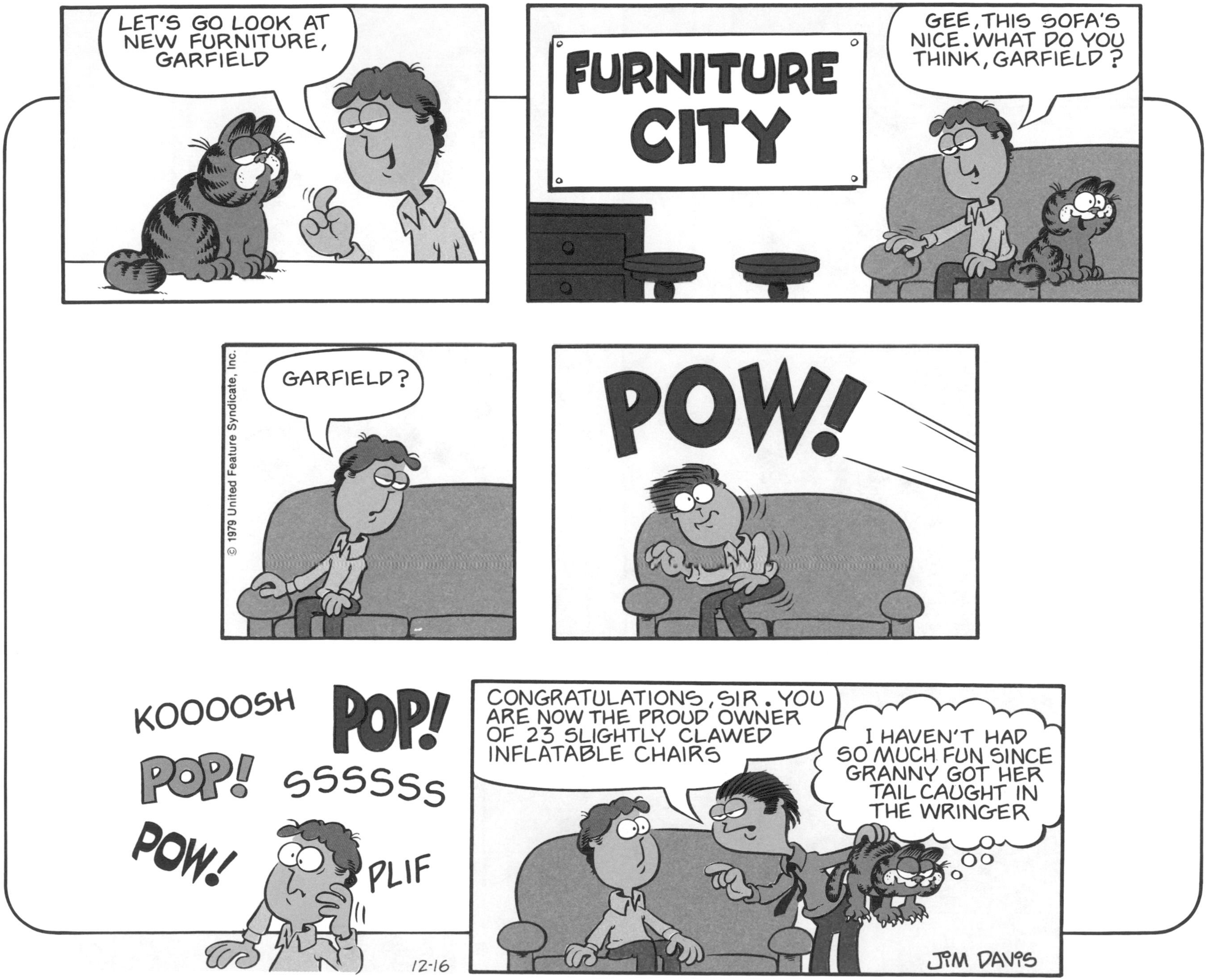

LET'S GO LOOK AT NEW FURNITURE, GARFIELD
FURNITURE CITY
GEE, THIS SOFA'S NICE. WHAT DO YOU THINK, GARFIELD?
GARFIELD?
© 1979 United Feature Syndicate, Inc.
POW!
KOOOOOSH
POP!
POP!
SSSSSS
POW!
PLIF
12-16
CONGRATULATIONS, SIR. YOU ARE NOW THE PROUD OWNER OF 23 SLIGHTLY CLAWED INFLATABLE CHAIRS
I HAVEN'T HAD SO MUCH FUN SINCE GRANNY GOT HER TAIL CAUGHT IN THE WRINGER
JIM DAVIS

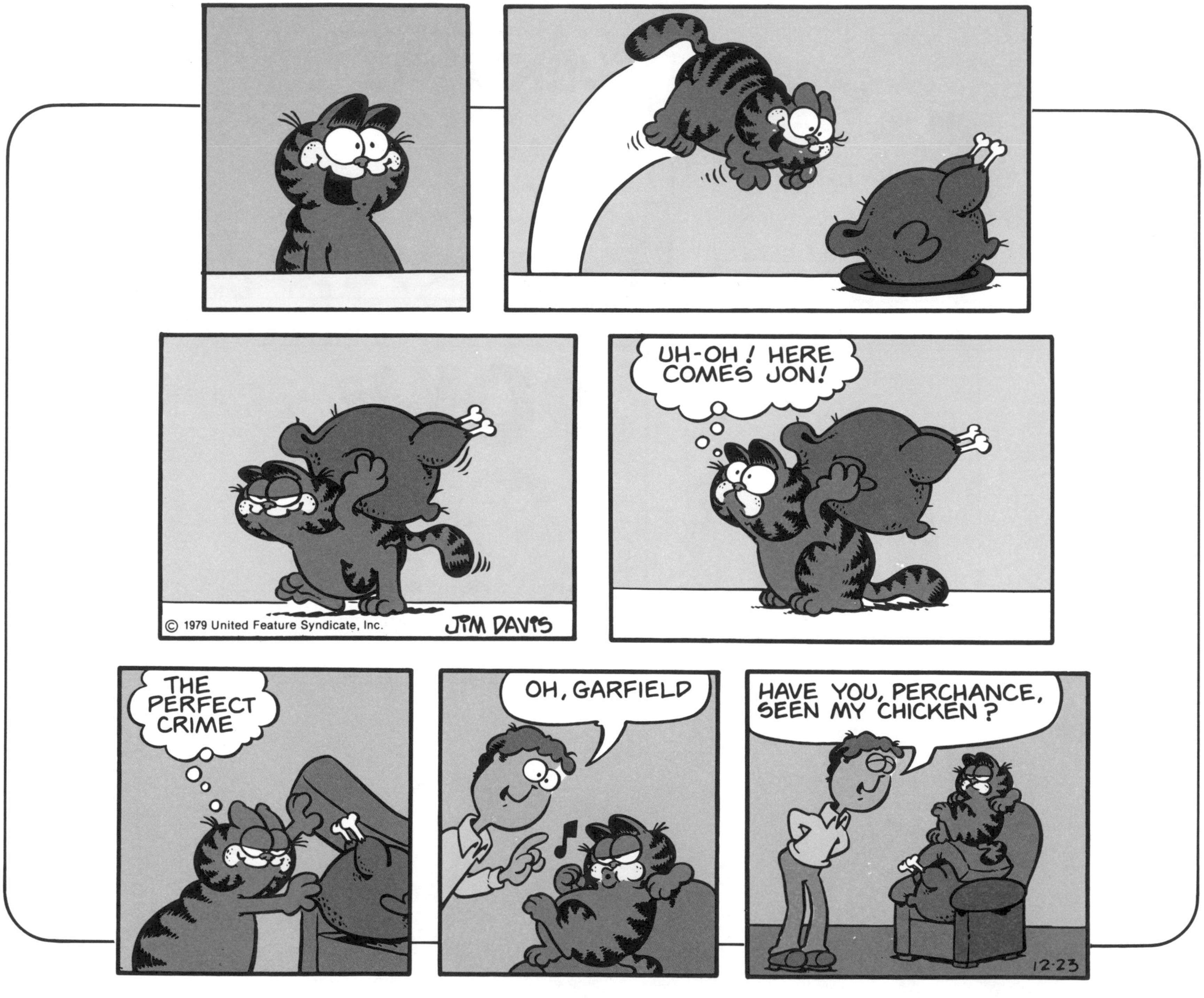
UH-OH! HERE COMES JON!
© 1979 United Feature Syndicate, Inc.
JIM DAVIS
THE PERFECT CRIME
OH, GARFIELD
HAVE YOU, PERCHANCE, SEEN MY CHICKEN?
12-23

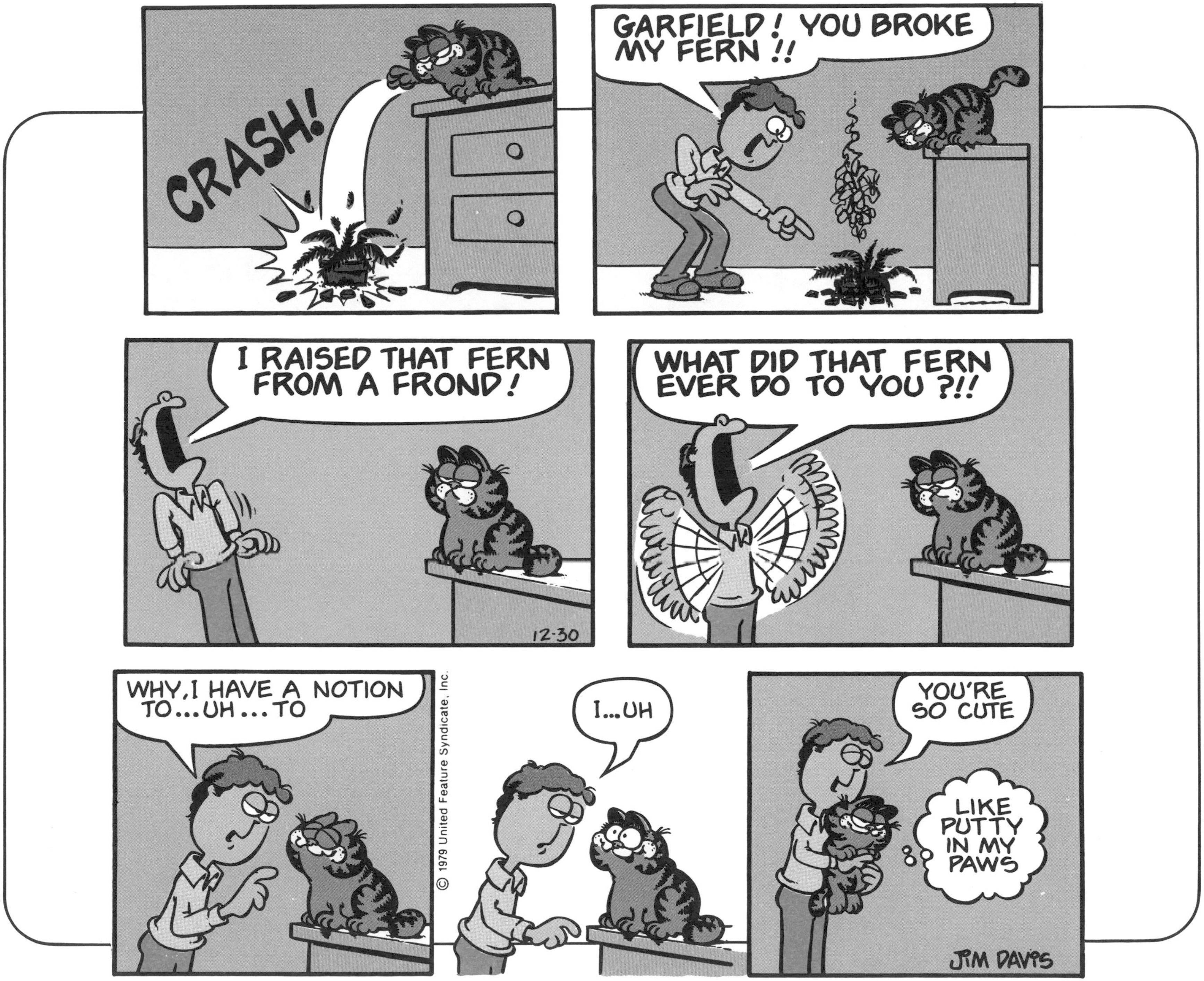
CRASH!
GARFIELD! YOU BROKE MY FERN!!
I RAISED THAT FERN FROM A FROND!
12-30
WHAT DID THAT FERN EVER DO TO YOU ?!!
WHY, I HAVE A NOTION TO... UH ... TO
© 1979 United Feature Syndicate, Inc.
I...UH
YOU'RE SO CUTE
LIKE PUTTY IN MY PAWS
JIM DAVIS

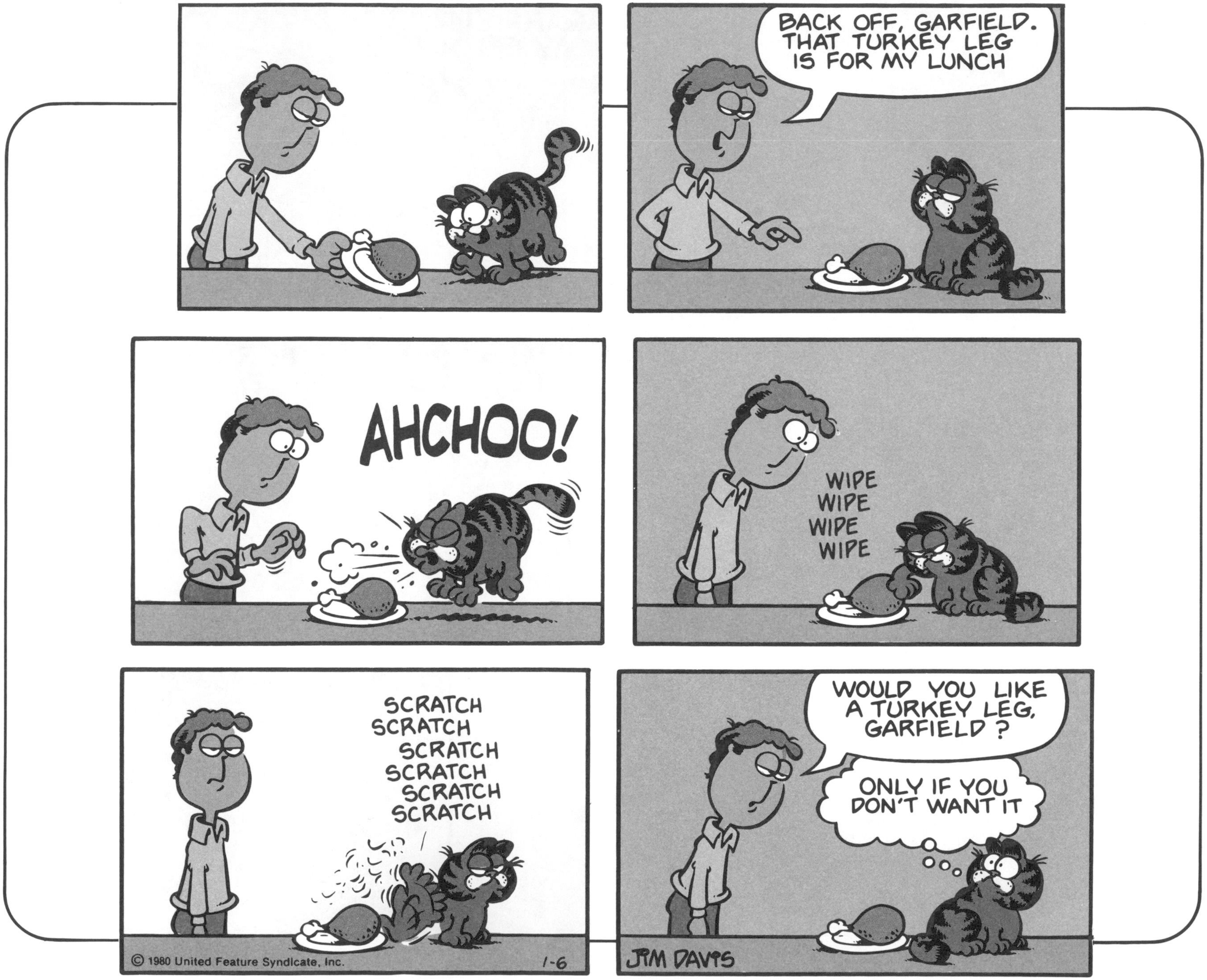
BACK OFF, GARFIELD. THAT TURKEY LEG IS FOR MY LUNCH
AHCHOO!
WIPE WIPE WIPE WIPE
SCRATCH SCRATCH SCRATCH SCRATCH SCRATCH SCRATCH
© 1980 United Feature Syndicate, Inc.
1-6
WOULD YOU LIKE A TURKEY LEG, GARFIELD ?
ONLY IF YOU DON'T WANT IT
JIM DAVIS

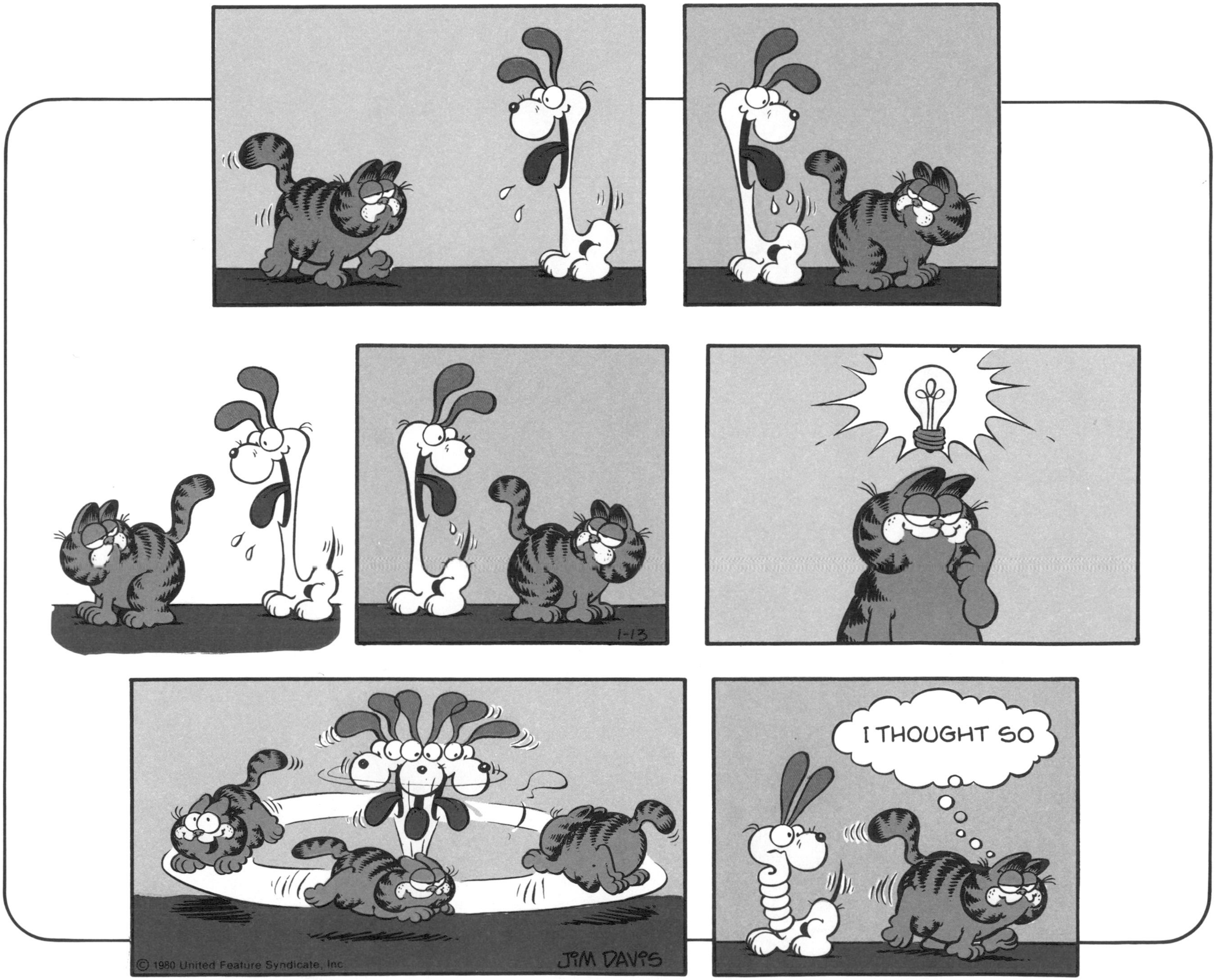
1-13
I THOUGHT SO
JIM DAVIS
© 1980 United Feature Syndicate, Inc

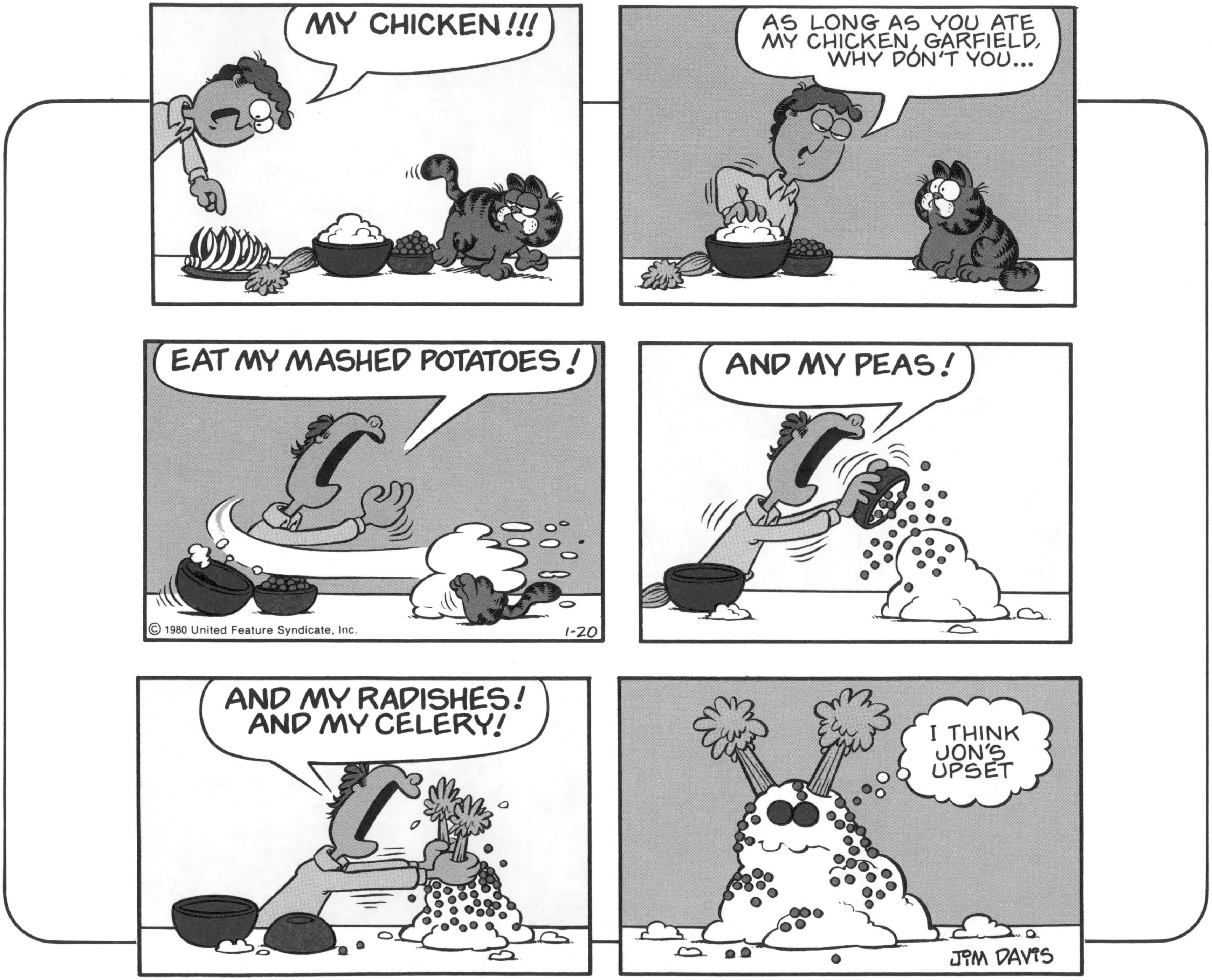
MY CHICKEN!!!
AS LONG AS YOU ATE MY CHICKEN, GARFIELD, WHY DON'T YOU...
EAT MY MASHED POTATOES!
© 1980 United Feature Syndicate, Inc.
1-20
AND MY PEAS!
AND MY RADISHES! AND MY CELERY!
I THINK JON'S UPSET
JIM DAVIS

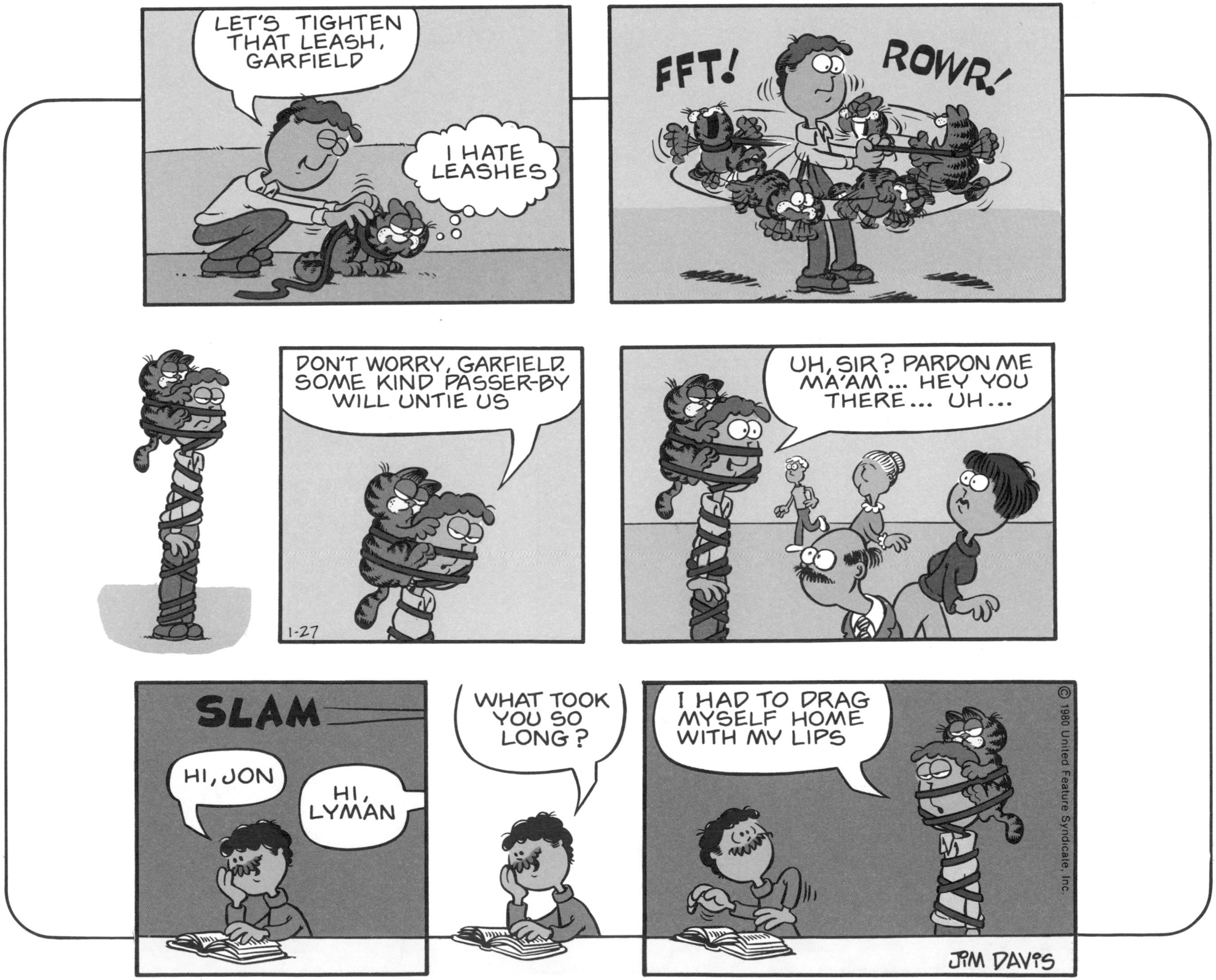
LET'S TIGHTEN THAT LEASH, GARFIELD
I HATE LEASHES
FFT!
ROWR!
DON'T WORRY, GARFIELD. SOME KIND PASSER-BY WILL UNTIE US
1-27
UH, SIR? PARDON ME MA'AM... HEY YOU THERE... UH...
SLAM
HI, JON
HI, LYMAN
WHAT TOOK YOU SO LONG?
I HAD TO DRAG MYSELF HOME WITH MY LIPS
© 1980 United Feature Syndicate, Inc.
JIM DAVIS

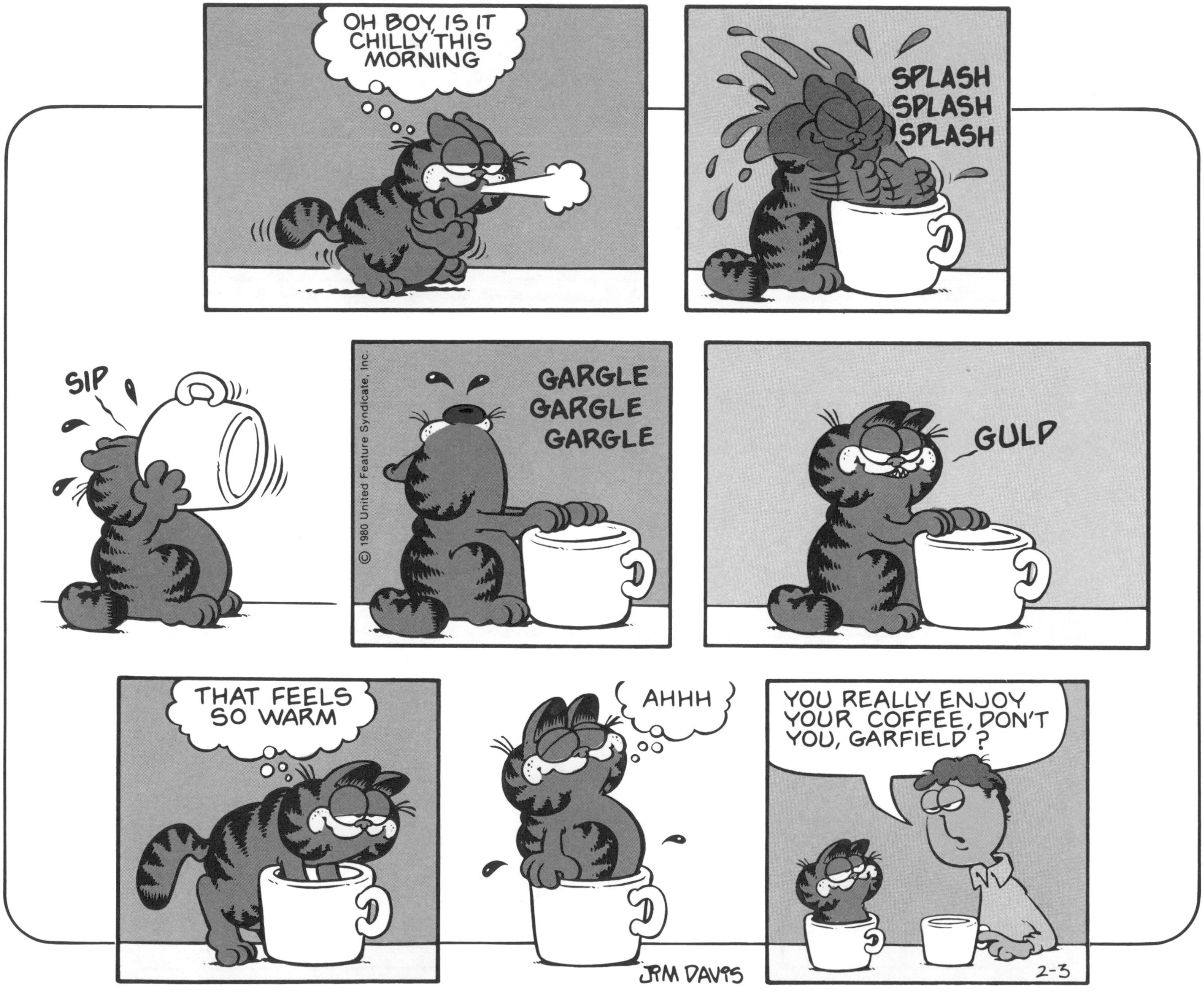
OH BOY IS IT CHILLY THIS MORNING
SPLASH SPLASH SPLASH
SIP
GARGLE GARGLE GARGLE
© 1980 United Feature Syndicate, Inc.
GULP
THAT FEELS SO WARM
AHHH
YOU REALLY ENJOY YOUR COFFEE, DON'T YOU, GARFIELD?
JIM DAVIS
2-3

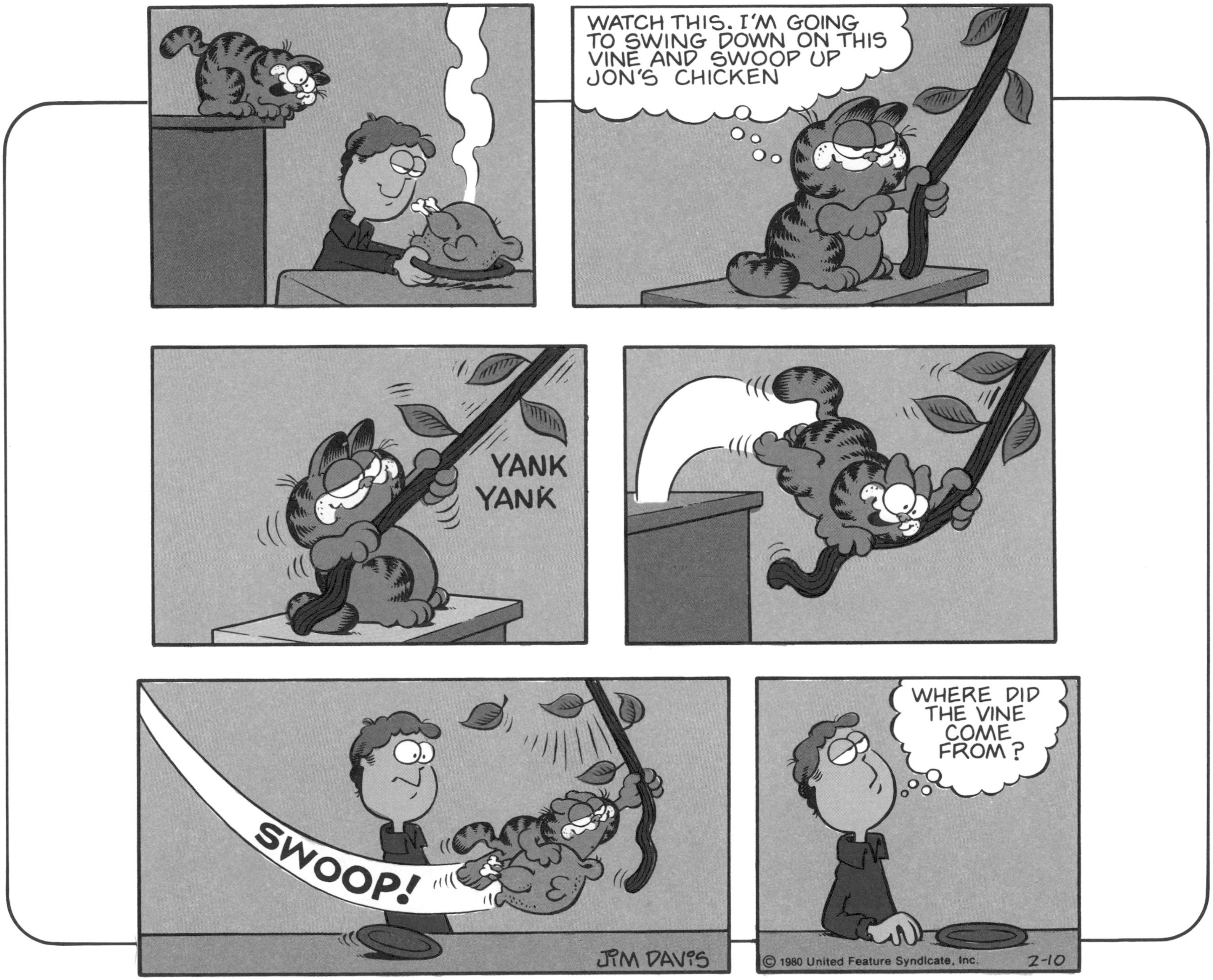
WATCH THIS. I'M GOING TO SWING DOWN ON THIS VINE AND SWOOP UP JON'S CHICKEN
YANK YANK
SWOOP!
WHERE DID THE VINE COME FROM?
JIM DAVIS
© 1980 United Feature Syndicate, Inc.
2-10

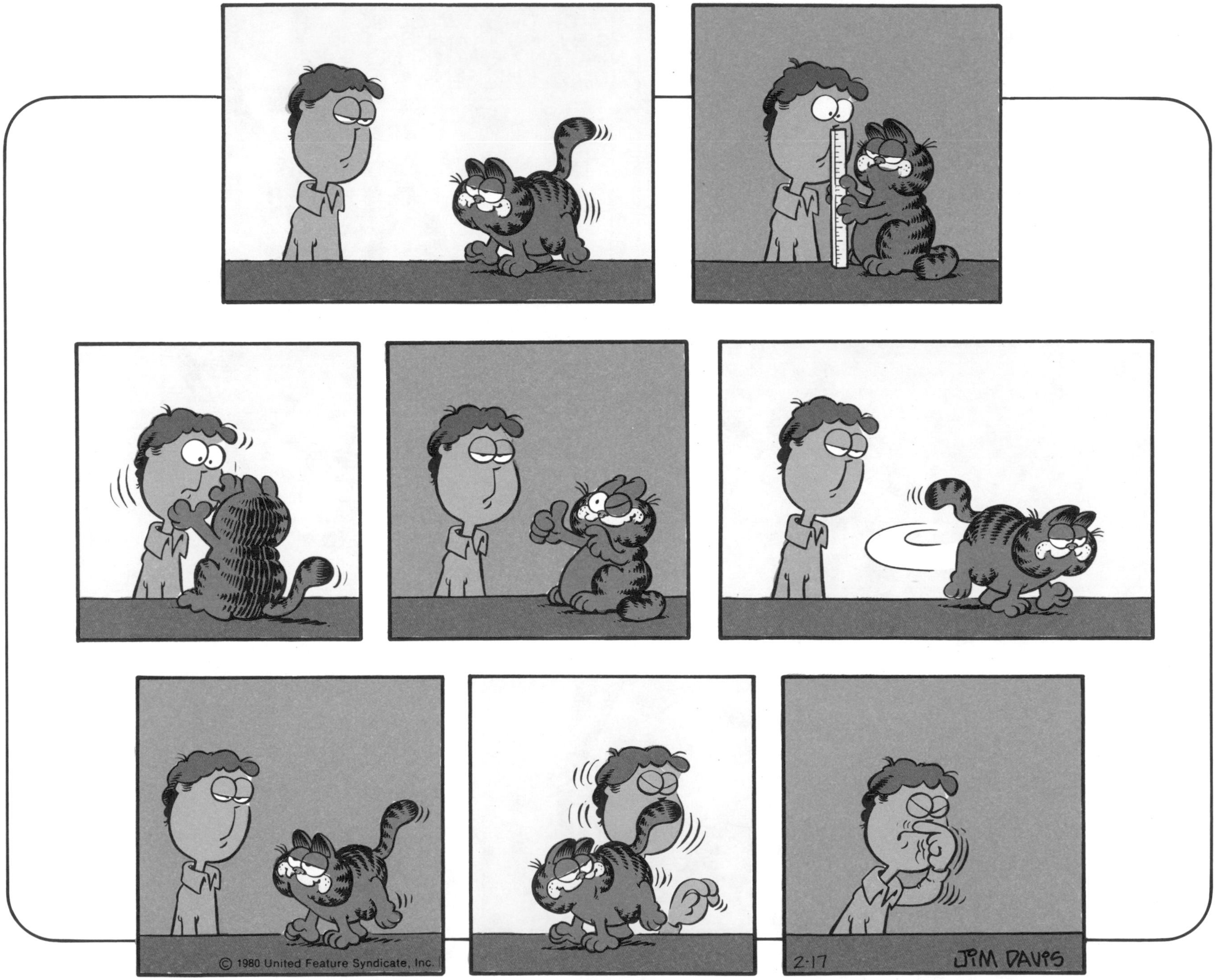
© 1980 United Feature Syndicate, Inc.
2-17
JIM DAVIS

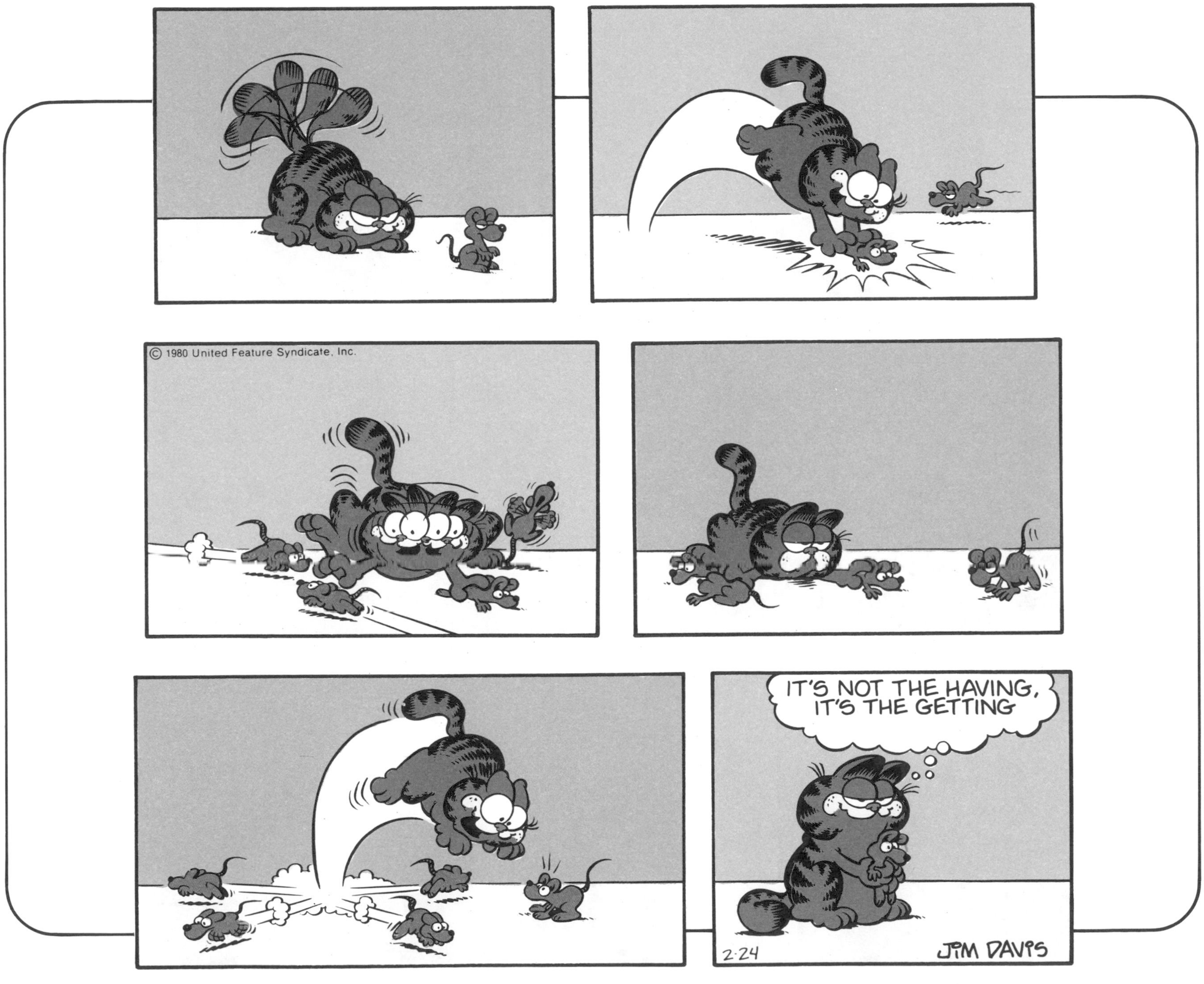
© 1980 United Feature Syndicate, Inc.
IT'S NOT THE HAVING, IT'S THE GETTING
2·24
JIM DAVIS

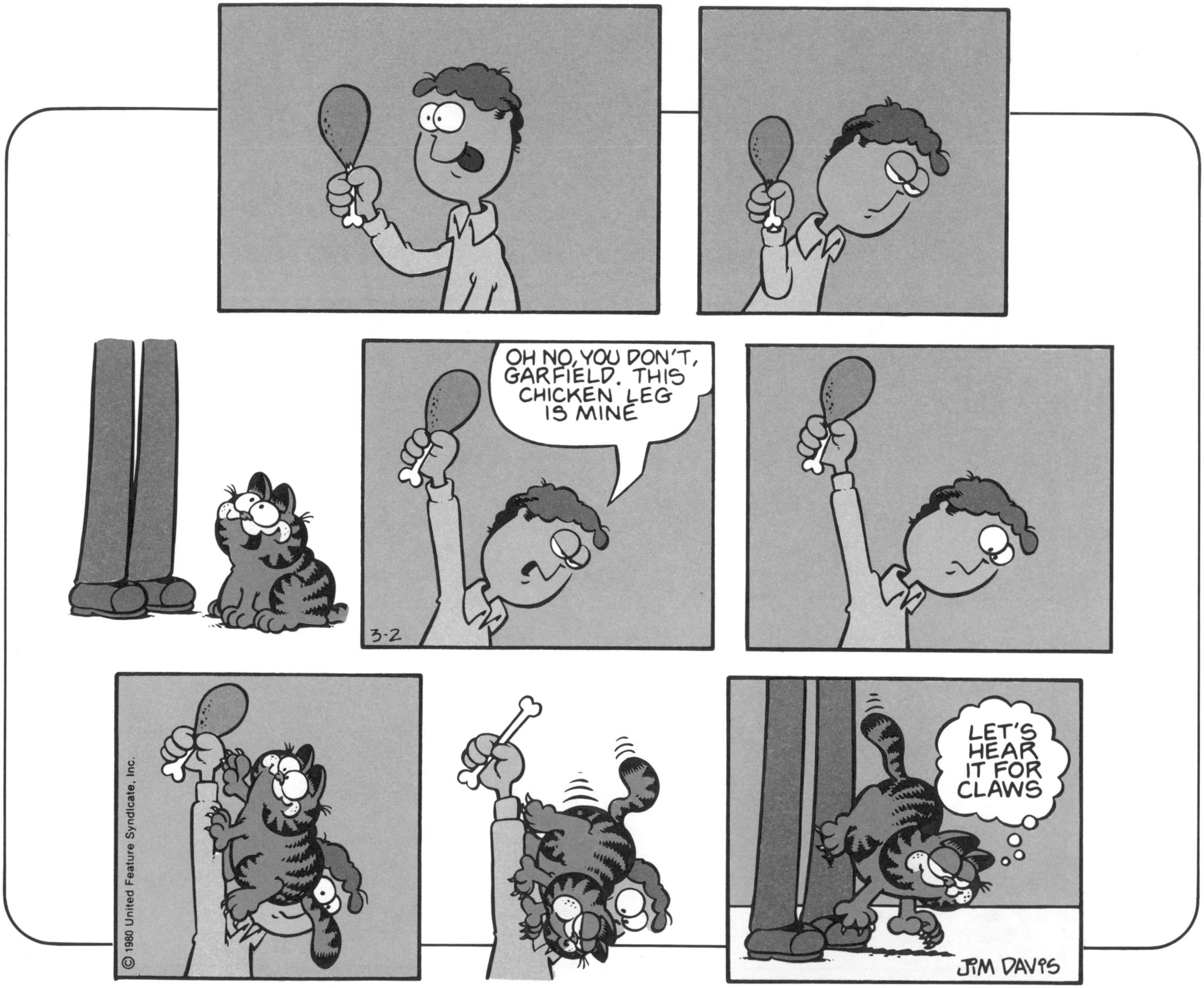
OH NO, YOU DON'T, GARFIELD. THIS CHICKEN LEG IS MINE
3-2
LET'S HEAR IT FOR CLAWS
© 1980 United Feature Syndicate, Inc.
JIM DAVIS

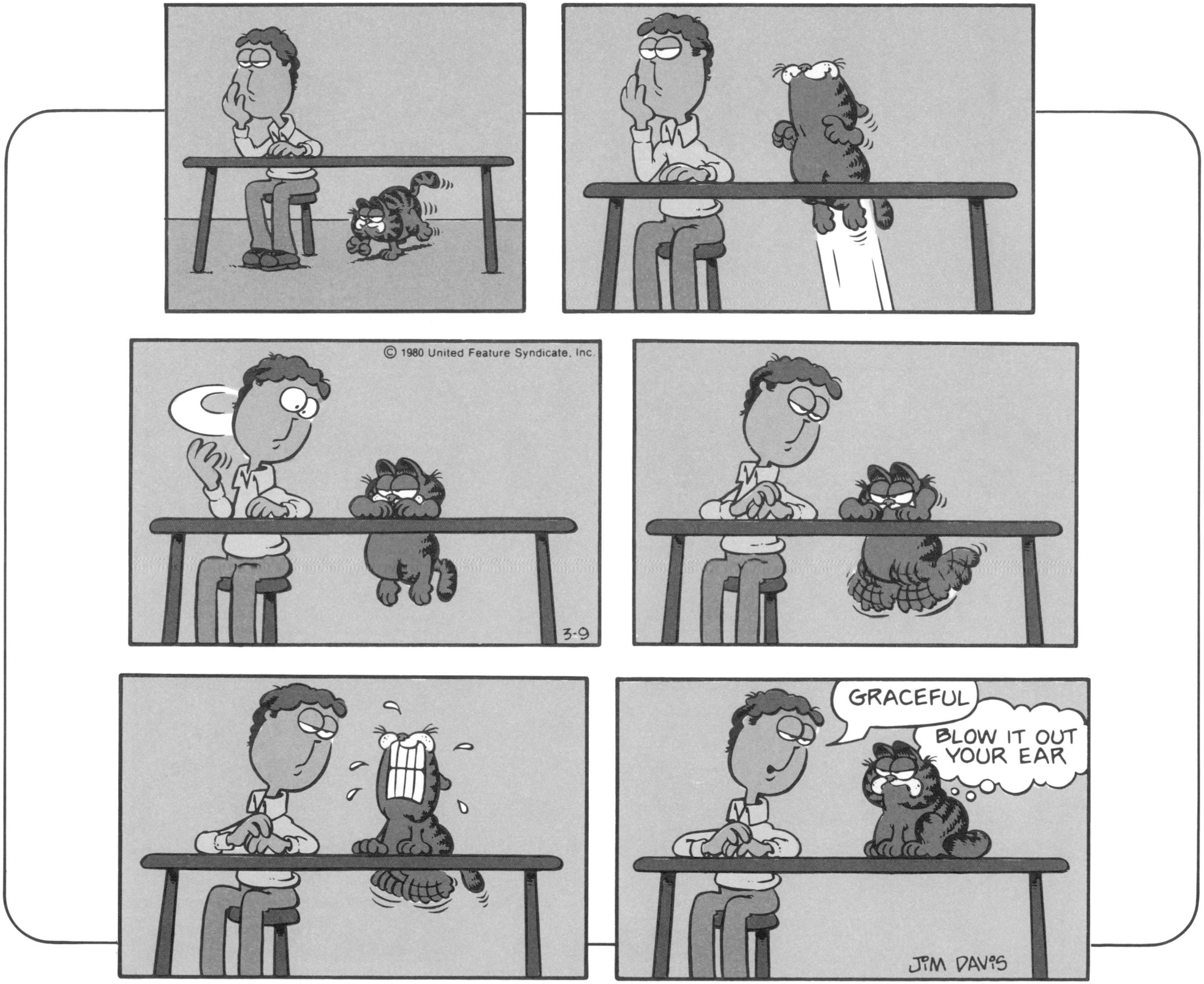
© 1980 United Feature Syndicate, Inc.
3-9
GRACEFUL
BLOW IT OUT YOUR EAR
JIM DAVIS

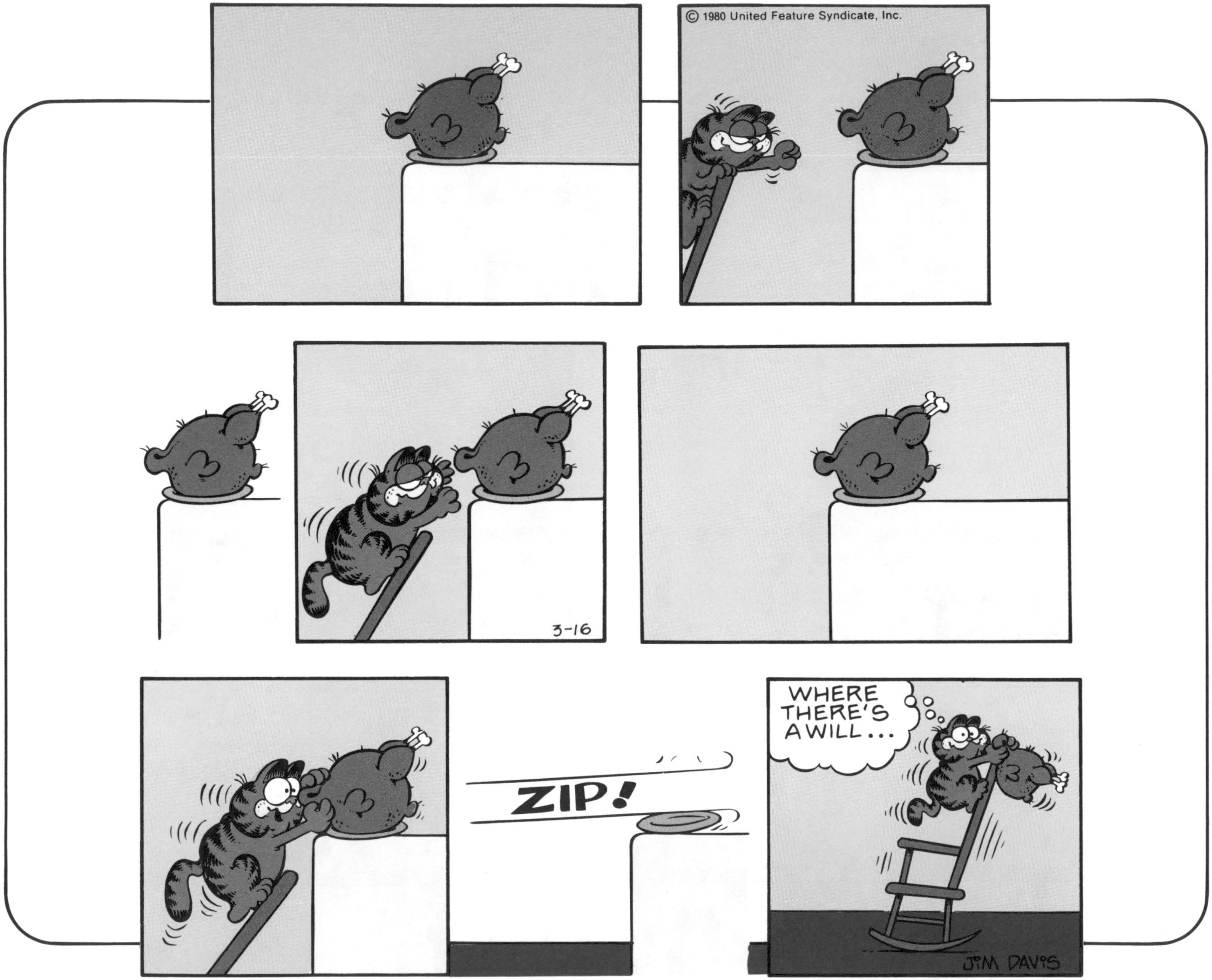
© 1980 United Feature Syndicate, Inc.
3-16
ZIP!
WHERE THERE'S A WILL...
JIM DAVIS

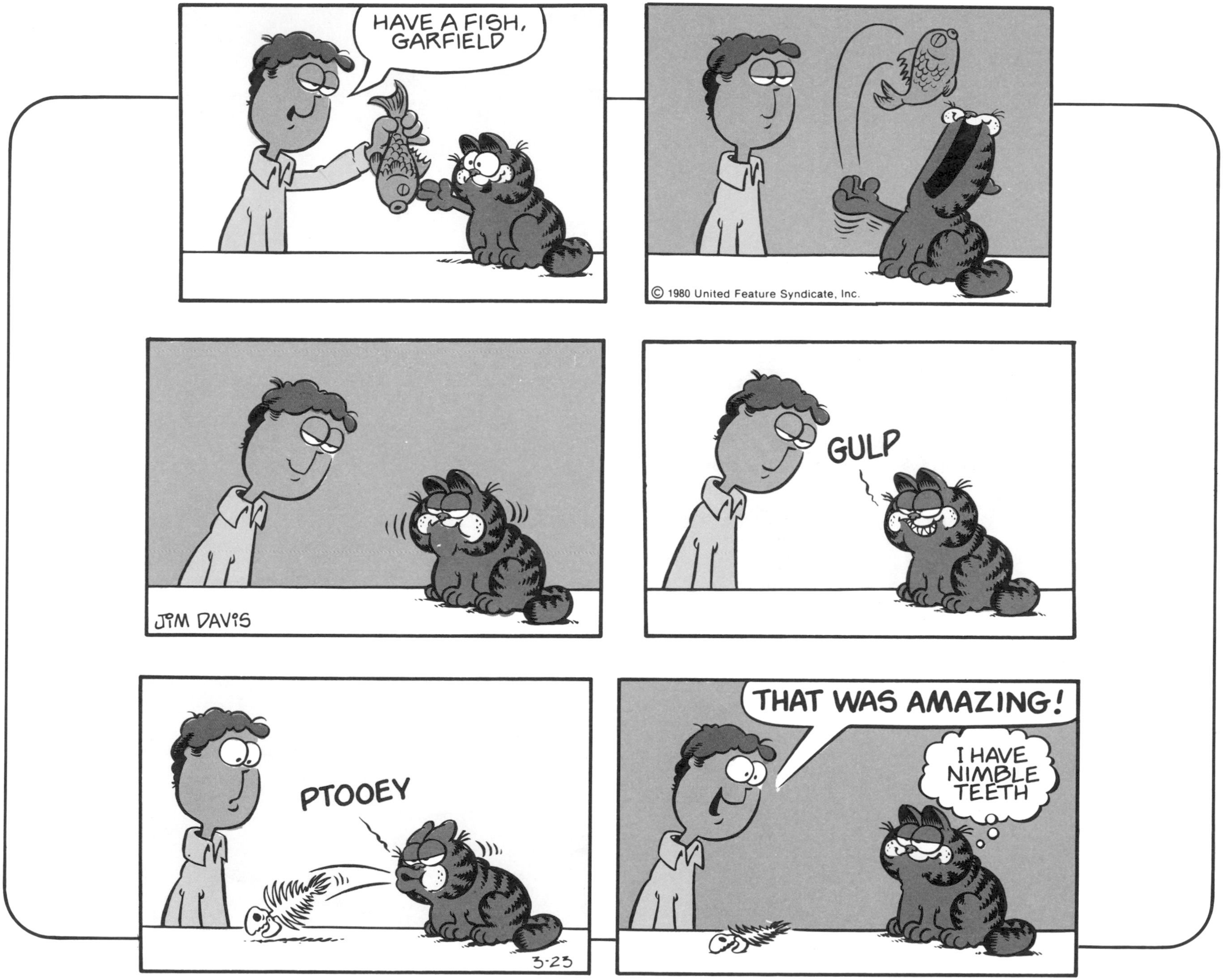
HAVE A FISH, GARFIELD
© 1980 United Feature Syndicate, Inc.
JIM DAVIS
GULP
PTOOEY
3-23
THAT WAS AMAZING!
I HAVE NIMBLE TEETH

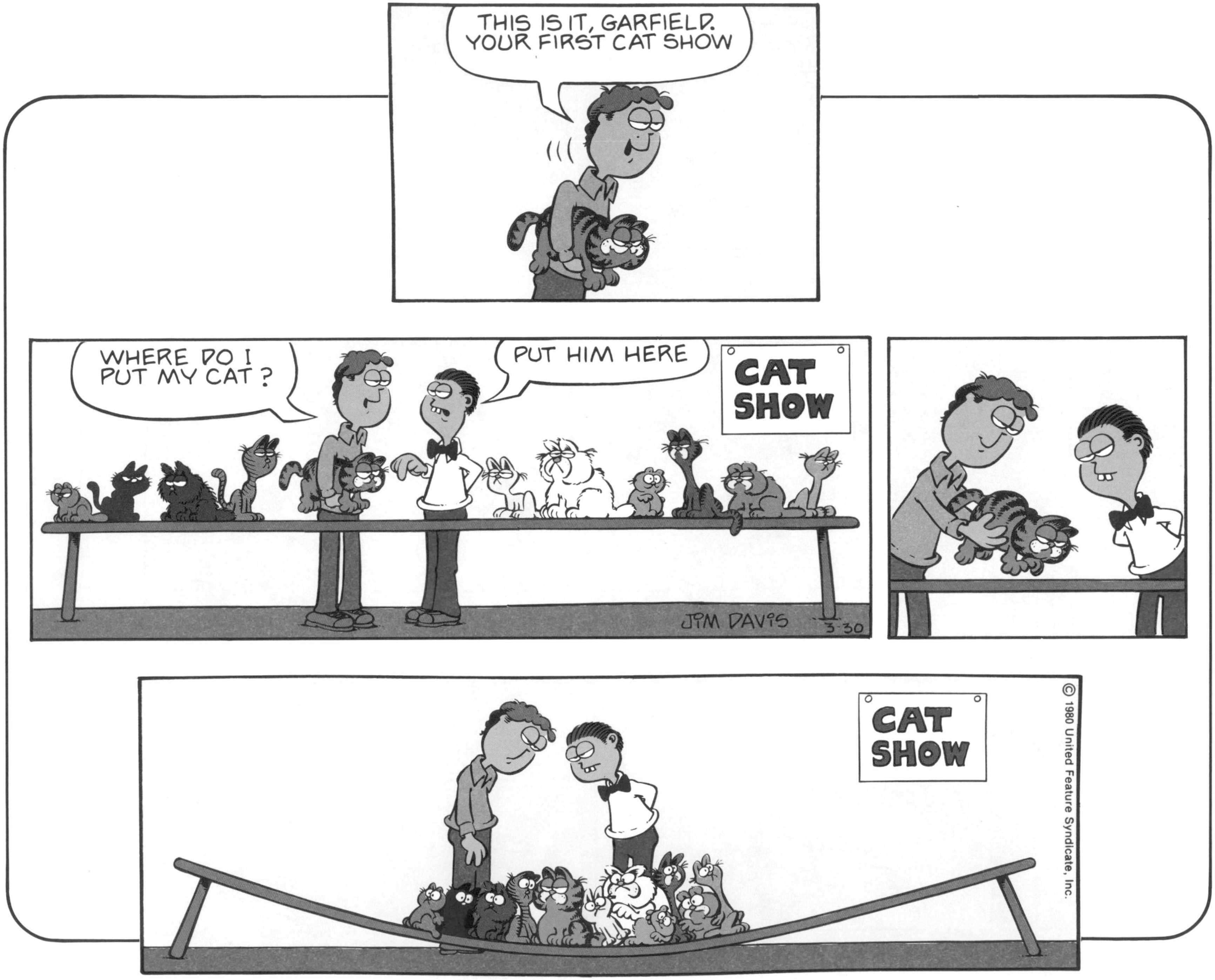
THIS IS IT, GARFIELD. YOUR FIRST CAT SHOW
WHERE DO I PUT MY CAT ?
PUT HIM HERE
CAT SHOW
JIM DAVIS
3-30
CAT SHOW
© 1980 United Feature Syndicate, Inc.

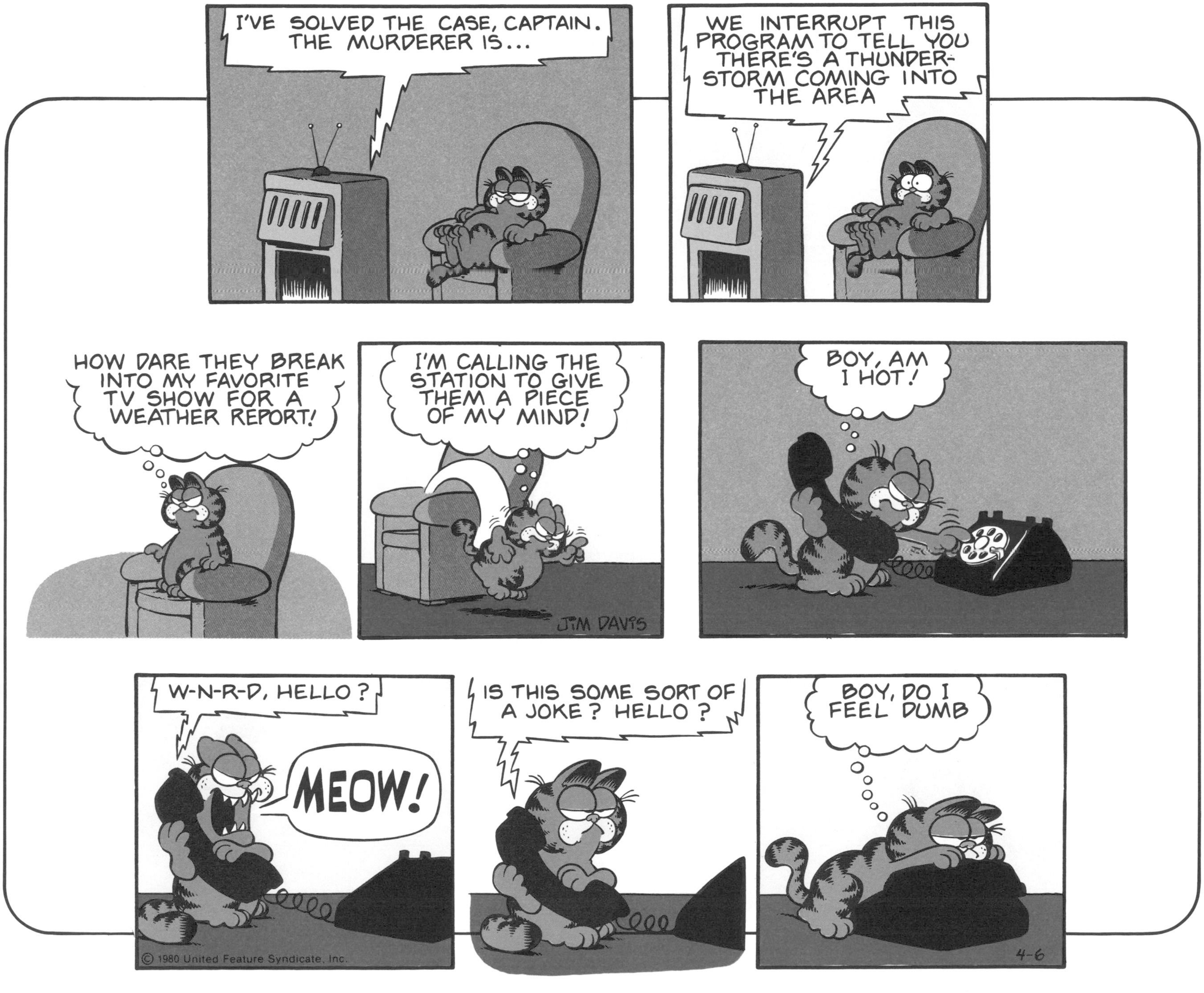
I'VE SOLVED THE CASE, CAPTAIN. THE MURDERER IS...
WE INTERRUPT THIS PROGRAM TO TELL YOU THERE'S A THUNDER-STORM COMING INTO THE AREA
HOW DARE THEY BREAK INTO MY FAVORITE TV SHOW FOR A WEATHER REPORT!
I'M CALLING THE STATION TO GIVE THEM A PIECE OF MY MIND!
JIM DAVIS
BOY, AM I HOT!
W-N-R-D, HELLO?
MEOW!
IS THIS SOME SORT OF A JOKE? HELLO?
BOY, DO I FEEL DUMB
© 1980 United Feature Syndicate, Inc.
4-6

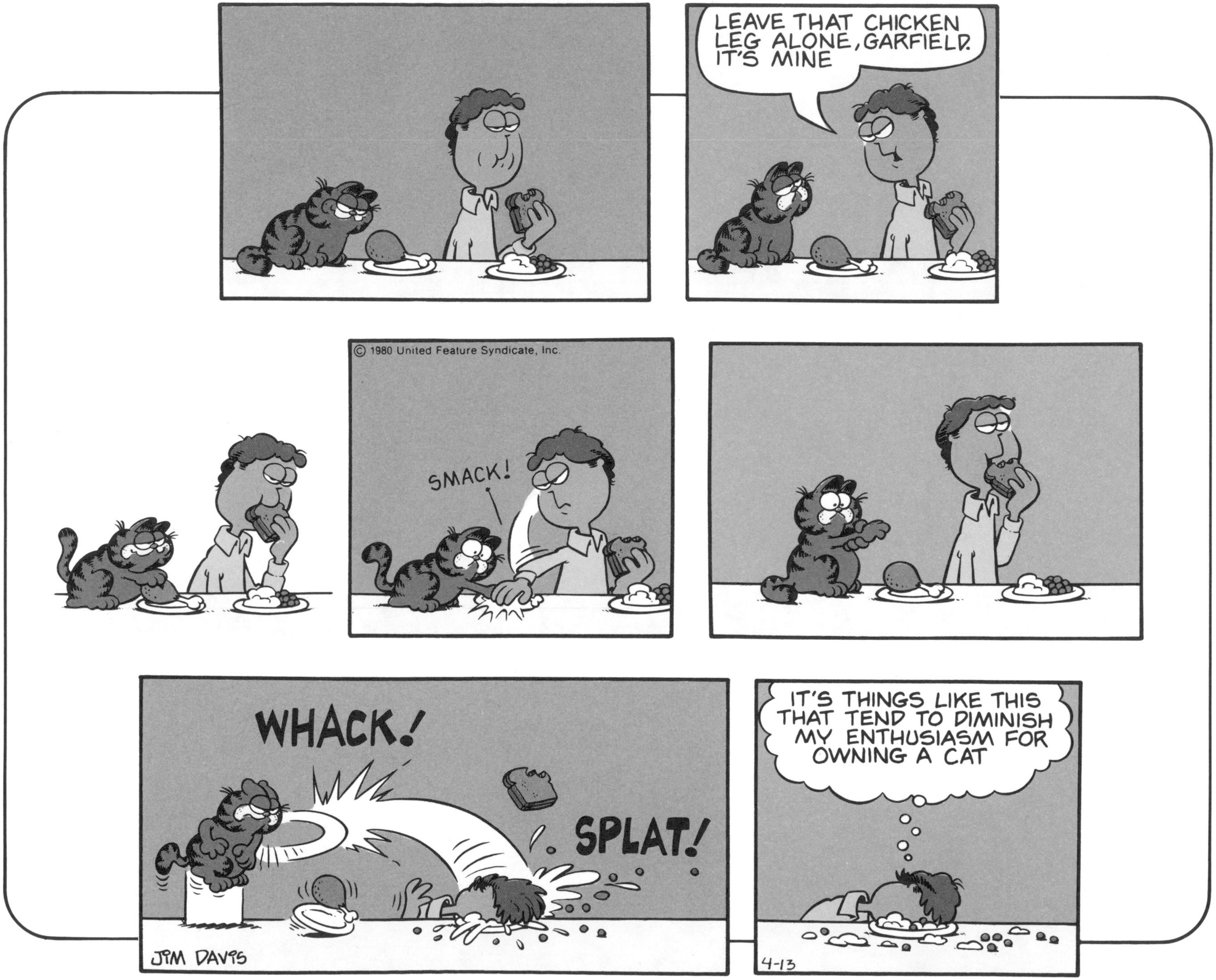
LEAVE THAT CHICKEN LEG ALONE, GARFIELD. IT'S MINE
© 1980 United Feature Syndicate, Inc.
SMACK!
WHACK!
SPLAT!
IT'S THINGS LIKE THIS THAT TEND TO DIMINISH MY ENTHUSIASM FOR OWNING A CAT
JIM DAVIS
4-13

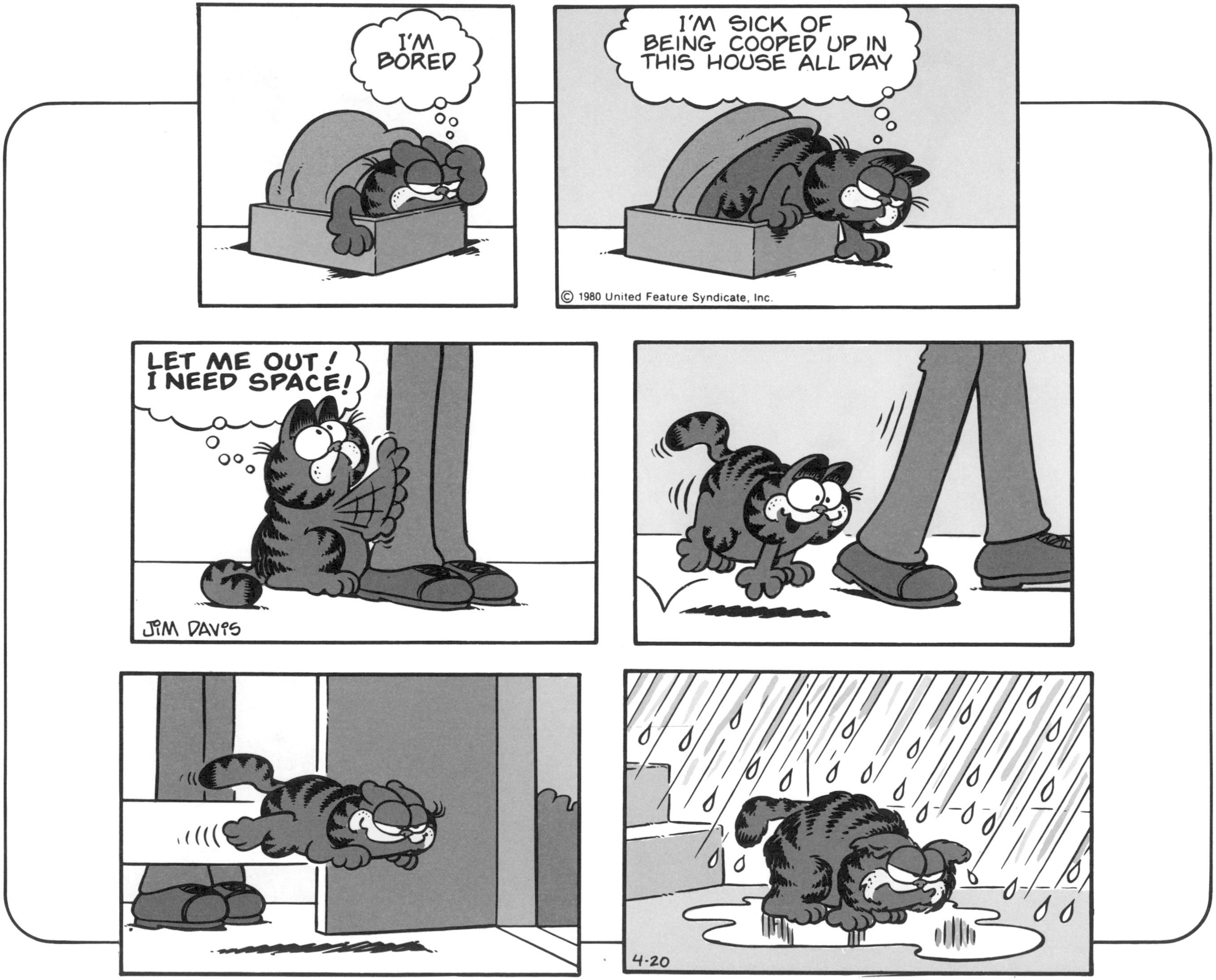
I'M BORED
I'M SICK OF BEING COOPED UP IN THIS HOUSE ALL DAY
© 1980 United Feature Syndicate, Inc.
LET ME OUT! I NEED SPACE!
JIM DAVIS
4-20

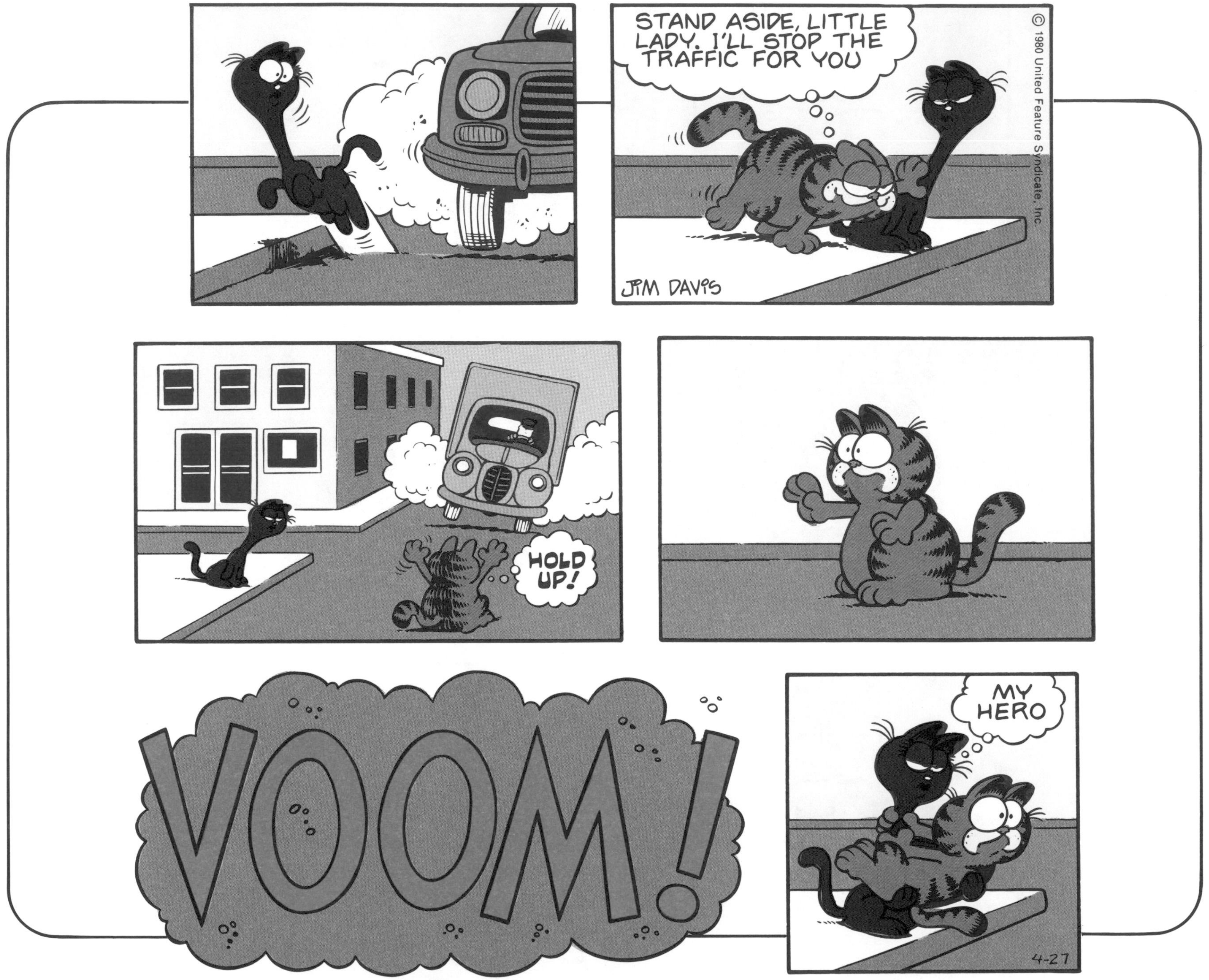
STAND ASIDE, LITTLE LADY. I'LL STOP THE TRAFFIC FOR YOU
© 1980 United Feature Syndicate, Inc.
JIM DAVIS
HOLD UP!
VOOM!
MY HERO
4-27

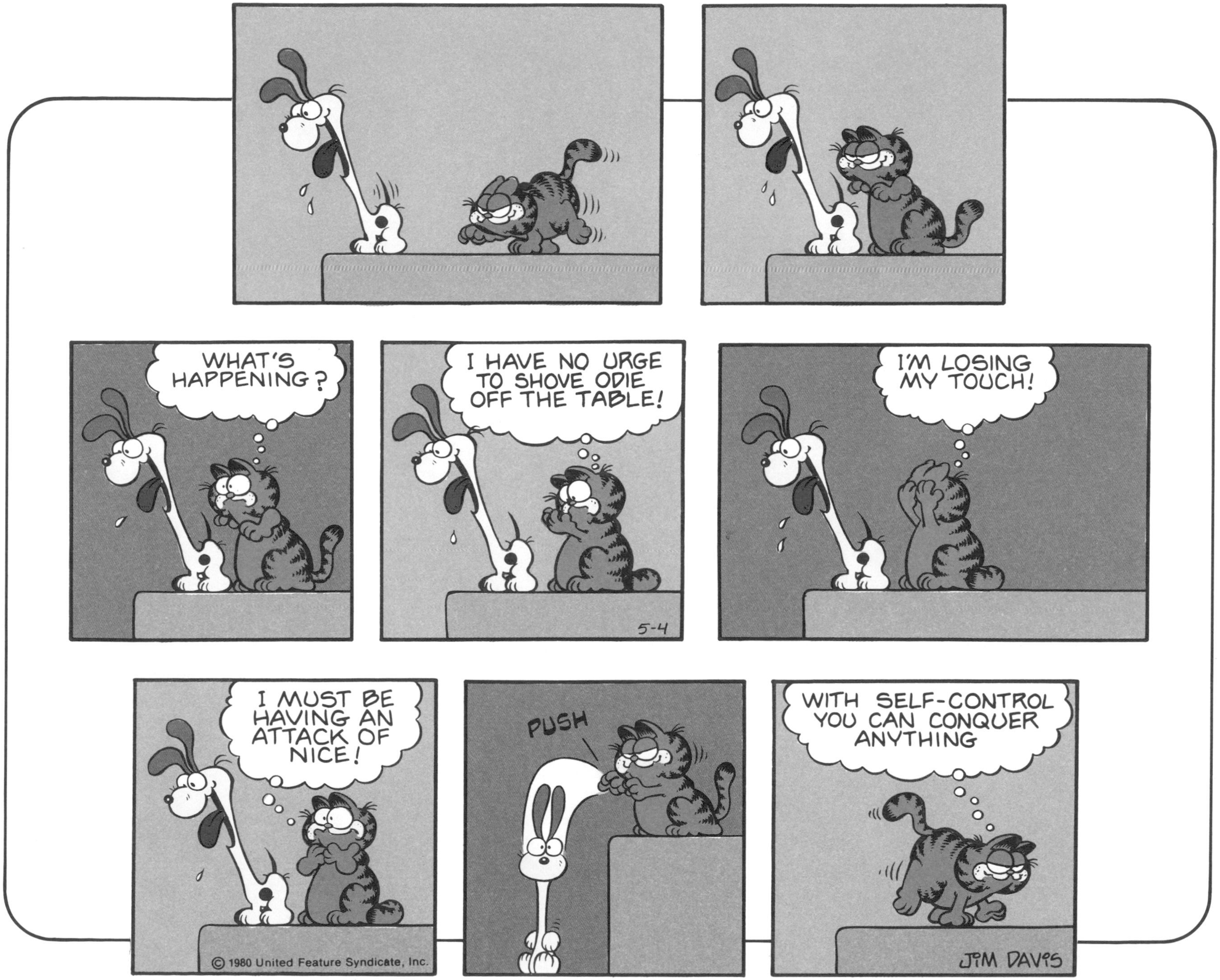
WHAT'S HAPPENING?
I HAVE NO URGE TO SHOVE ODIE OFF THE TABLE!
5-4
I'M LOSING MY TOUCH!
I MUST BE HAVING AN ATTACK OF NICE!
© 1980 United Feature Syndicate, Inc.
PUSH
WITH SELF-CONTROL YOU CAN CONQUER ANYTHING
JIM DAVIS

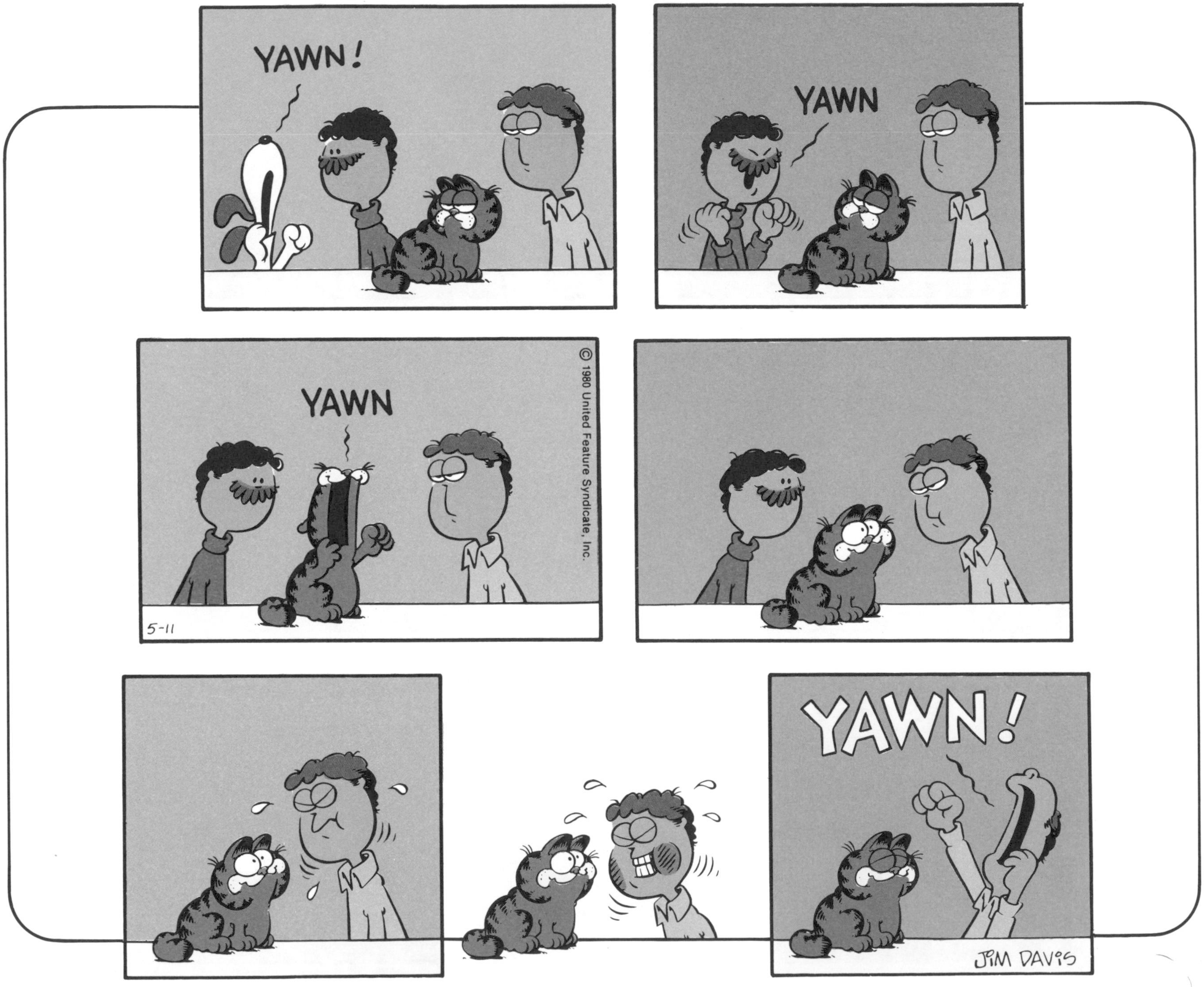
YAWN!
YAWN
YAWN
© 1980 United Feature Syndicate, Inc.
5-11
YAWN!
JIM DAVIS

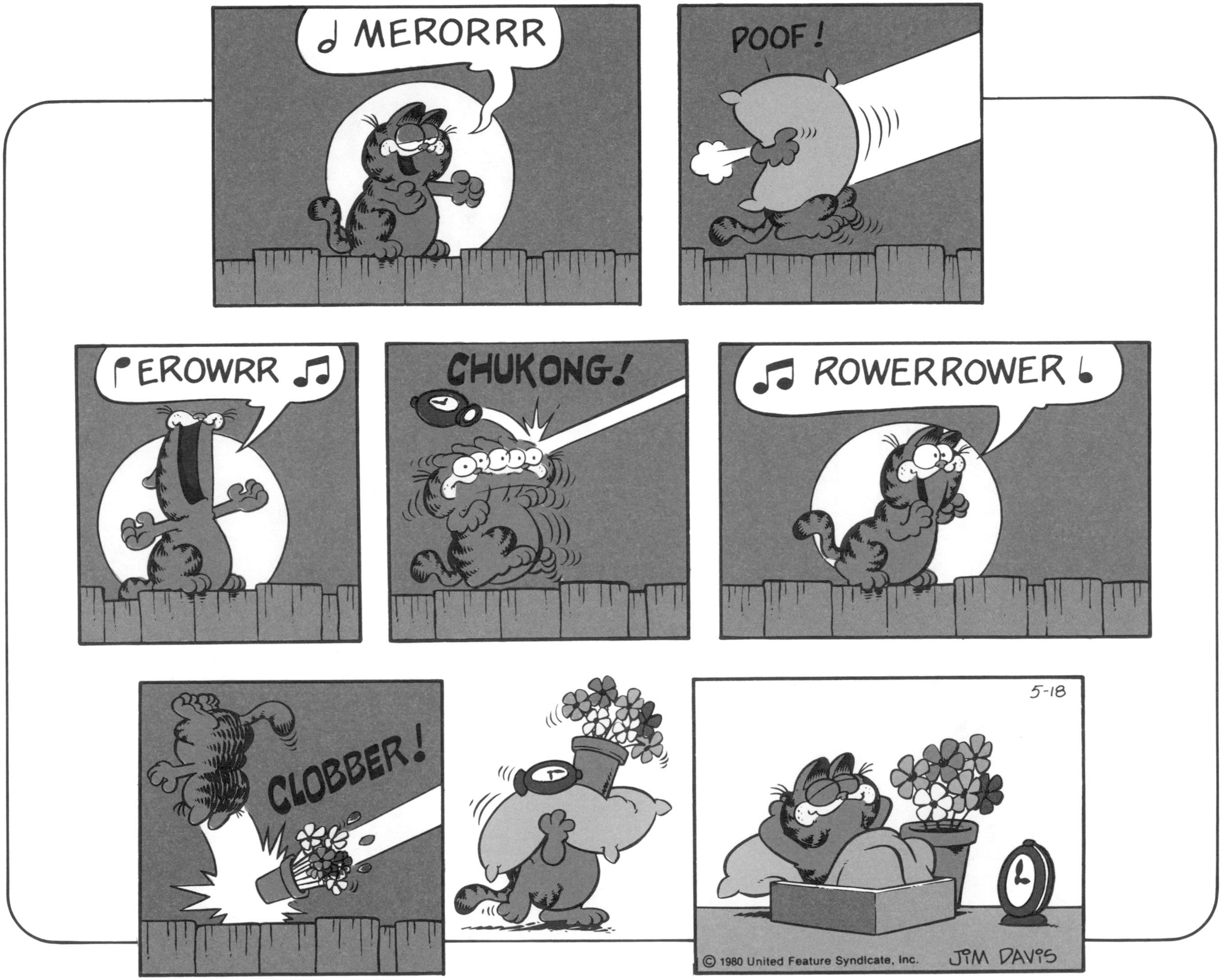
MERORRR
POOF!
EROWRR
CHUKONG!
ROWERROWER
CLOBBER!
5-18
© 1980 United Feature Syndicate, Inc.
JIM DAVIS

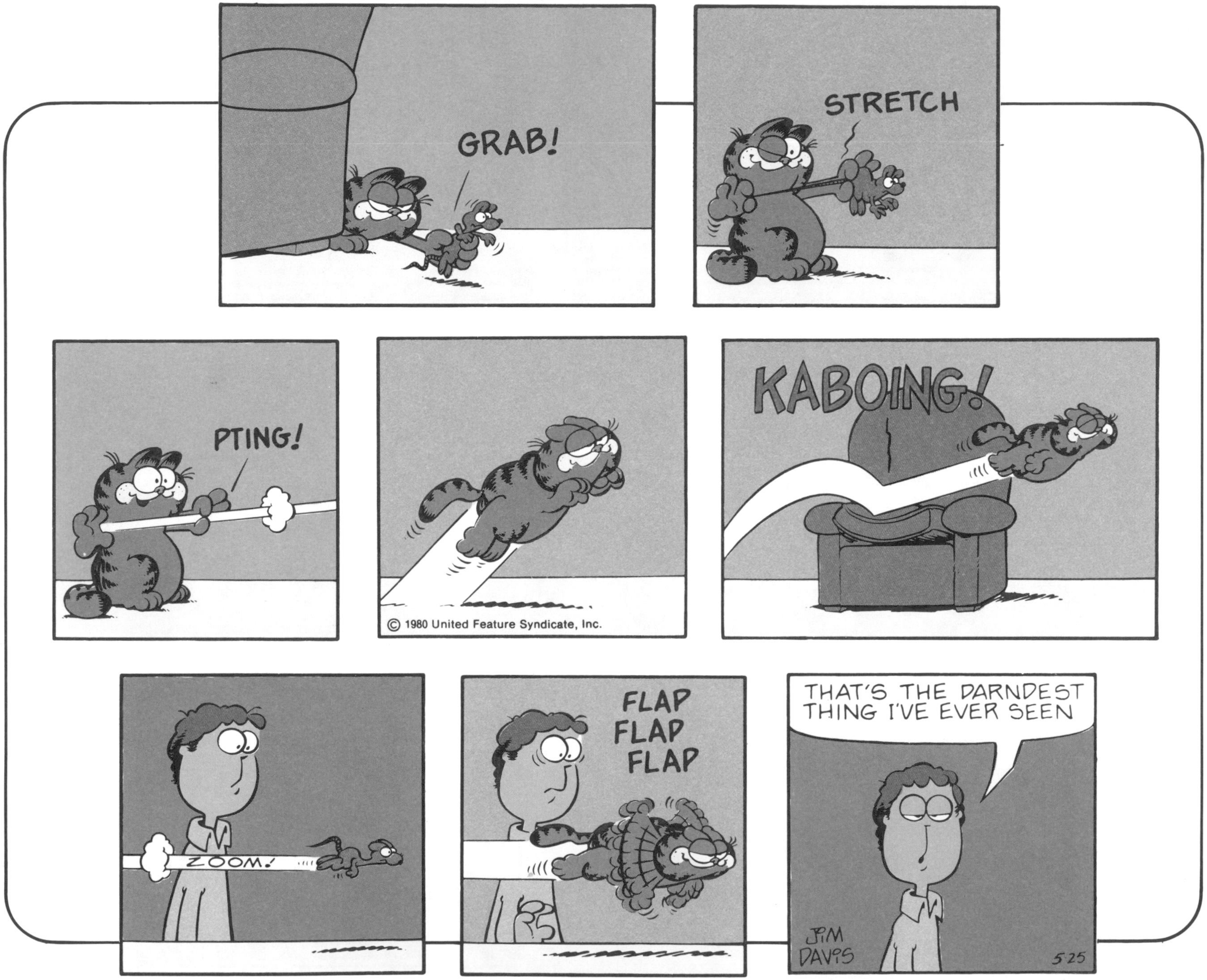
GRAB!
STRETCH
PTING!
© 1980 United Feature Syndicate, Inc.
KABOING!
ZOOM!
FLAP
FLAP
FLAP
THAT'S THE DARNDEST THING I'VE EVER SEEN
JIM DAVIS
5·25

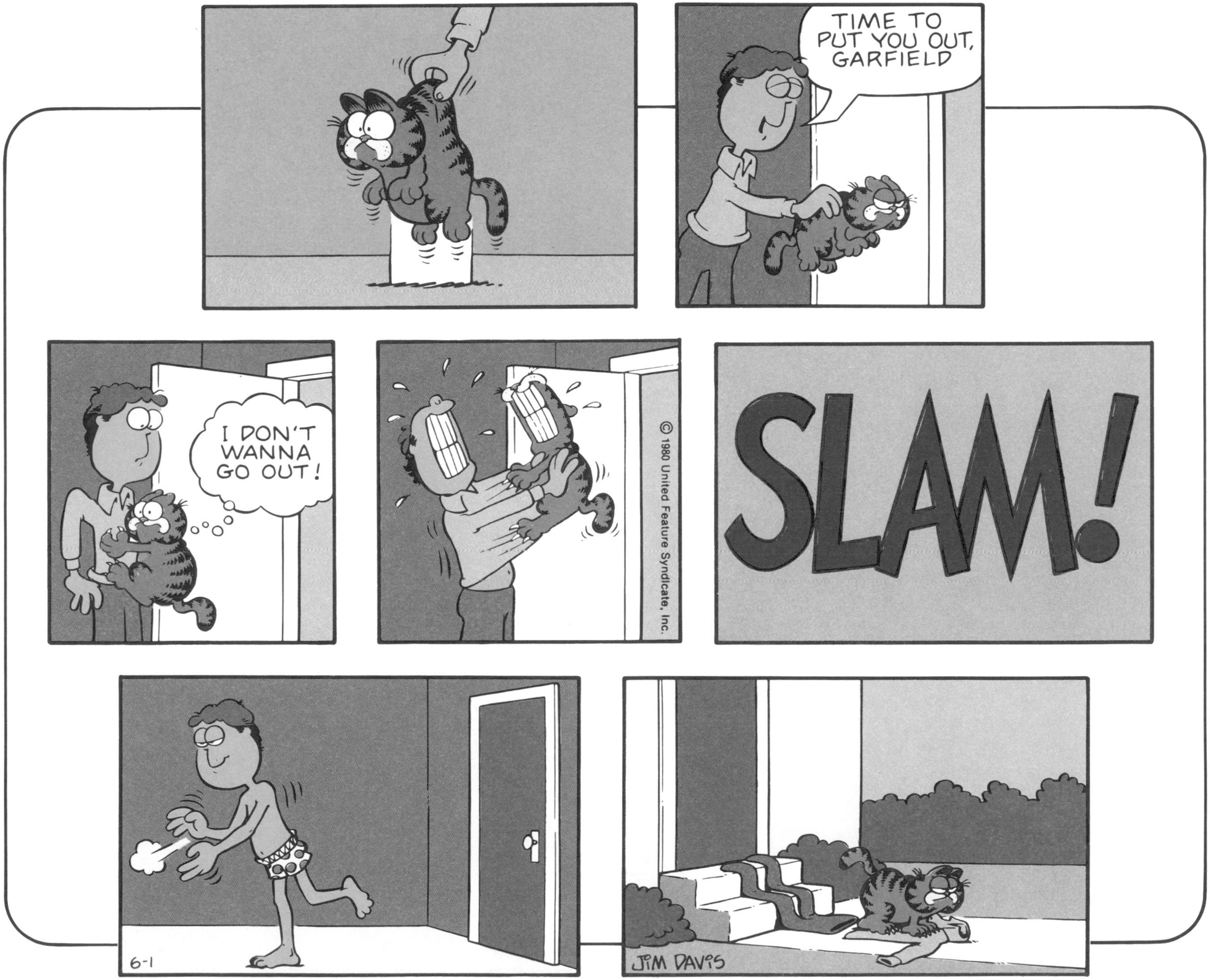
TIME TO PUT YOU OUT, GARFIELD
I DON'T WANNA GO OUT!
© 1980 United Feature Syndicate, Inc.
SLAM!
6-1
JIM DAVIS

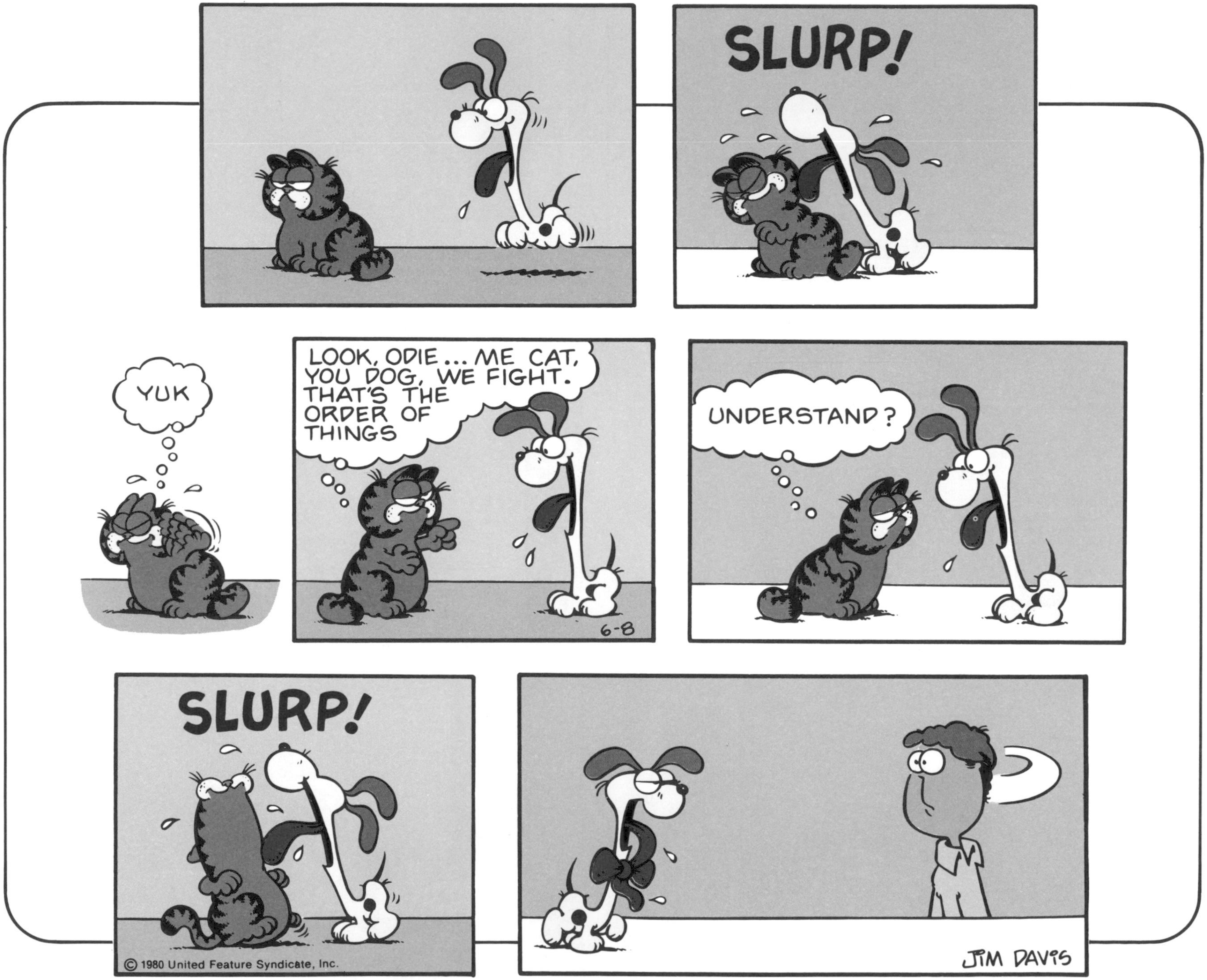
SLURP!
YUK
LOOK, ODIE ... ME CAT, YOU DOG, WE FIGHT. THAT'S THE ORDER OF THINGS
6-8
UNDERSTAND?
SLURP!
© 1980 United Feature Syndicate, Inc.
JIM DAVIS

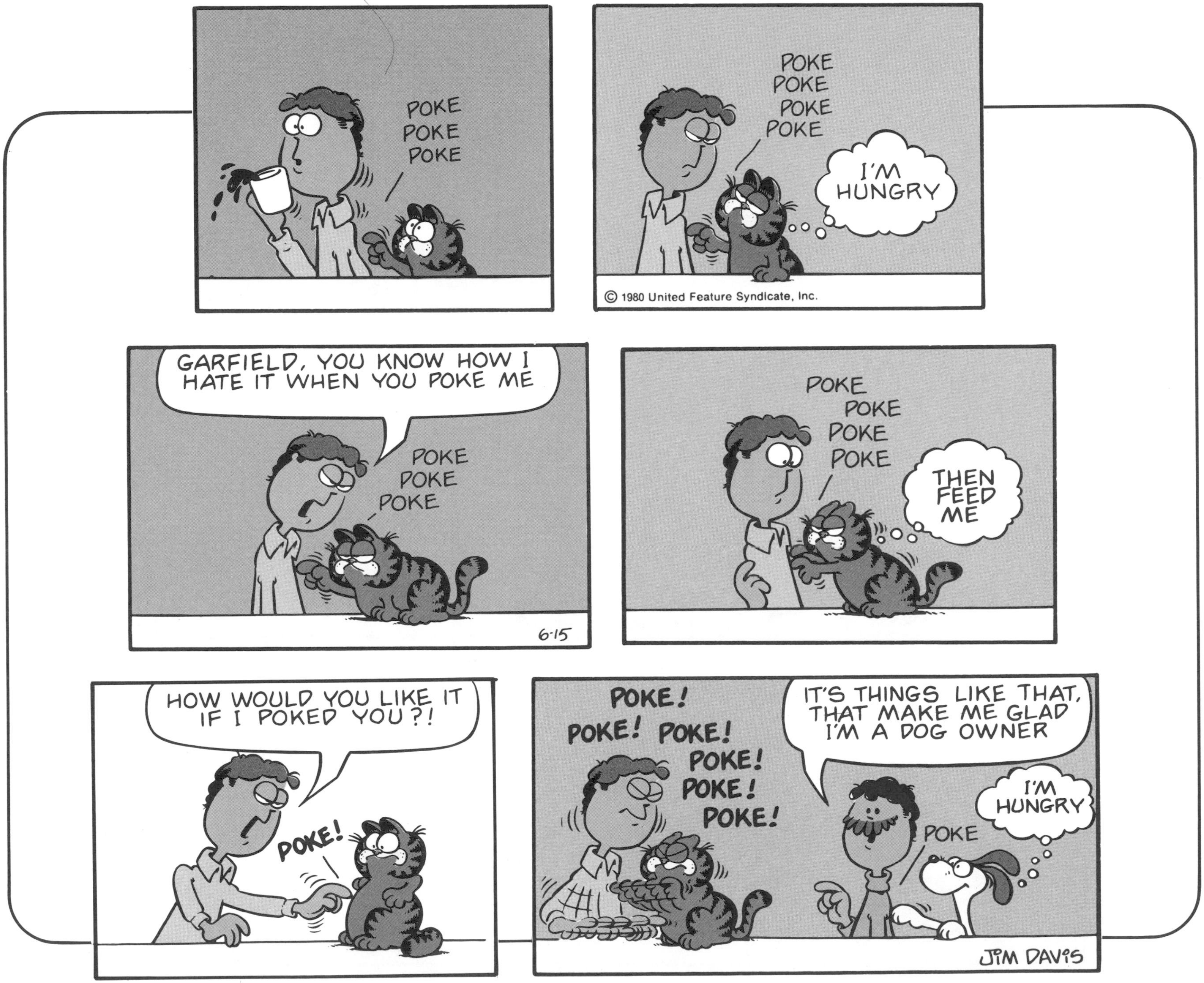

POKE
POKE
POKE
POKE
POKE
POKE
POKE
I'M HUNGRY
© 1980 United Feature Syndicate, Inc.
GARFIELD, YOU KNOW HOW I HATE IT WHEN YOU POKE ME
POKE
POKE
POKE
6-15
POKE
POKE
POKE
POKE
THEN FEED ME
HOW WOULD YOU LIKE IT IF I POKED YOU?!
POKE!
POKE!
POKE!
POKE!
POKE!
POKE!
POKE!
IT'S THINGS LIKE THAT, THAT MAKE ME GLAD I'M A DOG OWNER
POKE
I'M HUNGRY
JIM DAVIS

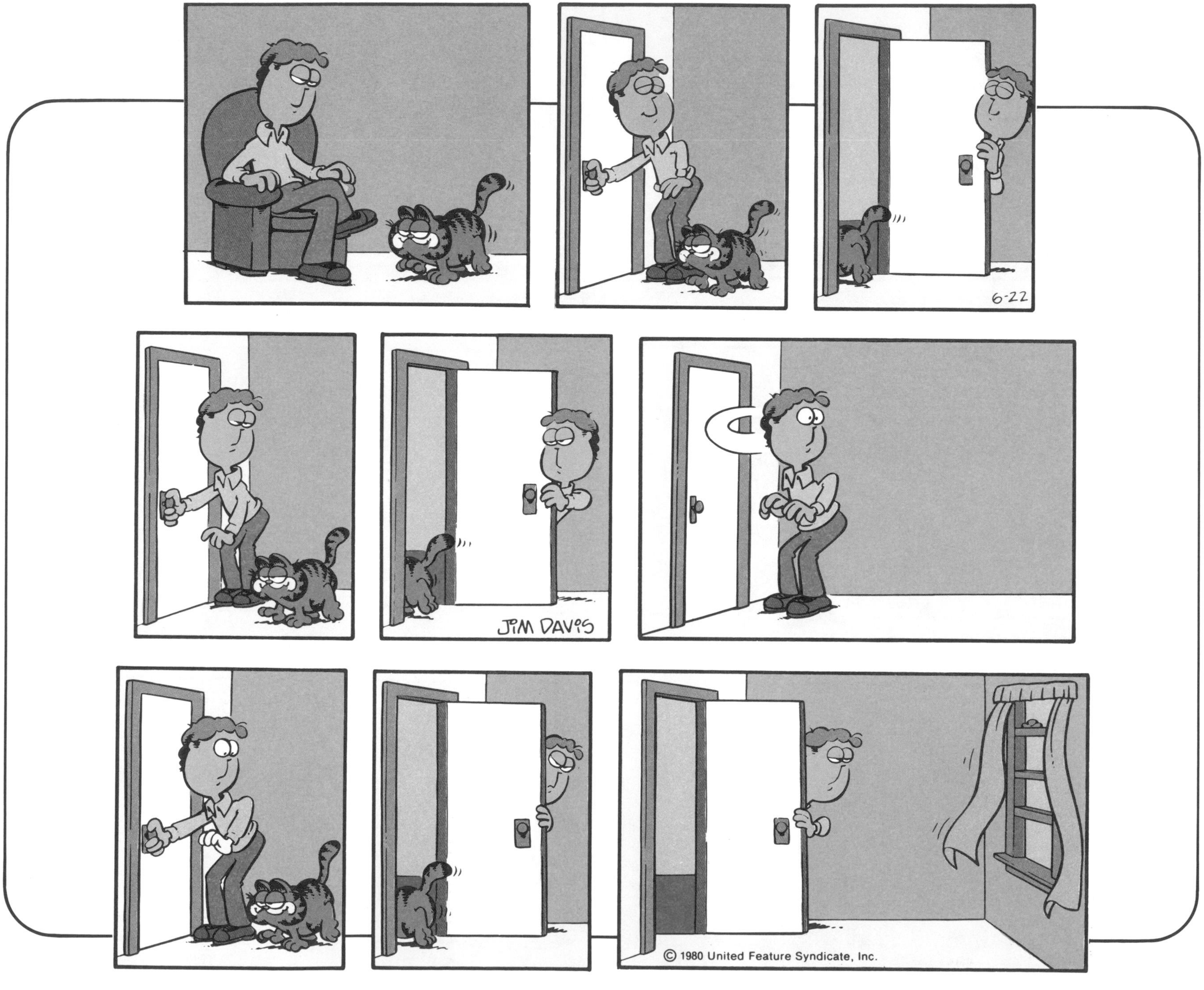

6-22
JIM DAVIS
© 1980 United Feature Syndicate, Inc.

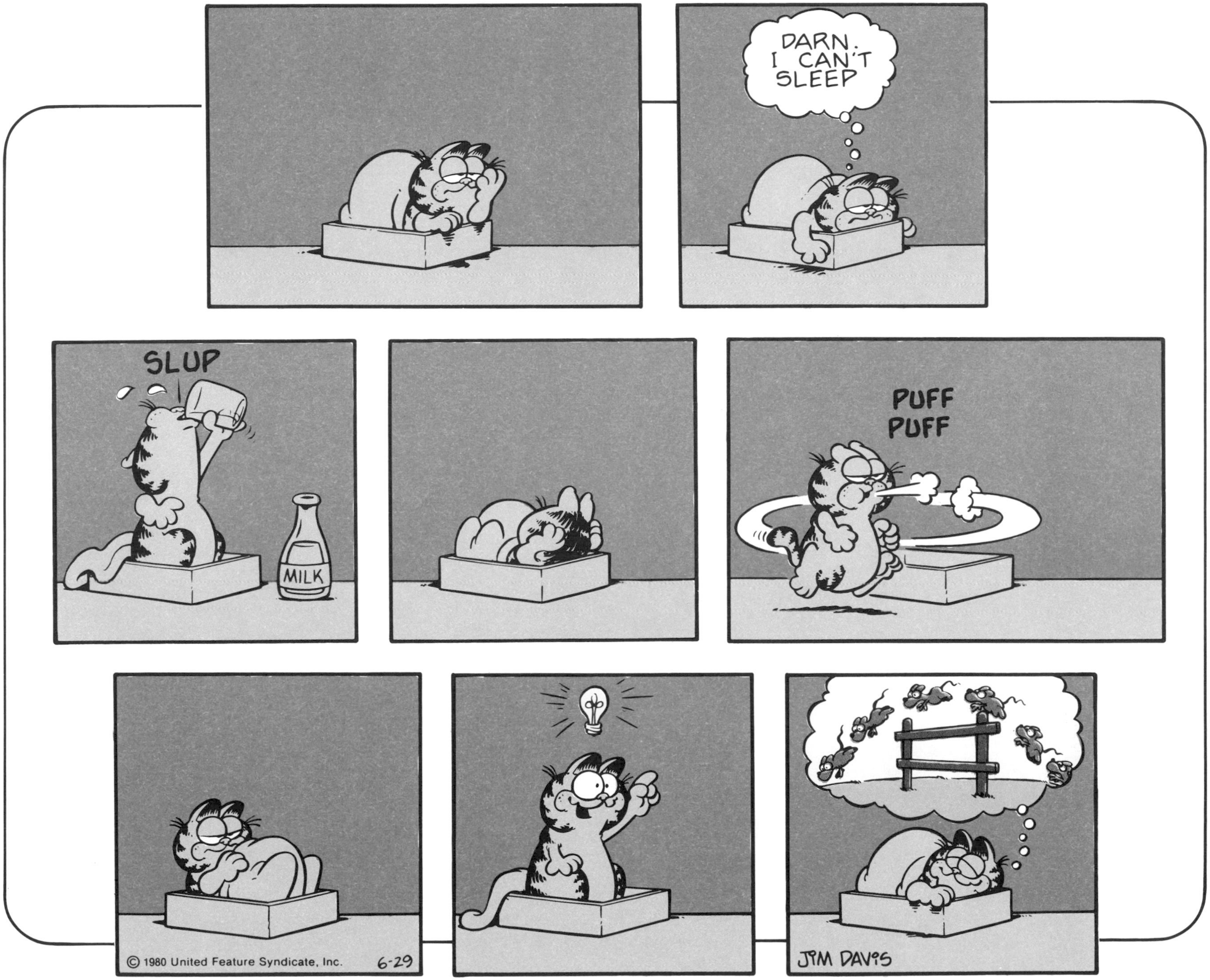
DARN. I CAN'T SLEEP
SLUP
MILK
PUFF PUFF
© 1980 United Feature Syndicate, Inc.
6-29
JIM DAVIS

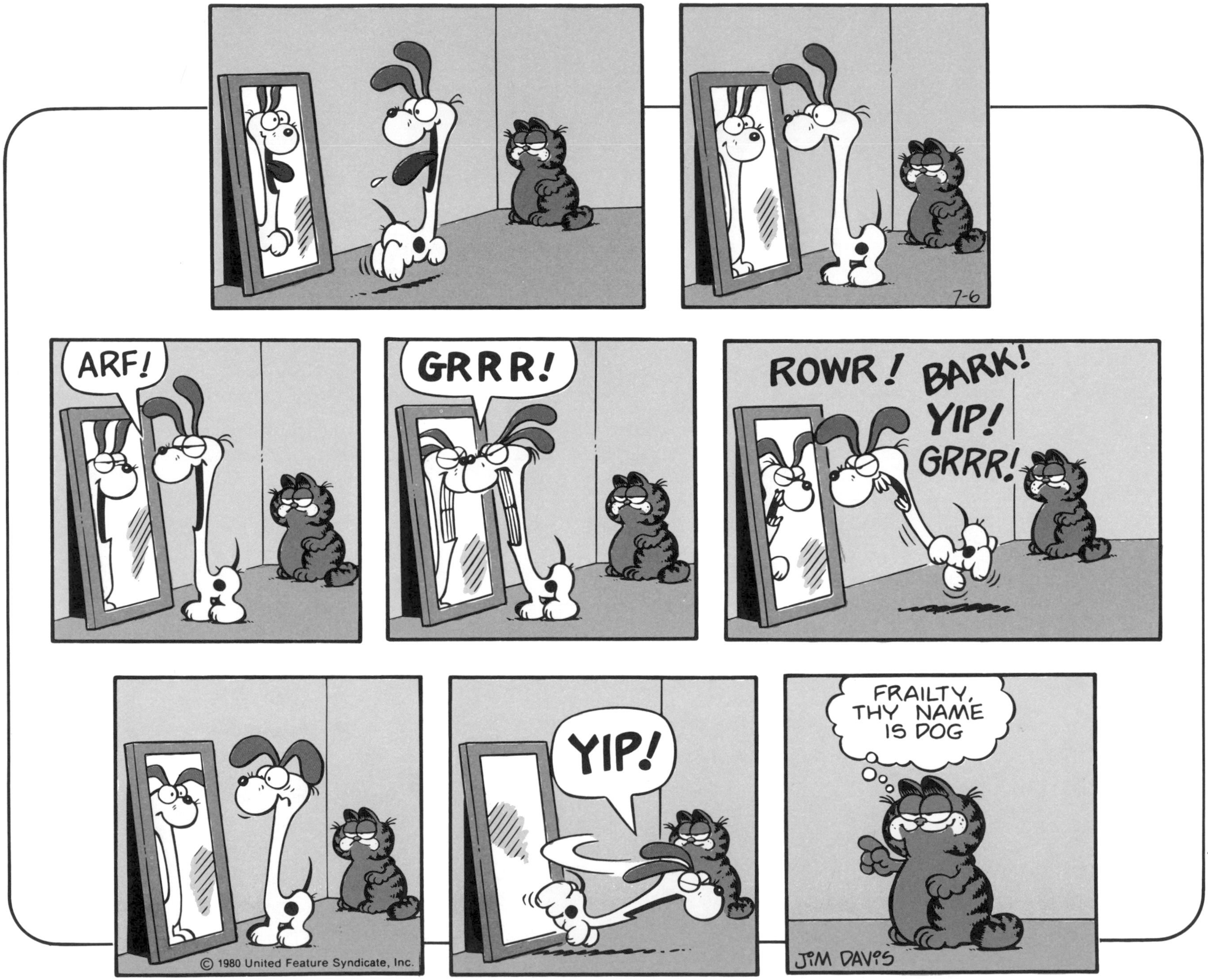
7-6
ARF!
GRRR!
ROWR! BARK! YIP! GRRR!
YIP!
FRAILTY, THY NAME IS DOG
© 1980 United Feature Syndicate, Inc.
JIM DAVIS

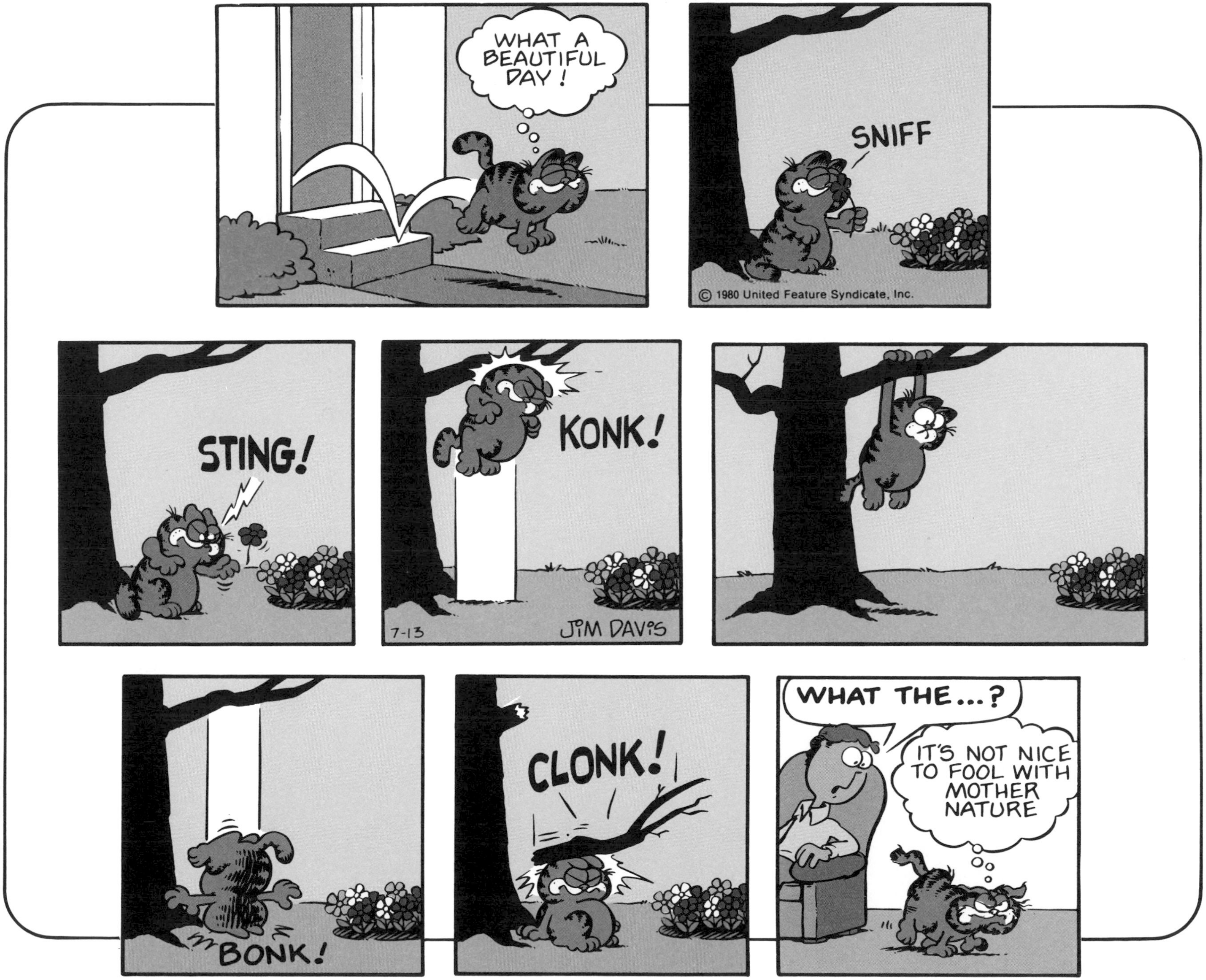
WHAT A BEAUTIFUL DAY!
SNIFF
© 1980 United Feature Syndicate, Inc.
STING!
KONK!
7-13
JIM DAVIS
BONK!
CLONK!
WHAT THE...?
IT'S NOT NICE TO FOOL WITH MOTHER NATURE

GARFIELD BEFORE & AFTER

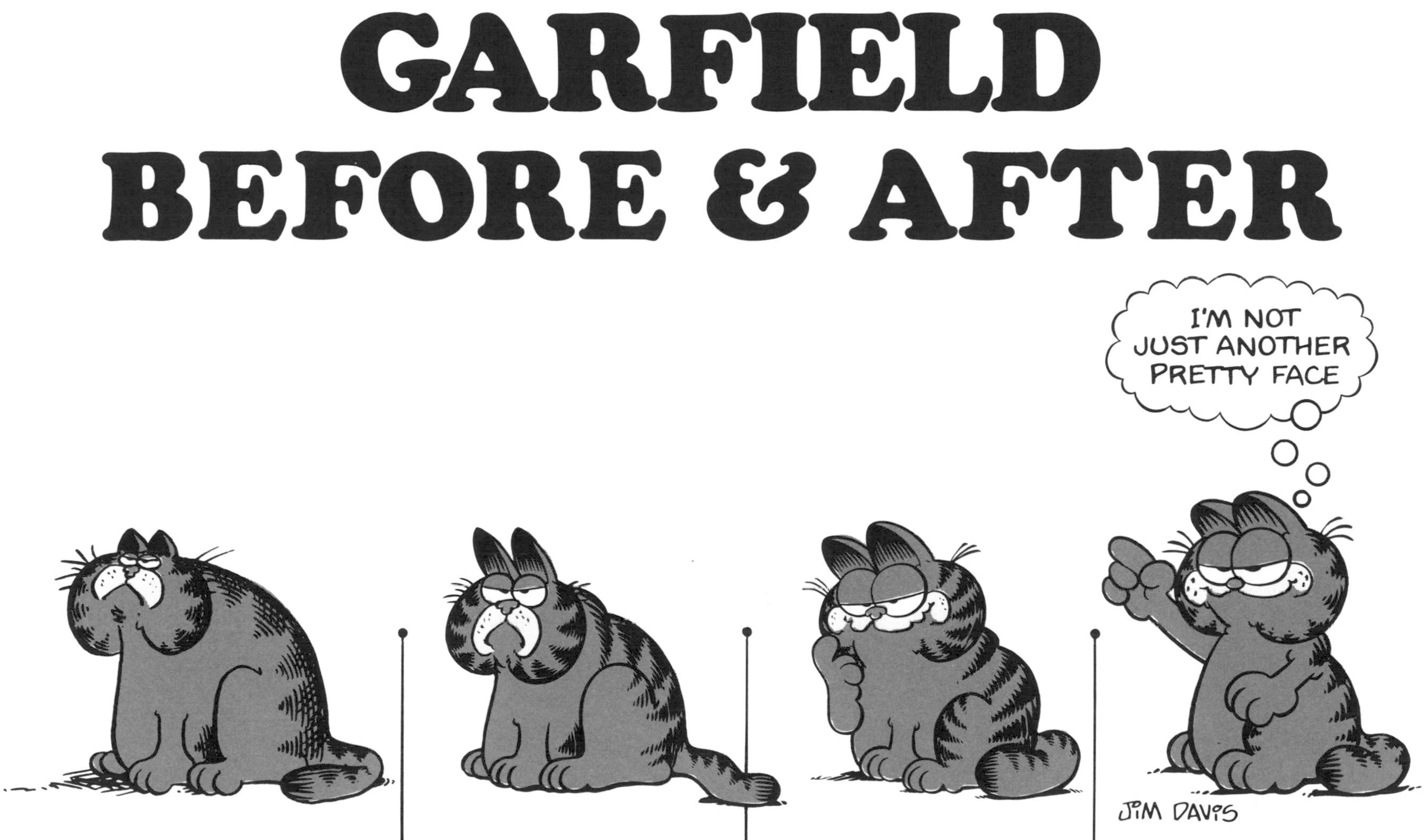
I'M NOT JUST ANOTHER PRETTY FACE
JIM DAVIS

1978 | **1978** *‹first brush drawing›* | **1979** | **1982**

About Jim Davis

Jim Davis was born July 28, 1945, in Marion, Indiana. After growing up on a farm near Fairmount, Indiana, with about 25 cats, Jim attended Ball State University in Muncie. As an Art and Business major he distinguished himself by earning one of the lowest accumulative grade point averages in the history of the university.

During the two-year stint at a local advertising agency Jim met and married wife Carolyn, a gifted singer and elementary school teacher.

In 1969 he became the assistant to Tom Ryan on the syndicated comic strip, TUMBLEWEEDS. In addition to cartooning, Jim maintained a career as a freelance commercial artist, copywriter, and radio-talent and political campaign promoter.

His hobbies include chess, sandwiches, and good friends. A new pastime is playing with his son, James Alexander.

In 1978 United Feature Syndicate gave the nod to GARFIELD.

Jim explains, "GARFIELD is strictly an entertainment strip built around the strong personality of a fat, lazy, cynical cat. It's the funniest strip I've ever seen. GARFIELD consciously avoids any social or political comment. My grasp of the world situation isn't that firm anyway. For years, I thought OPEC was a denture adhesive."

The strip is pumped out daily, in a cheerful atmosphere among friends. Valette Hildebrand is assistant cartoonist; artists include Kevin Campbell, Neil Altekruse, Mike Fentz, Brian Lum, and Dave Kuhn; Ron Tuthill is production manager; Jill Hahn is office manager; Dick Hamilton is business manager; Larry Carmichael is pilot for the group's corporate plane; and Julie Hamilton is president of Paws, Incorporated, the company that handles the merchandising of the characters in the strip.

"To what do I attribute my cartooning ability?" Jim asks. "As a child I was asthmatic. I was stuck indoors with little more than my imagination and paper and pencil to play with. While asthma worked for me, I wouldn't recommend it for everyone.

"Do I like cartooning?....It's nice work if you can get it."

STRIPS, SPECIALS OR BESTSELLING BOOKS . . .
GARFIELD'S ON EVERYONE'S MENU
Don't miss even one episode in the Tubby Tabby's hilarious series!

__GARFIELD AT LARGE (#1)   32013/$6.95
__GARFIELD GAINS WEIGHT (#2)   32008/$6.95
__GARFIELD BIGGER THAN LIFE (#3)   32007/$6.95
__GARFIELD WEIGHS IN (#4)   32010/$6.95
__GARFIELD TAKES THE CAKE (#5)   32009/$6.95
__GARFIELD EATS HIS HEART OUT (#6)   32018/$6.95
__GARFIELD SITS AROUND THE HOUSE (#7)   32011/$6.95
__GARFIELD TIPS THE SCALES (#8)   33580/$6.95
__GARFIELD LOSES HIS FEET (#9)   31805/$6.95
__GARFIELD MAKES IT BIG (#10)   31928/$6.95
__GARFIELD ROLLS ON (#11)   32634/$6.95
__GARFIELD OUT TO LUNCH (#12)   33118/$6.95
__GARFIELD FOOD FOR THOUGHT (#13)   34129/$6.95

Please send me the BALLANTINE BOOKS I have checked above. I am enclosing $_____. (Please add $2.00 for the first book and $.50 for each additional book for postage and handling and include the appropriate state sales tax.) Send check or money order (no cash or C.O.D.'s) to Ballantine Mail Sales Dept. TA, 400 Hahn Road, Westminster, MD 21157.

To order by phone, call 1-800-733-3000 and use your major credit card.

Prices and numbers are subject to change without notice. Valid in the U.S. only. All orders are subject to availability.

__GARFIELD SWALLOWS HIS PRIDE (#14)   34725/$6.95
__GARFIELD WORLDWIDE (#15)   35158/$6.95
__GARFIELD ROUNDS OUT (#16)   35388/$6.95
__GARFIELD CHEWS THE FAT (#17)   35956/$6.95
__GARFIELD GOES TO WAIST (#18)   36430/$6.95
__GARFIELD HANGS OUT (#19)   36835/$6.95
__GARFIELD TAKES UP SPACE (#20)   37029/$6.95
__GARFIELD SAYS A MOUTHFUL (#21)   37368/$6.95
__GARFIELD BY THE POUND (#22)   37579/$6.95
__GARFIELD KEEPS HIS CHINS UP (#23)   37959/$6.95
__GARFIELD TAKES HIS LICKS (#24)   38170/$6.95
__GARFIELD HITS THE BIG TIME (#25)   38332/$6.95

GARFIELD AT HIS SUNDAY BEST!
__GARFIELD TREASURY   32106/$11.95
__THE SECOND GARFIELD TREASURY   33276/$10.95
__THE THIRD GARFIELD TREASURY   32635/$11.00
__THE FOURTH GARFIELD TREASURY   34726/$10.95
__THE FIFTH GARFIELD TREASURY   36268/$12.00
__THE SIXTH GARFIELD TREASURY   37367/$10.95
__THE SEVENTH GARFIELD TREASURY   38427/$10.95

Name_____

Address_____

City_____ State_____ Zip_____
30   Allow at least 4 weeks for delivery   7/93

BIRTHDAYS, HOLIDAYS, OR ANY DAY...
Keep GARFIELD on your calendar all year 'round!

GARFIELD TV SPECIALS
___BABES & BULLETS   36339/$6.95
___A GARFIELD CHRISTMAS   34368/$6.95
___GARFIELD GOES HOLLYWOOD   34580/$6.95
___GARFIELD'S HALLOWEEN ADVENTURE   33045/$6.95
  (formerly GARFIELD in Disguise)
___GARFIELD'S FELINE FANTASIES   36903/$6.95
___GARFIELD IN PARADISE   33796/$6.95
___GARFIELD IN THE ROUGH   32242/$6.95
___GARFIELD ON THE TOWN   31542/$6.95
___A GARFIELD THANKSGIVING   35650/$6.95
___HERE COMES GARFIELD   32012/$6.95
___GARFIELD GETS A LIFE   37375/$6.95

BALLANTINE SALES
Dept. TA, 201 E. 50th St., New York, N.Y. 10022

Please send me the BALLANTINE BOOKS I have checked above. I am enclosing $ .... (add $2.00 for the first book and 50¢ for each additional book to cover postage and handling). Send check or money order—no cash or C.O.D.'s please. Prices are subject to change without notice.

GREETINGS FROM GARFIELD!
GARFIELD POSTCARD BOOKS FOR ALL OCCASIONS.
___THINKING OF YOU   36516/$6.95
___WORDS TO LIVE BY   36679/$6.95
___GARFIELD BIRTHDAY GREETINGS   36770/$7.95
___BE MY VALENTINE   37121/$7.95
___SEASON'S GREETINGS   37435/$8.95
___VACATION GREETINGS   37774/$10.00

Also from GARFIELD:
___GARFIELD: HIS NINE LIVES   32061/$9.95
___THE GARFIELD BOOK OF CAT NAMES   35082/$5.95
___THE GARFIELD TRIVIA BOOK   33771/$5.95
___THE UNABRIDGED UNCENSORED
  UNBELIEVABLE GARFIELD   33772/$5.95
___GARFIELD: THE ME BOOK   36545/$7.95
___GARFIELD'S JUDGMENT DAY   36755/$6.95
___THE TRUTH ABOUT CATS   37226/$6.95

Name _____

Address _____

City _____ State _____ Zip Code _____
30   Allow at least 4 weeks for delivery   3/90 TA-267